THE
LONG
HUNTER

THE
LONG
HUNTER

A New Life of Daniel Boone

LAWRENCE ELLIOTT

READER'S DIGEST PRESS
Distributed by Thomas Y. Crowell Company, New York, 1976

Frontispiece portrait of Daniel Boone
by Chester Harding, *Courtesy of The Filson Club,*
Louisville, Kentucky

Map by George Buctel

Copyright © 1976 by Lawrence Elliott

Designed by Abigail Moseley

Manufactured in the United States of America

Library of Congress Cataloging in Publication Data

Elliott, Lawrence.
    The long hunter.

    Bibliography: p.
    Includes index.
    1. Boone, Daniel, 1734–1820.   I. Title.
F454.B736   976.9′02′0924 [B]   75-30688
ISBN 0-88349-066-8

1 2 3 4 5 6 7 8 9 10

For Jenny and Mildred, with love;
and for
Nicholas, who arrived in the middle of it all.

Books by Lawrence Elliott

The Long Hunter: A New Life of Daniel Boone
I Will Be Called John: A Biography of Pope John XXIII
The Legacy of Tom Dooley
Journey to Washington (*With Senator Daniel K. Inouye*)
On the Edge of Nowhere (*With James Huntington*)
George Washington Carver: The Man Who Overcame
A Little Girl's Gift

Contents

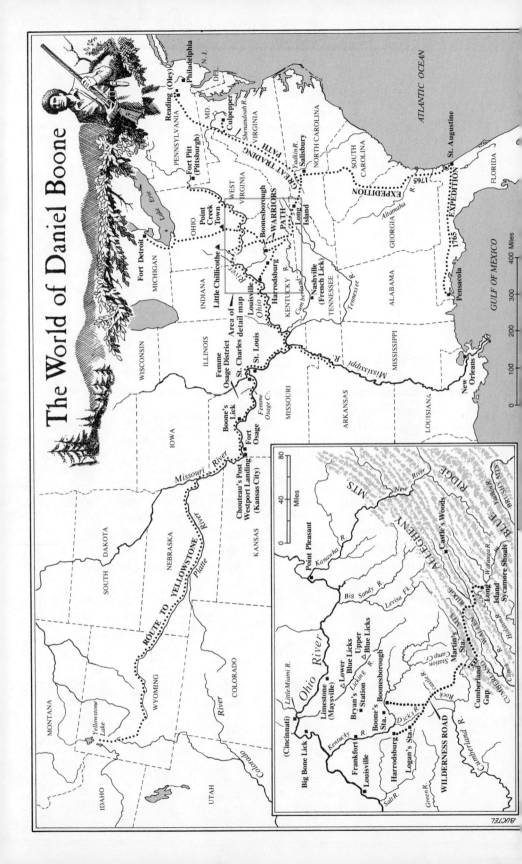

The World of Daniel Boone

ATLANTIC OCEAN

GULF OF MEXICO

Reading (Oley) · Philadelphia
PENNSYLVANIA · N.J.
MD. · DEL.
Fort Pitt (Pittsburgh)
Culpeper
VIRGINIA
Shenandoah R.
WEST VIRGINIA
Yadkin R. · Salisbury
NORTH CAROLINA
SOUTH CAROLINA
GREAT TRADING PATH
WARRIORS PATH
Point Creek Town
Boonesborough
Long Island
OHIO
Little Chillicothe
Louisville
Harrodsburg
Kentucky R.
Nashville (French Lick)
Cumberland R.
Tennessee R.
GEORGIA
Altamaha R.
ALABAMA
St. Augustine
FLORIDA
Pensacola
EXPEDITION 1765
INDIANA
Area of St. Charles detail map
MICHIGAN
Fort Detroit
Lake Erie
WISCONSIN
ILLINOIS
St. Louis
Femme Osage District
Boone's Lick
Fort Osage
Femme Osage C.
MISSOURI
Chouteau's Post Westport Landing (Kansas City)
KANSAS
Mississippi R.
ARKANSAS
MISSISSIPPI
LOUISIANA
New Orleans
IOWA
Missouri River
SOUTH DAKOTA
NEBRASKA
Platte River
ROUTE TO YELLOWSTONE
WYOMING
COLORADO
River
MONTANA
Yellowstone Lake
IDAHO
Colorado River
UTAH

400 Miles · 300 · 200 · 100 · 0

Detail map:

MTS.
New River
ALLEGHENY
BLUE RIDGE
BRUSHY MTS.
Yadkin R.
Point Pleasant
Kanawha R.
Big Sandy R.
Levisa Fk.
Castle's Woods
Watauga R.
Holston R.
Long Island
Sycamore Shoals
WILDERNESS ROAD
Ohio River
Little Miami R.
(Cincinnati)
Limestone (Maysville)
Lower Blue Licks
Upper Blue Licks
Licking R.
Bryan's Station
Boone's Sta.
Boonesborough
Castle's R.
Station Camp C.
Martin's Sta.
MALDEN MTS.
CUMBERLAND MTS.
Cumberland Gap
Rock Castle R.
Dick's R.
Big Bone Lick
Kentucky R.
Frankfort
Louisville
Salt R.
Harrodsburg
Logan's Sta.
Green R.
Cumberland R.
Clinch R.

80 · 40 · 0 Miles

BUCHTEL

Foreword

During the War of 1812, when the British were again inspiring Indian raids against the westernmost settlements, a man named Flanders Callaway was forced to flee his Missouri farm. The episode was not unique and would have been lost in history, except that Callaway was Daniel Boone's son-in-law. While Boone led his daughter and grandchildren to safety overland, Callaway filled a canoe with the family belongings and started down the Missouri River. He had not gone far, however, when the heavily loaded boat struck a rock and capsized; Callaway managed to scramble to safety, but lost forever, along with his family's most precious possessions, was Boone's own account of his adventures and personal history, dictated over a long period of time and painstakingly written down by a grandson.

The old frontiersman has had bad luck with those who have sought to convey his life story ever since.

Narratives of Daniel Boone come in two styles. There are those built on a skeleton of fact fleshed out by the authors' flights of fancy; they are the sheerest entertainments, romances of the frontier that were immensely popular in all the decades before movies and television—which, historically, have done no better by Boone. One of the earliest of such works was by a border preacher named Timothy Flint who actually interviewed Boone on several occasions; it was written, as Flint cheerfully conceded, "to sell, not use."

More recently, most Boone literature derives, at least in part, from the pioneering research of Dr. Lyman C. Draper, who made America's first significant collection of frontier manuscripts and reminiscences. Starting in 1838, when he was twenty-three, Draper roved the West for half a century rescuing family records from abandoned cabins and carefully writing down the recollections of aging frontiersmen and their kin, the sum of his incredible effort eventually filling nearly five hundred volumes. Still, it was not until 1939 that a Boone biography largely based on the Draper collection first appeared, a sound and documented work by John Bakeless. There has been no important book about Boone since.

Yet the intense historical scholarship of the past thirty-five years, the extraordinary interest in the Revolutionary frontier sparked by the American bicentennial, has produced more fresh studies toward a definitive Boone biography than had all that intervening period since Draper put up his pen. The present book is an attempt to make use of these new materials, to bring Boone up to date.

I undertook it for the most familiar of reasons—I liked Daniel Boone. I finished it liking him even more. It is true that throughout the writing he refused to stay put for me, never wholly and simply either the daring wilderness scout or the failed land speculator, but a complex amalgam of conflicting daydreams that goaded him into stunning acts both of bravery and foolishness, often at the most inconvenient moment for my narrative. But of course that was my problem, not his.

My debt to Draper and other historians of the nineteenth century will be recognized by the reader. But I also have had the advantage of current historiographic tools and research so that there is considerable material here that appears in a book for the first time; I am the beneficiary of a more reliable psychological concept of what life was like in America between 1734 and 1820 and, perhaps more important, a newly enlightened attitude that permits us to see our national legends as human beings. I *know* Daniel Boone drank whiskey, that during at least one period in his life he lived with an Indian girl, that his wife once bore an illegitimate child—and in 1976 these things can be told.

I have tried to make him real by reckoning with these frailties, this humanity. It has always saddened me that a historical figure as appealing as Daniel Boone had to be lost in legend, mythologized beyond recognition, for his story is more astonishing than any fiction. When he was born, Americans paid obeisance to the English king; by the time he died there was a westering nation called the United States, and it was Boone, foremost among an inspired handful of Long Hunters who opened the land. But it is also true that between the great adventures his life was hard and sometimes demeaning, that in a lusty, acquisitive era he was moved by the same human longings as any other man.

The title of this book derives from the name given to those men who were gone from their homes months, even years at a time, wandering far beyond the frontiers into the great canelands and over the mountains in search of game and adventure. They preferred hunting to plowing corn, but of course they were more than hunters. They were naturalists without knowing the meaning of the word, explorers unaware that they were blazing the westward trails of the unborn nation. As the historian Thomas D. Clark put it, "They were the forerunners of Anglo-American civilization who searched out the courses of streams, tested the quality of the land, learned the location of salt licks, and spied out Indian and game trails."

Daniel Boone was one of them, perhaps the most important, certainly the most interesting.

I would like to say a word about my methods. The Boone tradition is full of tales that stretch the imagination. Although not even Boone scholars are willing to ignore them all, they have come to us circumscribed by the writer's hesitation, labeled as legend and conveyed with a conspiratorial wink, or told in the text and denied in the chapter notes. I have tried not to do that. In almost every case, it seems to me, there is evidence enough on which to base a judgment between what actually happened and what did not. And so I have left out the stories I did not believe in, but offer the others without apology, including those from the less well-known source material and obscure Draper passages that, until now, appear to have gone undiscovered. Obviously I could be mistaken about one or another, but I invite the reader to join me in taking comfort from the certainty that in that lost Boone journal alone there must have been never-to-be-known adventures more fantastic than any that have come to light.

I have also parted company with my predecessors in the matter of Boone's spelling. Having described his meager schooling and quoted an example or two of his uninhibited orthography, I have transcribed the balance of his letters and military orders into serviceable English. I do not see any point in challenging the reader to do this for himself; nor do I want to make a public joke of the earnest efforts of an uneducated man who, for all the tortured spelling, always expressed his written thoughts forcefully and well.

I would like to express my appreciation to those who have offered aid and encouragement in the writing of this book. I must begin with my wife who was with me along every step of the long route I followed retracing Daniel Boone's meanderings; who did the tedious work of poring over the nineteenth-century scripts of Draper, Durrett, Shane and the others, searching out items I may have missed, organizing a mountain of books and documentation and suggesting still new sources. Her chronology of Boone's life, year by year and often day by day, has been invaluable to me and, as part of my Boone research now at the New York State Library in Albany, should be useful to Boone scholars of the future. Given her incredible memory, I have no doubt that she now knows more about the facts of Boone's life than I do.

I have had the kindest personal assistance in the public and private libraries of ten states, the Library of Congress in Washington, D.C., and the Public Archives of Canada, and my letters to dozens of others have been given generous attention. My first thanks in this regard go to Dr. Josephine L. Harper, reference archivist at the State Historical Society of Wisconsin, repository of the original Draper manuscripts. Dr. Harper, whose knowledge of the Draper material and other documents of the period is unique, was my first mentor on the Boone research. She gently steered me in all the right directions; she was an unfailing source of information and sound advice, and ultimately helped arrange the microfilming of those Draper volumes I required so that I could complete the writing of this book at home.

At the Filson Club in Louisville, which has a superior collection of historical materials about Kentucky and the colonial frontier, I had the benefit of long conversations with the late Robert Emmett McDowell, then editor of the *Filson Club Historical Quarterly*, and a longtime Boone student. I am indebted to him, and to Evelyn Dale, curator and librarian, now retired, for sharing her expertise and providing patient help.

Sincere thanks, too, to Mrs. Anne McDonnell, librarian of the Kentucky Historical Society, and to Kay Rouse in the publications department; to Sharon Brown McConnell in the John Grant Crabbe Library at Eastern Kentucky University, who provided me with copies of the Tipton papers; to Mrs. Oliver Howard and Mrs. Elizabeth Comfort in the reference library at the State Historical Society of Missouri, who answered my innumerable queries about the many excellent articles in the *Missouri Historical Review*.

I am grateful to Robert W. Allison, MSS Research Specialist of the

Joseph Regenstein Library at the University of Chicago, who was of particular help with the codices and copies from the Durrett Collection; to C. MacKinnon, head of the Research and Inquiries Section of the Public Archives of Canada, for his help with the Haldimand papers; to Mrs. Nancy P. Speers at the Friends Historical Library at Swarthmore College, for answering my questions about the Quaker Meetings to which the Boones belonged in Pennsylvania; to Mrs. Mary Jane Hubler of the Lincoln National Life Foundation; to Robert H. DuVall, Historian of the Boone Family Association; and to Gail A. Jacobson, librarian of the Columbia Greene Community College.

Getting books of the colonial period, most long out of print and some exceedingly rare, was a continuing problem. Martin Brown of the W. K. Stewart Bookstore in Louisville ultimately provided the lion's share of those available for purchase and I herewith express my appreciation for his special efforts. For the others, I am deeply indebted to Mrs. Ethel Gold, reference librarian at the New York Institute of Technology, whose expert knowledge of the vast and, to me, mysterious interlibrary loan system produced books I was able to track down nowhere else. Thanks, too, to her able assistant, Harrison Stewkesbury, for many kindnesses.

Anyone who has ever had able and intelligent help with the typing of a long manuscript will understand my final acknowledgment of appreciation. It is to my secretary, Mrs. Jean Leith, who typed her way through the many drafts of this manuscript without audible complaint, beginning with my hand-written scrawls that started it all.

Naturally I am hopeful that everyone who was interested enough to help me with this book will think well of it. But it must also be said that if there are errors or other shortcomings in it, the fault is not theirs but mine.

LAWRENCE ELLIOTT
Ghent, N.Y.
April 28, 1975

Come my tan-faced children
Follow well in order, get your weapons ready,
Have you your pistols? Have you your sharp-edged axes?
Pioneers! O pioneers!

WALT WHITMAN

PENNSYLVANIA

The Boones: Moving West

In the year 1717, a Devonshire Quaker named George Boone set out across the Atlantic with his family to make a new life in America. He was fifty-one years old and had already spent an eighteenth-century lifetime in one English west country village or another, a simple weaver, seemingly neither more nor less content with his lot than his neighbors. But until the day he sailed, George Boone had never been content. He was a dissenter—a restless, unfulfilled man constantly reaching out for a freedom just beyond his grasp.

Fifteen years before, he had quit the Church of England to become a member of the Religious Society of Friends—a Quaker. It was the act of a brave and independent spirit, for the established authority looked with understandable exasperation on a sect that refused to take oaths or bear arms and that addressed everyone, even the nobility, as "thee" or "thou."

But not even this Quaker equality, and the assumption that no man needed another to intercede with God, was enough to appease George Boone's undefined longings. Something kept tugging at him, souring the peace that other men found in a respected trade and a good home, something, though he may not have known it, that ran in his blood.

He began to hear tales of a haven for Quakers in America, in the colony founded by William Penn. Though harried for his beliefs, Penn had become one of the very few Friends to be tolerated, thanks in part to the influence of his father as the King's admiral. When the elder Penn died in 1681, King Charles II, out of regard for the "memorie and meritts" of the late Admiral—and in settlement of the sixteen thousand pounds owed him in back salary—gave the son a huge land grant in America. It consisted of 28 million acres and came to be named Pennsylvania.

A lust for land—to beguile Boones westward for generations to come—had taken strong hold of George Boone. The extravagant size of Pennsylvania, largely unsettled, stirred his imagination. He had ambitions for himself and his sons. And in Pennsylvania it was also said that every man was the equal of every other and for all men there was justice and freedom.

But even more than this opportunity, the thing that would ultimately draw George Boone across the sea was his innate wanderlust. His Norman ancestors had left their homeland in the time of William the Conqueror for the Devon coast, which then thrust out toward the westernmost limits of the known world. Now the world's horizons had expanded again—America!—and again fired that Boone passion to move on.

To understand all this about George Boone is already to know a great deal about his grandson, Daniel Boone.

Thousands envisioned themselves in the New World but only a handful ever went. For most, to have dreamed the dream was adventure enough. America beckoned, yes, but America was a long and hazardous sea journey away. And what if the glowing stories one heard about it were not true?

George Boone clung to his dream for seven years. He lived then in a village called Bradninch, near the county town of Exeter. He was of hardy stock—a family Bible records that his mother lived to the age of eighty and "never had an aching bone or a decayed tooth." Alone, he would have sailed at once. But he had nine children, two of them still infants. Nor did he presently have the money to pay for such a voyage. But in 1712 he made a first commitment: he sent his three eldest children, George, Sarah and Squire, to see America and to report to him its possibilities.

His children's letters, and others that now came to George Boone's notice, were full of enthusiasm. They said that good land could be had for the cost of a survey and a quitrent of a penny an acre; a hundred pounds in cash would buy five thousand acres outright.

> Because one may hold as much property as one wishes and pay when one wishes, everybody hurries to take up property. The farther the Germans and English cultivate the country the farther the Indians retreat. They are

agreeable and peaceable. . . . . In summer one can shoot a deer, dress the skin, and wear pants from it in twenty-four hours.

That the new land pleased his children was otherwise evident. Sarah soon married and Squire, growing to young manhood, never returned to England, and though George did, he stayed only long enough to urge his father to join them. But still Boone stayed, biding his time. Soon the youngest children would be grown enough to bear the rigors of the crossing. Though the woolen trade had fallen off, he was managing to accumulate some small capital, and he needed to prepare himself spiritually, too. Early in 1717, he wrote out and signed a remarkable public confession, preserved in the Devon Hall of Records:

> Dear Friends, being duly sensible of my transgressions and sins against God, I do therefore after a long time make my humble confession. . . . From this my wickedness—which was the keeping of wild company and drinking by which I sometimes became guilty of drunkenness—I fell into another gross evil, by which the honour due unto marriage was lost, for the marriage bed was defiled. Oh, what shall I say, Lord, wash me and cleanse me, I beseech thee.

That summer, George Boone, his wife Mary, and their six remaining children went on foot to the port city of Bristol, a matter of some seventy miles. There he paid out thirty-five pounds, the cost of six full fares and two half-fares, for the passage to America. When the "next good wind and weather" came on August 17, the Boones set sail for the New World.

In the first years of the eighteenth century, the white population of the English colonies in North America numbered fewer than three hundred thousand. It was a thin strand of humanity set down in the wilderness, a scattering of souls strung out between Nova Scotia and the Carolinas and contained in a span of land that nowhere reached more than fifty miles from the seacoast or some navigable river. Beyond, to the west, there rose the great barrier spine of the Appalachian Mountains, and beyond that a vast and little-known country claimed by the French.

But the tide of immigration was rising. There were three cities with at least ten thousand inhabitants, and a dozen other fast-growing towns. A heady sense of promise emanated from this New World, dreams of a fresh start, fortunes lying in wait. Some were lured by gaudy tales of adventure and discovery. Others came searching for a land where they could practice their religion freely. And a goodly number, criminals, vagrants, paupers and prostitutes, came because even the most arduous manner of existence seemed preferable to the one they were leaving behind.

Life *was* hard in America, and sometimes dangerous. Whatever it was the immigrants sought, not one in ten found it in the towns. Adventure, cheap land, independence—all that began where the King's highways ended. And so despite the risks, nearly all moved out toward the farther settlements and beyond, following a buffalo trace out in the back country. And there, sensing the promise that had brought them, they built a cabin and began clearing the virgin land, tree by tree. Nowhere in the silent surrounding wilderness was there any assurance against marauding Indians, nor much organized defense when the Indians struck.

The Boones landed on this alien shore after an eight-week nightmare of a voyage. The hot, overcrowded holds had been rank with the smell of vomit, the water barely potable and the salt meat putrid. But the Boones survived and landed in Philadelphia, "600 miles nearer the sun," in William Penn's exuberant words, on October 10, 1717.

Carrying the few household goods they had been able to bring, they went first to the community of Abington, just north of the city, where Squire and young George awaited them, and spent the winter in nearby North Wales. But George Boone could see that the best land was already spoken for; in the spring of 1718, the Boones moved on again, settling some fifty miles west in Oley Township, a Quaker stronghold on the Schuylkill River, where Sarah and her husband, Jacob Stover, had established themselves. There, with very nearly the last of his money, George Boone bought four hundred acres of land.

The earliest settlers had come only a few years before and even the cleared land was studded with stumps and boulders. But there were fish in the fresh-running streams and a plentiful supply of game.

Soon George Boone built a good sound log house. He became a founder of the Oley Monthly Meeting and gave the land for a burial ground and the first meeting house; as a prominent member of the little community, he was chosen to be Justice of the Peace. Later, when new land divisions were made and a separate township cut from the southern portion of Oley, it was named Exeter after the county town near his home in the old country.

Squire Boone, the second son, had been taken with a girl named Sarah Morgan in North Wales and had remained behind. In 1720, having observed the decent interval of courtship prescribed by Quaker custom, and a convocation having certified his "Clearness from Other Women," he married her. Squire was then nearly twenty-four years old, "a man grown to but small stature," and his bride was four years younger, with black hair and the snapping black eyes of the Welsh. In accordance with the tradition of the Friends, there was no minister; the austere ceremony is described in its entirety in the *Gwynedd Friends Meeting Book*:

> At a solemn assembly of ye people called Quakers . . . the said Squire Boone took the said Sarah Morgan by the hand (and) did in a solemn manner declare that he took her to be his wife, promising to be unto her a faithful and loving husband, until death should separate them, and then and there in the said assembly the said Sarah Morgan did likewise declare.

Afterward, a certificate of the proceedings was read aloud and signed by each of the thirty-nine witnesses. Among them was the bride's brother, Daniel, for whom the sixth of eleven children eventually born to the couple was named.

For a time the young married couple continued to live on rented land in North Wales where Squire Boone worked as a weaver and blacksmith, and did some farming. But he was his father's son—he moved several times in search of a better life—and by 1730, he had settled on a farm adjoining the Boone tract in Oley. In the spring he planted a small crop.

When Sir William Penn came to Pennsylvania in 1700, the resolute old Quaker got down on his knees and gave "thanks to God for such a peaceful and excellent shelter in the wilderness." The proprietor of a domain as large as England itself, Penn could have become an American feudal lord, but he had a higher vision. He framed a government that was "free to the people under it, where the Laws rule, and the People are a Party to those Laws." Pennsylvania became the first social order in a thousand years to afford equality to different nationalities and different religions under the same government. And Pennsylvania set a standard for the nation.

In Oley Township, where the Boones were thriving, German Mennonites, Swedish Lutherans, Scotch-Irish Presbyterians, Huguenots and Moravians all lived in comparative harmony alongside the Quaker majority from the British Isles. And the friendship extended by Penn was accepted, as well, by still another immigrant group—a band of Shawnee Indians from the Illinois country.

Then, in May 1728, trouble flared. A misunderstanding over some meat led to angry words and suddenly the tentative friendship between alien races was shattered. Shots were fired; a Shawnee brave fell wounded. Soon the district was swept by panicky rumors of an imminent Indian attack. Forbearance was in short supply on the frontier, and fear stifled reason. Before long the whites had worked themselves into such a state that Justice of the Peace George Boone himself had to rush out and save two Indian girls from some hotheads agitated enough to kill them in cold blood. Boone sent an urgent call for help to the Royal Governor in Philadelphia:

> Our Condition at Present looks with a bad Vizard. . . . our Inhabitants are Generally fled (and) there remains about 20 men with me to guard my mill. . . . we are resolved to defend ourselves to ye last Extremity. Wherefore I desire ye Governor & Counsel to Take our Cause into Consideration; And speedily send some Messengers to ye Indians, And some arms and ammunition to us, with some strength allso, otherways we shall undoubtedly perish and our province laid desolate and destroyed.

This time it did not come to a fight. But George Boone's allegiance to his Quaker faith was undergoing new strains on the harsher soil of this frontier world. In England, the Friends' pacifism had seemed godly; at the edge of the wilderness, in his view, it was delusive and downright dangerous. The stanchest members of the Oley Meeting had fled the Indian threat rather than take up arms in violation of their principles. The defense of their community was left to those few brethren, mainly George Boone and his sons, who would not be run off their land.

There were other trials. Though the Friends were a good and compassionate people, they held their own faith under stern precepts and this led to difficulties for the lusty Boones. "There were several notices of *male Boones* in the records, as being occasionally unruly members, some being over belligerent and self-willed, calling for the Meeting to deal with them. . . ." George Boone had once been obliged to acknowledge his forwardness in giving his consent to John Webb to keep company with his daughter. The Friends' objection to Webb, a Philadelphian, was that he was not one of them. But as he seemed otherwise worthy, and perhaps not wishing to further test the doughty father of the clan, the Meeting relented and gave its blessing. Webb and Mary Boone were married and an uneasy truce prevailed.

In 1733, George Boone built a large stone house, befitting his station, next to the log house he'd lived in for thirteen years. Soon after, his son Squire was building himself a more substantial home too. He and Sarah now had five young ones and were expecting a sixth the following winter. One of his near neighbors was Mordecai Lincoln, and there were to be close ties between the Boones and Lincolns of Berks County, including five intermarriages. Mordecai's grandson, Abraham, would become a warm friend of Squire's son, Daniel. And it was Abraham's grandson who became the sixteenth president.

Daniel Boone was born on November 2, 1734. In boyhood he was particularly close to his mother, who seems to have known from the first that there was something different about her Daniel, that certain behavior for which she would have punished the other children was instinctive and unchangeable in him. He wandered. He turned fretful under confinement. At the monthly Meeting of the Friends, he stayed only as long as she held him by the hand; when she let go he disappeared, though no one ever saw him leave.

Once, when an epidemic of smallpox struck in Oley Township, the Boone children were kept at home to minimize the danger of exposure. Daniel, perhaps six years old, bore the restraint only a short time, then persuaded his older sister Elizabeth that if they caught the disease they would be free to come and go as they pleased. The two promptly slipped away to a neighbor's house, got into bed with a stricken child and returned home, still undiscovered, to await their own eruption of red spots. It came soon enough, and Sarah Boone wondered aloud, how could such a thing have happened? She had been so careful to protect the children. And Daniel, now feeling guilty as well as sick, told her. "Thee naughty boy," she said without anger, "why did thee not tell me before so I could have had thee better prepared?" And she fell to work nursing her brood.

Daniel Boone was lastingly touched by the Quaker spirit. Unlike most on the frontier, he would never be possessed by the "war spirit." But neither would he suffer indignity lightly. There are accounts of fistfights in which he defended what to others were the odd ways of the Friends—that they dyed their clothes black; that they said "thee" and "thou" instead of "you." In one of these fights he acquired a loose front tooth that wobbled in its socket ever after.

One summer day, two neighbor girls came to fetch some fresh shad that his mother had offered to their family. Returning, they spied young Daniel dozing under a tree. There was a whispered conference, then the pan containing the slimy fish entrails, already separated out for their dogs, was dumped over the boy's head. It was an unwise move. The girls enjoyed only an instant of howling glee before Daniel sprang to his feet, bloodied both their noses and sent them home wailing. When their mother came storming up to the Boone kitchen to protest that "this is unchivalrous conduct, madam," Sarah Boone, though the most devout Quaker in the family, rose to her son's defense, her black eyes flashing: "If thee has not brought up thy daughters to better behavior, it is high time they were taught good manners. And if Daniel had given them a lesson, I think that in the end it will do them no harm. And I have only to add that I bid thee good day."

It was as though he were born to the outdoors. Sent to chop wood, he made the ax fly, even when he was so small that the handle stood almost as tall as he did. He walked miles without tiring and swam the first time he tried. He could outrun his cousins and, slender as he was, down every one of them when they wrestled. If they shot at targets with bow and arrows, Daniel scored best. If they played "Hunt the Indian," Daniel led the hunters; when it was his turn to be the Indian, he always got away. No mother worried when the children were in the woods—Daniel knew the way home.

It is said that a few years later, when he and his friends were old enough to carry rifles, they once surprised a wildcat sunning on the river bank. It turned with a snarl to charge and the others fled in all directions. But Daniel stood his ground, peering over the rifle sight, waiting. At the last moment, in the split second before the wildcat left the ground to spring, he pulled the trigger and shot it dead in its tracks.

The best friend of his boyhood was Henry Miller, who was two or three years older and was apprenticed in Squire Boone's smithing shop. Daniel was put under his instruction to learn the repair of rifles and traps, essential skills of the frontier. There is evidence that the two also found time for pranks. One spring, townsmen who had voiced objection to the boys' lively spirits found their wagon wheels on the barn roof or dangling from a tree.

When they were a bit older, they learned of a frolic in a distant settlement. Quaker stricture forbade their attendance but they slipped a horse out of Squire's barn and set off anyway. Returning, they tried to coax the poor animal into a leap over some sleeping cows. The horse stumbled, fell hard and broke its neck. The boys were shaken but worried less about their bruises than what would happen if they were discovered. With fumbling fingers they undid the saddle and carried it back to the barn, then slipped away to their beds. For weeks after Squire Boone puzzled aloud over how his horse could have gotten out of a locked barn and broken its neck in a fenceless field.

Old George Boone, the patriarch, died at the age of seventy-eight, on February 2, 1744. In keeping with Quaker custom there was no gravestone but his memory was kept nonetheless: the family Bible noted that "when grandfather died he left 8 children, 52 grandchildren and 10 great-grand-children living, in all 70, being as many persons as the house of Jacob which came into Egypt."

By this time, Exeter had begun to take on the feel, if not the look, of an established community. The farmers were shipping sizable quantities of grain up the Schuylkill River to market in Philadelphia, and in return got gunpowder, wagons and a few delicacies like chocolate to brighten their meals of pork and wheat-flour pudding or, in season, venison and wild turkey. But the proximity of Indian villages, the constant presence of the Shawnee and Delawares who came to trade or just pass the time, made it plain that Exeter was still hard by the frontier.

Daniel Boone's earliest memories were of Indians calling on the family, squatting in a cluster outside the stone house and talking with words and hand signs, and of the Quaker neighborliness shown them by the elder Boones. Indians fascinated him. He knew from the first that they were better at tracking game than the best white hunters; he sensed that the white man was an alien creature in the woods but that an Indian, like some sleek and powerful animal, was in his natural element. Without even being aware of it he began following them, studying their ways, asking them questions. How did they make a fire without flint or steel? What tree bark made the best overnight shelter?

All his life he would find it easier to talk to Indians than to most of his own people, and the Indians responded to his openness with affectionate regard. Soon he was learning Indian hunting techniques and the uniquely Indian way of thinking, their reactions to the countless challenges of the forest, that later enabled him to predict with stunning accuracy what they were likely to do in a given situation.

The Indians were taken by this guileless boy. Other whites, even the best-natured, tolerated the red men but were forever trying to convert them to the white man's ways. But the young buck with the wide mouth seemed to regret that he hadn't been born Indian. And so they answered his endless questions and shared their woodland secrets, as though he were one of their own. His neighbors naturally thought this all very peculiar. When one asked Daniel why he spent so much time trailing after Indians, he replied that they had taught him to walk through the woods so that now, retracing his steps, he could not find even a single track. Well, why was that important? Daniel thought the answer obvious and said no more.

His Uncle George, who did some surveying, also had to contend with Daniel. When he was out marking boundaries or laying out lots the boy dogged his footsteps. Before long Daniel could place the flag, draw the chain without getting off the mark, and blaze the trees. He could also make a readable map and figure the enclosed acreage.

Only his formal learning was wanting. Dr. Lyman C. Draper, who spent a lifetime amassing a treasure of Boone biographical data, summarized Daniel's education in a single paragraph:

> When he was about fourteen years of age, his brother Samuel, nearly seven years his senior, married a very amiable and intelligent young lady named Sarah Day, who taught her young brother-in-law Daniel to read and spell a little, and in a rude manner to form letters. He could at first do little more than write his own name in an uncouth and mechanical way. To these humble beginnings, he added something as he grew up, by his own practical application. . . . His compositions bear the marks of a strong common sense, yet as might be expected, exhibiting defects in orthography, grammar and style, by no means infrequent.

This was a graceful way of saying that though Boone could express himself forcefully in letters and military orders, his written style remained wildly at variance with all known rules. Even his Uncle John, a teacher who tried to temper Daniel's heedless spelling and sentence structure, could not hold his attention indoors. Soon he confessed to the boy's father that the task seemed hopeless. Unperturbed, Squire replied, "Let the girls do the spelling; Daniel will do the shooting."

Thus, of all George Boone's fifty-two grandchildren, Daniel was easily the least schooled. In middle life he could certify a legal record by noting at the bottom, "This was coppyed by the Clark and is awl Wright. Daniel Boone." But unhappily for a number of historical societies still cherishing segments of ancient tree bark with what is said to be Boone's carved inscriptions—"D. Boon killa bar on this tree 1773," or, "D. Boon cilled a bar on tree in the year 1760"—he did know how to spell his name properly. The wide-ranging woodsman, it is true, often cut his graffiti into trees from Virginia to the Yellowstone. But his undisputed signatures on letters, deeds and claims make clear that he always wrote his family name with an "e" at the end.

There is also no basis for the legend that he once taught school in Kentucky, thereby supporting his family through some hard winter months. He used to tell his children that he never spent a single day inside a schoolhouse, in any capacity, and there is no reason to doubt their recollections.

The plain fact is that Daniel Boone's head and heart were pledged to the open land and he was only really at peace when he was alone in the astonishing forest. There he was a most earnest student indeed. He followed the Indian paths or deer paths or no path at all to unfamiliar streams and surprising meadows. He learned to move silently through the tangled growth, the way the Indians did, so he could hear the slap of a beaver's tail on the water, and to lie hidden and still on the downwind side of a pond so that deer, buffalo and even bears came almost within touching distance to drink. He crossed the Schuylkill to climb Flying Hill, named for the flocks of wild turkeys that gathered there in early autumn. He seems to have been born with a longing for virgin woods and the farthest reaches of land, for a screen of trees to put between himself and the tedious chores of farming and blacksmithing, for an unending wilderness in which neither the sight nor the sound of other humans could touch him. Perhaps it was a singular expression of that same spirit of independence that brought the Boones to America. Whatever it was, it was in the very essence of his being and it never went away. And he was only ever unhappy when out of some mistaken notion that he must learn to live like other men, he betrayed it.

Squire Boone continued to farm his land and to work as a weaver and blacksmith, even turning his hand to gunsmithing. In 1744, when Daniel was ten, he bought a twenty-five acre grassland about four miles away in which to pasture his cattle. As that was too far to bring them in each night, Daniel was designated herdsman, with his mother to do the milking and keep a tiny summer cabin for the two of them; his sister Elizabeth would look after the others. So one day in late spring they set out, Sarah leading a packhorse and Daniel driving the cows from behind. They did not return until autumn. Every week or so one of the Boone boys brought news of the family and took back the cheese and butter Sarah churned.

So Daniel spent the next six summers, looking after the bony, barely domesticated herd. It was a glorious, unrestrained time and he never forgot it. All day he wandered the woods and hillsides, returning at dusk to drive the cows to the cabin for milking. His first hunting weapon was a sapling with a cluster of gnarled roots at the end that he'd shaved smooth and learned to throw with such accuracy that he could kill a rabbit at ten yards. When he was twelve, his father gave him a rifle, a short barreled European model. He took to it at once, his skill as a marksman almost as natural to him as breathing, and from that time on he became the main provider of wild game for his family.

The game was abundant. It was a time when wildcats and buffalo still roved eastern Pennsylvania, and the forests and stream banks abounded with bears, deer, beaver and otter. He prided himself on his speed in cleaning and dressing a turkey and in early fall, when turkeys were fat and plentiful, he loved to cook one outdoors for his mother. He would hang it by the neck over a fire, turning it with a stick so that it roasted evenly on all sides. Under it he put a piece of curved bark to catch the drippings; with this he basted the turkey.

"Where did thee learn to do that?" Sarah once asked him.

"An Indian told me," he replied.

Through those six summers Daniel grew closer to his mother than did any of her other children. Sarah Boone forthrightly admitted that he was her favorite, and he responded to her Quaker calm and clemency. Some say that his inability to hate another human, even an Indian and even in the face of terrible provocation, came from Sarah.

Yet the other edge of his character would not be denied. His yen to wander was irrepressible and much as he loved his mother, and much as he later loved his wife, that came first. It is not hard to understand that a boy dazzled by nature's wild places and creatures and fascinated by the peculiarities of animals and birds as Daniel Boone was, would sometimes lose interest in a placid herd of cattle. Once he forgot them altogether, and his mother, as well. It was evening and he failed to return with the cows. Sarah fetched and milked them, busied herself churning butter, and tried not to be concerned about her thirteen-year-old alone in some distant darkening forest.

When he did not return that night or the following morning, a worried Sarah Boone walked back to the town to get help. A search party was quickly organized and set off across the Oley hills, continuing south toward Neversink Mountain. They found no trace of Daniel that day but the next, traveling still further afield, they spied a plume of smoke rising into the clear summer sky. It was nearly dark by the time they reached it and found there a sturdy bark shelter. Daniel was inside, sitting on a bearskin and roasting a piece of fresh meat at the fire. The rest of the neatly skinned bear hung nearby.

Was he lost? they asked him.

No, he knew where he was—on the south shoulder of the mountain, nine miles from the cabin.

Well, what was he doing there? And what about the grief he had caused his mother?

Oh. He regretted that, but he had been tracking the bear and thought he might as well take it before turning back. And look—now there was fresh meat for all!

By the time he was fifteen he was the best shot in Exeter and his prowess as a woodsman was known across the township. By observation and trial and error, by persistent self-reliance, he had taught himself to live congenially in the wilds and to profit from its bounty. From early spring to late fall, one eye on the cows, he kept the family table supplied with meat. In the winter, when the furs of the beaver and otter were heavy and rich, he was off trapping. Twice he went with Henry Miller to Philadelphia where he exchanged his pelts for gunpowder, flints and hunting knives, enough for himself, his father and all his brothers.

Once again the Boones fell out of harmony with the Friends. Sarah, Daniel's eldest sister, had fallen in love with a young man named Wilcoxen, and in 1742 married him though he was not a Quaker. She was promptly censured by the Exeter Meeting for "marrying out," as were her mother and father for allowing it, and all three expressed contrition. But Squire Boone said "that he was in a great streight in not knowing what to do, seeing he was somewhat Sensible that they had been too Conversant before."

That Sarah and her young man had been "too Conversant" was already a community rumor and, if true, a transgression the Meeting could hardly overlook. A committee of Quaker ladies was appointed to look into the question and counting backward, "found the truth of a former suspicion vis., that Sarah Wilcoxen, daughter of Squire Boone, was *with child before she was married.*" The ladies listened solemnly to the paper Sarah "produced to this Meeting condemning the said action," then they expelled her.

It was a trying time for Squire Boone and his wife. Exeter, a small settlement with little enough for diversion, kept few secrets. Nor was Sarah's their only disgrace. "The Boones were active for good," the Meeting book notes around this time, "but sometimes overcome with evil. Strong drink, so common, overcame one or more who had to be dealt with."

Squire began thinking about leaving Pennsylvania. And though trouble with the Friends prodded him, it was not the only reason. His free spirit, his wanderlust, was at large again. He wanted to be where the forest was outside his front door.

The countryside was changing. Even the border towns seemed to be striving to outdo Philadelphia, with yesterday's fancy notions suddenly become tradition and a self-important society laying down rules right and left. Was that why the Boones had come to America—to be told what they would be allowed to do? And still people kept streaming in, thinning the game, taking up the land. The best of it was already gone so that his own children surely would have a hard time finding a decent homestead. His farm would not long support them, for as he used up the richness of the soil, his harvest dwindled.

During those years Daniel remembered sitting by the hearth while the Boone men gazed into the fire and talked of moving on. Sometimes they discussed the territory to the west, for it was known to be an open and untouched land. But it was otherwise uninviting: between rose the stark Allegheny Mountains and, beyond, Indian tribes whose hostility to white settlers had already been bared in blood. There was talk too of another place, to the southwest, the Yadkin River valley of North Carolina. It was a long way, perhaps five hundred miles, but the route followed the valley of the Shenandoah, a natural passageway between the Blue Ridge and the Appalachians. Squire's sister Sarah and her husband Jacob Stover had gone south early on and eventually came to own ten thousand acres in the Valley of Virginia. As for the Yadkin, the Boones had heard that it was a beautiful country with a warm, sunny climate and abundant wild game. There were said to be "so many bears in autumn that common hunters could kill enough to make 2,000–3,000 weight of bear bacon."

Daniel daydreamed of such a journey but his father could not decide. Then in 1747, Israel, the oldest son, also "married out" and was disowned by the Exeter Meeting. Though the Meeting sent a delegation that included his own brother James to speak to him about "countenancing his son's disorderly marriage," Squire refused to humble himself again. He insisted that there was nothing wrong with the girl other than that she was a "worldling" and he said that his children must marry as they pleased. Half a century before his father had dissented from the Church of England; now Squire Boone braced himself to reject the dissenters.

On March 17, 1748, the Friends gathered to invoke the inevitable judgment:

Whereas Squire Boone hath of late fallen from that good order and Discipline of Friends. . . . Therefore, this meeting thinks themselves engaged to give public testimony against him as not being a Member with us until such time as we may be sensible of his coming to a Godly sorrow in himself.

Thereafter the name of Squire Boone is never again mentioned in the minutes of the Exeter Friends.

Now Squire decided to go. There was a family conference, and the lure of the new frontier won over two of Daniel's cousins, John and George Boone, and the apprentice, Henry Miller. Thereafter Squire busied himself disposing of his land, his holdings, and everything that was too bulky to fit into a covered wagon. That he had as yet no fixed idea about where they were bound is made clear by the fact that Sarah, who clung to her faith, armed herself with letters from the Exeter Friends attesting to her merits and orderliness and addressed to Meetings in Maryland, Virginia and North Carolina. But they set off bravely on the morning of May 1, 1750, some wagons and a straggle of cows. The children rode, legs dangling, and the women walked alongside. Most of the older boys were at the rear, shooing the cattle along, but Daniel was up front with the men.

Many apart from the Boone kin were sorry to see them go. Among these was John Lincoln, son of Mordecai, who had been a near neighbor to Squire Boone and a good friend. It may be that the sight of the little caravan wending its way westward through the town first planted in young Lincoln's mind the notion that would eventually persuade him to take his own family to Virginia, just as, years after, John's son, Abraham, would follow his friend Daniel Boone into Kentucky. And there were voices: "Goodbye. Godspeed."

They crossed the Susquehanna and continued west to Carlisle, then followed the crudely cut road south into the Cumberland valley. Beneath the bluffs where the Shenandoah joins the Potomac, at a ford that was to be consecrated in history by the abolitionist John Brown and by the bloody battles of the Civil War, a ferryman named Robert Harper took them across into Virginia.

Daniel Boone walked in advance of the jouncing wagons as they pushed on, between the dark mountains and the sloping forests, camping, breaking camp and moving on again. He carried his long Pennsylvania rifle cradled in his arms and his sharp blue eyes searched out the trail and the slopes, watching for signs of game or any stirring in the brush that might give them a moment's warning against an Indian ambush. He was six months short of his sixteenth birthday, a boy of medium height and slim build, with his brown hair tied behind in a neat club. But the people had confidence in him; even the older men listened when he spoke. And so his heart soaring at the great adventure, he led them on into the Shenandoah valley.

NORTH CAROLINA

II

The Pride of Kings

Sometimes they stayed a few days with friends, for a number of Pennsylvania families had settled along the route. When they reached Opequon Creek near Winchester, where a Quaker Meeting had been established some years before, they unpacked the wagons. They had covered a fair distance and as the land seemed generous and the people hospitable the Boones decided to stay on for a time.

Squire set up as a blacksmith and probably farmed some rented land as well. As for Daniel, he and his friend Henry Miller were off roving the country, stalking game all the way to the headwaters of the Yadkin, more than a hundred and fifty miles to the southwest. They did well—after a year's hunting and trapping they took their catch back to Philadelphia and sold it for thirteen hundred dollars. But they stayed on in the city and in three weeks of wenching and merrymaking spent every penny. Daniel, who returned laden with gifts for his family, does not seem to have regretted the spree, although he never went on another. But he would live a long lifetime impervious to the craft of money management, always confident that as long as there was game in the forest he could recoup any loss, repay any debt.

That was not Henry Miller's way. He was nearing twenty years of age and it soon became clear that Philadelphia had been only a final frolic before he settled down. Long afterward one of his descendants told of this turning point in the lives of the two friends:

> Our grandfather told Boone if he chose he could go on hunting and trapping—but for his part he intended to quit and settle down, make money and keep it, which he did.

When in the autumn of 1751 Squire decided to move on—partly because of his son's enthusiastic description of the Yadkin's bounty—the boyhood comrades said goodbye. Henry remained in Augusta County, there to found the first iron works in Virginia and to become very rich indeed. And the Boones took up their journey.

In 1746, it was estimated that "there were not above one hundred fighting men in all western North Carolina." Five years later, when the Boones arrived, there were twenty-five thousand in the colony and Acting Governor Matthew Rowan was reporting that "Inhabitants flock in here daily, mostly from Pennsylvania and other parts of America, and some directly from Europe." It was a land to stir a pioneer's blood. Rising up from the coastal plain, sheltered by the thickly forested Blue Ridge to the west, it stretched away in luxuriant grasses, fertile, free of the rocks that plagued the farmers of Pennsylvania. Cold clear streams pounding down from the mountains nourished the bottomland and the canebrakes, those great overspreading stands of reed thickets twelve, even sixteen feet high, so rich in wild game.

This was a country! Squire Boone was elated by what he saw as his little party moved down the east bank of the Yadkin. His Daniel had not told him any tall tales. On a height above what is still known as Boone's Ford they took shelter in a cave, their first home in North Carolina. There they spent the winter, and in spring built a crude cabin. They were squatters for a year or more; it would be that long before Squire had the cash to buy some land of his own.

A considerable part of that cash came from Daniel's rifle and trapline. His older brothers were now married and Squire preoccupied with blacksmithing and scratch farming. Daniel was left to do the thing he loved best, to lose himself in the hunt, and he turned those next months to good account. Border farming yielded a subsistence living at best, but a clever hunter with a packhorse or two could come out of the woods with a handsome profit. Otter and beaver furs brought a good price and a buck deer, prized for the leather that went into men's breeches, was as good as currency: One buck would buy a dollar's worth of salt or gunpowder anywhere and eventually the words "buck" and "dollar" came to mean the same thing on the frontier. Daniel, who brought down his share of deer, soon became a familiar figure at the trading post in the market town of Salisbury, some log cabins and the courthouse, twenty miles away.

A story is told of his arriving there one spring afternoon, his horse laden with the catch from his winter trapline. Two men loitering outside asked if he'd care to join them in a shooting match, with perhaps a small wager to lend. interest. That sounded friendly, Daniel said, and the three went to a nearby field where, to the apparent chagrin of one of the men, Daniel soon won ten dollars shooting at tree targets. "Look here," that one said, "I'll bet you a hundred dollars against your furs on one more shot." "If you're sure you want to," Daniel replied.

The man was quite sure. It was the old story of the country bumpkin as intended victim. The target cut into the next tree had been prearranged, with a bullet hole emplanted only a hairbreadth from the bull's-eye. All the townsman had to do was pull his shot wide and claim the prepared one.

Daniel dutifully congratulated him on the shot. But he was not taken in. He had seen the muzzle swerve and knew at once that he had been assigned a fool's role. Putting his rifle to his shoulder with particular care, he drove his bullet straight through the bull's-eye.

That month, April 1753, Squire was able to buy 640 acres on Buffalo Creek from agents of the Earl of Granville. By grant of the King, Lord Granville owned all the northern half of the colony, twenty-six thousand of the fifty-two thousand square miles that comprise the present state of North Carolina, although he had never set foot on its soil. Even after Squire bought the land, the deed stipulated that he was obliged to pay Granville an annual quitrent of more than eight pounds, that he must hand back three-quarters of any gold or silver mined there, and that if he failed to clear and cultivate at least twenty acres every three years, the sale was voided and his money forfeit. These were typical conditions set by the lords-proprietor and they would be fuel for the revolutionary fires.

Meanwhile, in December Squire bought another 640-acre tract. Here, on the west side of the Yadkin, on land that rose up gently from the generous bottomland of a lively creek, he built the family home. It was characteristic of the more substantial border cabins of the time: a single story, single room structure about twenty feet square built of faced logs with a pitched roof, deep fireplace, oak floors, the whole curtained in two for sleeping.

In season, the business of clearing the land—felling trees, digging up stumps, chopping down canebrakes—back-breaking work even in the amenable North Carolina country, engaged the attention of all the Boone men. Daniel was required to participate at harvest time too, and to ride the farm's produce into Salisbury for sale. But anyone could see his heart was never in that sort of drudgery. In rainy weather, when it was not possible to work the fields and other men were glad to stay inside, Daniel would take his rifle and slip away into the woods. Deer was the most important game, not only for its hide but for the venison that could be cured with saltpeter or cut into "jerk," small strips of meat smoked over a low fire for preservation. Along the creek bottom near the Boone home a heavy stand of beech trees dropped a carpet of nuts that attracted countless bears. Buffalo came regularly to the salt licks. And fish were so plentiful at the shoals above Dutchman Creek that Daniel fed shad, mullet and catfish to the entire community. In all, he was in the woods more than he was at home.

His reputation as a marksman and hunter was now well founded. Someone said that he could lick a tick off a bear's snout at a hundred yards, and he took to calling his long Pennsylvania rifle Ticklicker. Among the Catawba Indians of the Yadkin valley was a sharpshooter named Saucy Jack who was galled that the whites talked only of Daniel Boone's prowess as a hunter. Jack fed his frustration with whiskey and one day announced that he was going to track Boone down and kill him. Then they would all know who was the better shot. Daniel was off on a hunting trip at the time but the threat was relayed to Squire and the lapsed old Quaker saw red. "Well," he roared, rushing off in search of Saucy Jack, "if it has come to this, I'll kill first." Luckily the intemperate Catawba was forewarned and fled the valley. But it would not be the last time that Boone's skills incited an Indian's envy.

As they had in Exeter, the Boones became central figures in the emerging homespun society of Rowan County. They were not so prosperous as the Carters or the Bryans but were esteemed as good hunters and ambitious farmers. Morgan Bryan, a Quaker who had also emigrated from Pennsylvania, was the most prominent settler on the Yadkin. His land holdings stretched into two counties and though past eighty years of age, he continued active in the management of the sprawling Bryan settlement and in county affairs. He took a liking to the Boones—no doubt his influence was responsible for Squire's appointment as a justice of the Rowan County Court—and encouraged the several intermarriages between the two families that soon began and were to have such a profound effect on frontier America.

In 1754, Daniel's sister Mary married William Bryan. It was at this wedding that Daniel, now twenty years old, first saw Morgan Bryan's granddaughter, Rebecca, a slender slip of a girl, fifteen years old, dark-haired, dark-eyed. Her likeness would linger in his mind through some difficult days just ahead. He didn't speak to her that first day, but he didn't forget her. After the wedding there was a shooting match. Daniel won—he almost always did—and perhaps Rebecca remembered him too.

One drowsy afternoon that summer, a session of the County Court at Salisbury was gaveled into abrupt recess when someone brought word that a Shawnee band was attacking a settlement not two miles away. The whites and some friendly Catawbas rushed over to drive the raiders off, killing five of them. But it was a bad omen that the rifles they took from the dead braves, and some beads and looking glasses, were all of French manufacture. It meant that the Indians and white settlers alike were now pawns in the struggle between France and England that had fumed and flared for the past sixty-five years. At issue was the question of which nation, language and culture was to dominate North America; which of two mutually exclusive ambitions for the empty land—a dynamic, proliferating society of loyal subjects abroad, or an Arcadian wilderness— would prevail.

The British had fostered the colonization of the eastern coastline mindful that the mother country would reap the rewards of a flourishing commerce with her overseas dominion. They did little to dampen the colonists' westward urge and eventually the Pennsylvanians and Virginians who had been confined to tidewater by the mountain barrier began moving up the eastern slopes and finding a way through the gaps, filtering at last into the western country.

On the far side of the mountains were the French, claiming all that immense territory known as Louisiana that reached out from the Appalachians to the Rockies. But the French king, Louis XV, had no desire to build a colonial empire in the New World. His interest could be summed up in a single word: fur. There were no expanding colonies and the French presence was barely felt in the lonely land, their empire in America fragilely founded on a string of isolated strongholds and trading posts between New Orleans and Quebec. Only the yellow Bourbon lily on the white flags flying above the stockades connected the fur-rich regions of the Mississippi, the Ohio and the St. Lawrence, and commanded the passage between.

The French strategy was plain: they had to keep the Ohio valley open at all costs; the British had to be contained on the seaboard side of the mountains. If their colonial settlements kept pushing westward, they would drive out the wildlife; they would cut the lucrative trade route in two. And then what was to prevent them from turning north into French Canada?

As France and England moved inexorably toward war over a country neither was destined to possess, the French made an invaluable alliance. The northern Indians feared new settlements along the upper Ohio, too, settlements that were to be hewn right out of the Indian hunting grounds. The French at least left them their land and way of life. It did not take much French persuasion to win the Indians' support, nor much urging to send Shawnee war parties down through the mountains along the mysterious Warrior's Path to inflict bloody punishment on the Catawbas and Cherokees friendly to the white settlers and on the settlements themselves.

So the border raids began. The scout Christopher Gist, returning to his home on the Yadkin after making one of the first explorations of Kentucky, found his family gone. "The Indians had killed five people in the winter near that place," he noted in his journal, "which hastened my wife and children away to Roanoke." Once the Shawnee struck a settlement at Buffalo Creek, close to Squire Boone's land, killing thirteen and taking ten prisoners. No one could know when death in a painted face would come darting from the forest. There were fresh reports of attacks on white settlers at every meeting of the Rowan County Council. Wrote Draper:

> The frowns of war at length fell heavily upon the border settlements. . . .
> Though the kings and courts had no small pride and interest at stake in this
> war of personal ambition, yet the people of the colonies generally had little or
> nothing to gain, and those especially along the frontier had to bear the
> crushing miseries of the contest.

Indian raids were but the shock waves of the closing foreign armies. The war itself would be fought far from the Yadkin, in Canada, and in that contested upper Ohio valley. There, heedless of Indian rights and French claims, the British Board of Trade in 1752 had granted a group of prominent Virginians five hundred thousand acres of rich land conditional on their building a fort and settling a hundred families. In time Governor Robert Dinwiddie sent a patrol under the command of a twenty-one-year-old major of the Virginia militia, George Washington, to warn the French that they were trespassing on English land. The reply, as Major Washington soon reported, was succinct: the French considered the land *theirs*. "They told me, That it was their absolute design to take possession of the Ohio, and by G— they would do it."

He was sent back the following spring with 150 men to garrison an unfinished fort at the Forks of the Ohio. Halfway there he met the retreating construction detachment. They had been driven out by the French, who proceeded to destroy their fort and were building a more substantial one in its place, to be called Fort Duquesne.

To Washington, this was an act of war and he went looking for the enemy. Some fifty miles southeast of the Forks he flushed out a small French reconnaissance force, killing ten and capturing the rest. It was only a preliminary skirmish but Horace Walpole assessed it with stark precision: "The volley fired by a young Virginian in the backwoods of America set the world on fire." A tinderbox of grievances was about to explode, turning North America and Europe into a battleground; the fighting would last nine years and leave a million dead.

Anticipating a strong counterattack, Washington withdrew to a valley grassland and hastily threw up a square log enclosure aptly named Fort Necessity. And there the French and their Indian allies, five hundred strong, struck on a gray, wet morning, pouring round after round into the confined militia. The bloody battle raged all day, the rain pelting down, the toll in dead and wounded mounting until, toward nightfall, Washington yielded. He was granted the honors of war and the following morning the decimated militiamen marched out, colors flying. But they went on foot, their horses having been slain, and carried the wounded in a long line of improvised litters. It was July 4, 1754. The French and Indian War had begun.

Daniel Boone signed up with the North Carolina militia and rode off to camp at Fort Cumberland on the Maryland border. In February 1755, a major general named Edward Braddock arrived there from England to assume command of all His Majesty's forces in America. He was a vain and contentious man, a parade-grounds soldier ever aware that he, who had served with the Coldstream Guards, was now in the company of immigrants. In the face of better advice he was preparing to fight the coming battle with the courtly tactics devised for the open plains of Belgium. When Benjamin Franklin warned him against the danger of an Indian ambush he replied with the arrogance of a man who has spent forty-five of his sixty years in the military and become immune to any other influence: "The savages may be formidable to your raw American militia; upon the King's regulars and disciplined troops it is impossible they should make any impression." He said that capturing Fort Duquesne, key to the entire upper Ohio valley, could hardly detain him three or four days.

It took all spring to muster the striking force. The British regulars were augmented by seven hundred militiamen, among them the company from North Carolina in which the twenty-one-year-old Daniel Boone served as teamster and blacksmith. Despite the rough country to be traversed, Braddock had scorned the use of packhorses, insisting instead on a great wagon train for supply. The countryside had to be scoured and the farmers intimidated so that he could be furnished with five hundred draft horses and 150 heavy Pennsylvania wagons, to be loaded with baggage, wheat, cannon and ammunition. Early in June the awesome legion, largest ever assembled in North America, lumbered off to war.

George Washington, recently promoted to lieutenant-colonel in the Virginia militia, commanded the colonials. Christopher Gist was lead scout. Another among the Americans was Dr. Thomas Walker, commissary general to the Virginia troops, who had already distinguished himself by his explorations in Kentucky. He had preceded Gist by almost a year and was first to make a detailed record of the journey.

In all America only a handful of whites had ever found a way into the untracked plain called Kentucky, yet there was still a third in Braddock's company. His name was John Findley, a trader now serving as a teamster with a company of Pennsylvanians. In the long evenings, when the expedition ground to a halt and gathered strength for the next day's assault on the blind forests, John Findley invariably drew a campfire crowd with his tales of Kentucky, for its legend haunted the frontier. He said the land was so rich that the Indians grew corn without effort and told how once, unpacking some trading goods in an Indian village, he had thrown aside the dried English bluegrass in which the goods were wrapped and that the grass had sprouted and spread. A man could take a stand and have the game come to him, he said, great herds of deer and buffalo, a veritable treasure in furs and skins just for the taking.

Inevitably some cynic then asked why he was flogging a team of horses in the Pennsylvania wastes instead of spending his riches in Philadelphia. Findley, whose good nature hadn't deserted him though "Death (was) always snapping at his heels and Loss his constant companion," ruefully explained that the trick was to bring the profits home. His always seemed to be seized by plundering Indians or lost in some wilderness disaster. But at least he still had his scalp. He told of one trader who had made the mistake of offering a Wyandot Indian a charge of powder and a single bullet in exchange for a beaver skin, so enraging the brave that he split the trader's skull with one swing of his tomahawk.

No one listened more avidly to Findley's stories than did Daniel Boone. The appeal of this hunter's paradise, the promise of adventure in a new land, so fired Boone's imagination that half a century later he still vividly recalled his excitement. He now knew that he would never be content until he saw Kentucky, and he questioned Findley closely about his route. How had he gotten over the mountains when so many others had to turn back? Had he found some secret way through? No, Findley told him, he had come down the Ohio with the Shawnee. But he had heard of a way overland following the Warrior's Path that was said to open west at a gap in the Cumberland range called Ouasioto. He believed he could find it and if Boone wanted to go, he would go with him.

There was ample time for campfire talk. A month after leaving Fort Cumberland, the ponderous force was still breasting its way through the stream-slashed timberland and over the Endless Mountains, as the men took to calling the Alleghenies. Few among them had ever seen such a primeval wilderness, covered with forests so dense that the flank scouts went from dawn to dark without catching a glimpse of the sky.

Finally, early on the morning of July 9, the long column began crossing the Monongahela to do battle. Washington, ill with fever, rose from his wagon bed to watch the regulars pass, "colors flying, drums beating, and fifes playing the *Grenadiers March*. . . . brilliant in their dazzling uniforms, their burnished arms gleaming in the bright summer's sun." Afterward the young Virginian would remember this spectacle as the most thrilling of his life. History does not record whether he noted, as did Daniel Boone, that Braddock had stationed the colonial companies, which alone had any experience fighting Indians, well to the rear; that engineers, not scouts, led the troops up onto the far bank of the Monongahela; and that even the flank guards had been pulled in tight to the main column. The army was moving into battle without eyes or ears.

It was midday before Boone and the last of the wagoners forded the river. They found themselves looking up a cramped, sloping ravine and hearing the thin crackle of rifle fire. Up ahead, the regulars saw only a haze of smoke as the enemy, hidden behind the thickly wooded ridges commanding the route of march, poured a devastating volley of hot lead into their stunned ranks. There were eight hundred Indians and French lying in ambush and they would never have better targets than the bunched and brutally exposed British troops in their luminous scarlet tunics.

Washington ordered his militia to the cover of the woods where they lost no time heeding the frontier admonition: every man to his own tree and the devil take the hindmost. Dispersed, the colonials fought back with good effect. But Braddock kept trying to whip his panicking redcoats into ranks and columns. But they were undone by the slaughter and the unearthly war whoops of the Indians; they were shooting back at specters and smoke, and finally they broke and ran. Galloping into the terrified mass in an attempt to rally them, Braddock was shot down, perhaps by one of his own men. "Who would have thought it?" he muttered as Washington placed him on a gun carriage and prepared to lead the haggard remnant of an army back across the river. The wagoners held out as long as they could in hopes of saving some of the provisions. But the Indians, emboldened by the headlong flight of the redcoats and eager for scalps and a share of the plunder, closed on the baggage train, tomahawks flashing.

Daniel Boone could not believe the spectacle unfolding before his eyes—the proud British general blundering into a ruinous ambush when any colonial recruit would have known better, his resplendent troops beaten into a shattered, stupefied rabble. Ordered not to leave his wagon, Boone waited as the shrieks of the Indians came closer, waited as long as he dared. Then he bounded onto a horse, slashed his team's harness straps and galloped for the river. Findley and the surviving wagoners did the same.

Inside Fort Duquesne an American named James Smith, who had been captured some days before, watched heartsick as the triumphant force of Indians and French returned with "a great number of bloody scalps, grenadiers' caps, British canteens, bayonets. . . ." Twelve of Braddock's men, still without any real comprehension of war in the wilderness, had surrendered to the Indians and were now led back, their faces painted black in stark signal of the fate that awaited them. Smith was witness to their bitter end:

> (They were) stripped naked, and with their hands tied behind their backs. . . . These prisoners were burned to death on the banks of the Allegheny River opposite the fort. I stood on the fort wall until I beheld them begin to burn one of these men. They had him tied to a stake and kept touching him with fire-brands, red-hot irons, etc., and he screaming. . . .

Meanwhile, the bewildered survivors mustered on the far side of the river. With Braddock dying and his senior aides dead, they began the long retreat under the command of Washington, the twenty-three-year-old lieutenant colonel of the Virginia militia. By now the full extent of the disaster was clear. The British had lost two-thirds of their force, a thousand men dead or disabled. And the French had reaffirmed their control of the Ohio valley.

Too late Braddock learned the bitter lesson. Four days after the battle, when the battered column was in sight of Fort Necessity, he roused himself from delerium to say, "We shall know better how to deal with them another time." But there would be no other time for the proud Briton. He died that same day and was buried in the middle of the road he had hacked through the wilderness.

Daniel Boone was back on the Yadkin before the end of summer, bringing with him a small walnut table and a desk carved by a fellow wagoner. He would not soon forget the catastrophic end of Braddock's expedition nor its lessons, but that was behind him. Now his thoughts were fixed on the future and buying the two pieces of furniture had not been an impulsive act. He was old enough to be thinking of a home of his own. Like many another young man home from war, he was thinking about a particular girl—Rebecca Bryan.

They met again at a cherry-picking picnic at the Bryan settlement. Rebecca was wearing a crisp white cambric apron, rarely seen in the backwoods, and Daniel, captivated anew, managed in some fumbling way to make his existence known to her. He would always be shy with ladies, but he did not lack courage to go after the things he really wanted. The two found themselves sitting together in the orchard, the girl lithe, serene, gazing at him with those frank dark eyes; and the young Boone dressed in buckskin, trying to conceal the intensity of his feelings, absentmindedly tossing his knife into the grass as they spoke. It may have been nervousness. Or, as Boone claimed years afterward, he may have been trying to test Rebecca's good temper, not an inconsiderable virtue in a frontier wife. Whichever, the fact is that as his knife went slicing through the grass it somehow cut a great gash in the girl's lovely apron. And as she neither wept nor scolded but told him to pay it no mind, he decided then and there to marry her.

He did not wait long to declare his intentions. Both the families were pleased and Rebecca, taken with the quiet-spoken young man whose hunting counsel was sought even by the elders, made no objection. In the year that followed, the frontier rituals of courtship were faithfully observed. One required Daniel to bring a deer to the Bryan home and cut up the meat in the family's presence, thereby demonstrating his ability to provide for the bride-to-be. This he did and with such gusto that his clothes were thoroughly greased and bloodied. He took some considerable teasing over this from Rebecca's sisters and friends but said nothing until all the young people sat down to eat. Then he lifted his bowl, regarded it silently until all eyes were on him, and, still staring into the bowl, said, "You, like my hunting shirt, have missed many a good washing." The score had been evened.

They were married on August 14, 1756, when Rebecca was sixteen years old and Daniel not quite twenty-two. As no church had yet been established on the North Carolina border, Squire Boone, in his capacity as Justice of the Peace, performed the ceremony according to the straightforward language of the Scriptures: "Daniel took Rebecca, and she became his bride and he loved her."

She had ridden to the wedding on her father's horse. She left on Daniel's horse, riding behind him to the tiny cabin he had built in Squire Boone's yard. There they would honeymoon, but first family and neighbors congregated for a roistering backwoods wedding party. There was venison and corn bread to feast on, and jugs of corn whiskey to move steadily from mouth to mouth. There were innumerable toasts to the bride and groom and to their expected aptitude in producing a bountiful progeny, and these led, inevitably, to chortling, good-hearted allusions to what would soon go on in the sleeping loft above.

Eventually Rebecca was obliged to climb into the loft, followed by the friends chosen to put her to bed, she silent, they giggling. Then Daniel went up the ladder, a clutch of young men just behind to haul the bedclothes back so he could get in, tucking them up around his chin, full of jokes and mischievous advice, and the bride and groom staring up at the roof in an agony of embarrassment.

The party went on. In time the celebrants brought food up to the newlyweds and there was more bantering, more jokes. Not until the small hours were they all gone, the cabin quiet at last, and Rebecca and Daniel turned to each other in the blessed darkness.

Their marriage was to last fifty-six years and in that long span of time they brought each other much happiness and some grief. Rebecca would often be alone for months and sometimes years, never sure whether her

Daniel was alive or dead, and once the crushing loneliness was more than she could bear. She was a simple woman—though reared in a well-to-do family she never learned to read or write and signed her name with an X—and was to know few comforts and little peace in her long life. But she made Boone a home and helped to defend it, becoming good enough with a rifle to inspire some teasing tales among the Boone and Bryan men—they loved to say that she once killed six deer with a single shot, and her own horse, as well. She bore ten children and reared nine, followed her husband from one wilderness cabin to another, and her devotion to him, and his to her, was strong and constant until the day she died, an old woman of seventy-three in a faraway place called Missouri.

Soon after the marriage the couple went to live at the Bryan settlement where Daniel cleared some land in a fork of Sugartree Creek and built a cabin. A neighbor came to watch him dig the well. It was hard, hot work, but the man made no effort to help. Finally he said, "If you go any deeper and do hit water, it'll be so hot a body can't drink it."

Understandably, Daniel did not laugh. But he was soon able to pay off the score; the same neighbor, noticing his new chimney of soapstone and wood, asked, "Does it draw good?"

"Sure does," Daniel said tartly. "You're the third danged fool it's drawed today."

He gained a local reputation for his way with words. People traded his little adages like bits of gossip. Once he was out hunting with a companion who wanted to stop and eat. Daniel said no, they'd go on: "Men are like horses: as long as you hold a lump of sugar in front of a horse he'll keep going, keep strong. But once he's eaten the sugar he's likely to want to stay where he's at."

Another time someone asked if he wasn't afraid to venture into an unknown part of the forest. "Sure am," he replied. "I wouldn't give a hoot in hell for a man who isn't sometimes afraid. Fear's the spice that makes it interesting to go ahead."

It was at Sugartree Creek that the first two Boone children were born and there, in time of peace, the family lived the next ten years. Little by little Daniel quit using the Quaker thee and thou and although he never joined a church, presumably unwilling to be bound even by rules of religion, he always retained a rugged personal faith in God.

He did a little subsistence farming and earned the cash he needed for powder, bullets, coffee and salt by turning his hand to some smithy work for the neighbors. Before, hunting and trapping had brought in all the money he needed; now, though, except for some pot hunts, he never seemed to get far from home. Occasionally he went to a militia muster in Salisbury, then spent the rest of the day with the other young married men of the community target shooting, at which he always won, or betting on cock fights, at which he almost always lost. Rebecca, meanwhile, joined the ladies in quilting parties and sewings. Together she and Daniel went to the neighborhood weddings, births and funerals.

Daniel lived out this domestic idyll—he didn't know how, he said later—nearly two years. He was ready for something more. He couldn't believe that he was destined to live and die a scratch farmer. But seventeen years were still to pass before he stepped into history. Meanwhile, in the spring of 1758, when he heard that three North Carolina companies would join the British in another campaign against Fort Duquesne, he promptly signed up as wagonmaster. Rebecca and the children, living among her relatives, would be well cared for.

Prime Minister William Pitt personally chose Brigadier John Forbes to lead the second attack on Duquesne. But unexpected problems assailed the new commander. The first was an illness that forced Forbes to conduct the campaign from a litter. The second was George Washington. As ranking colonial officer, Washington pressed Forbes to take Braddock's route west from a base in Virginia—for reasons that were largely political. A lively commerce was bound to follow the new road from its eastern terminus and Washington, having lately been elected to the House of Burgesses, was anxious to win the business for his fellow Virginians. When Forbes decided on the more direct route across Pennsylvania there was friction between the two men until the march actually began. Finally, as the weeks passed in tedious preparation, a sizable number of Indians recruited for the campaign lost their springtime enthusiasm and slipped away.

Late in July, the expedition got under way. It was a larger force even than Braddock's and its arduously cut route with a chain of protective forts would become the first national highway to the West. Over the high Alleghenies the army went, the draft animals struggling upward in the late summer rains and slipping and stumbling down to the creeks that separated each ridge. Many a larger stream had to be bridged and on one, over the Juniata River, Daniel Boone killed a man for the first time.

The advance had paused while Forbes and his staff sought the alliance of some local Indians. Boone, having crossed the bridge on business, was returning to the bivouac area when he overtook a big, bellicose, half-drunken Indian, who drew his knife and waved it about menacingly. He was angry that his chiefs would parlay with the English and "declared that he had killed many a 'long knife' and would kill another on his way home," thereby disrupting the negotiations.

Boone was unarmed and tried to keep a cautious distance. It was a delicate as well as a dangerous situation: he had to get past the husky warrior who seemed determined to fight, but even if he got the upper hand neither side would be pleased to learn that he had killed an Indian in the midst of peace talks. Then the blustering brave began to close on him and Boone decided that he had no choice. "That one," he later recalled, "had killed the last white man he would ever kill."

They were in mid-bridge with no one else in sight. As the Indian raised his knife with the clear intention of dispatching him on the spot, Boone suddenly lowered his shoulder and charged for his antagonist's waist, buckling him, driving him backward over the low guard rail and off the bridge, down to the rocks and water some forty feet below. "And that was the last of the big Indian," he said, recounting the story years later, "and though many inquiries were made for him next day, no one could give any intelligence as to what had become of him."

Meanwhile the tide of events was running against the French. Their Indian allies were deserting them. As Forbes pushed across western Pennsylvania, the English summoned the tribes to a great peace council at Easton and, passing out presents with a lavish hand, pledged that once the French were driven out, whites would be forbidden to settle west of the Alleghenies. The English promises—and their wampum and whiskey— were persuasive. The Indians vowed friendship and, as the news spread westward, the warriors at Fort Duquesne began melting into the woods.

In the Forbes encampment late on November 24, the night before the planned assault, the soldiers heard a booming explosion to the west. Some thought a French ammunition dump had been accidentally detonated. Not until the next day, when they finally reached the height commanding Fort Duquesne and looked across the cleared plain toward their prize, did they know the truth. Duquesne was a smoldering ruin, blown up and burned by the French commander, abandoned in the face of impossible odds by the last handful of defenders.

Forbes immediately set his men to work building a new stockade, which he named Fort Pitt in the prime minister's honor. The war now turned northward and within five years, France, with a stroke of the pen, gave up the rich domain she had cherished and struggled two centuries to develop; in another generation the British would be forced to do the same.

Boone, meanwhile, headed home for the Yadkin with some thought that his days of fighting were behind. He had left with one son, James, in the cradle; he returned to find that one walking and a second, Israel, just born. It was often to be that way. Nor were Boone and his young family spared any but the briefest interlude of peace in the cabin on Sugartree Creek. The beleaguered North Carolina frontier was smoldering again and, within months, burst into full flame with the Cherokee War.

The English had proved unable to live up to promises made to the Indians at Easton. Settlers, like a flooding tide, kept pouring into the western country, felling trees, raising cabins, sowing crops. The French, who had abandoned Fort Duquesne but not their hopes for the Ohio valley, continued to exploit the Indians' grievances, inciting them to take up the tomahawk against the sparse settlements in western Virginia and North Carolina. And the powerful Cherokees, who had long resisted all efforts to hound them into attacking the colonists, finally were goaded into taking the warpath by the colonists' own senseless cruelty.

There were always plenty of whites to whom the only good Indian was a dead one. In 1758, a band of Virginians murdered some Cherokee hunters without cause. A little later a party of braves, coming upon what they took to be stray horses, rode off with them. The white owners followed, caught up with the Cherokees and wantonly and without trial killed fourteen. The families of the slain Indians swore revenge. Soon war parties were again swooping down on the frontier settlements, leaving death and desolation in their wake. During the planting season of 1759, the South Carolina *Gazette* reported that twenty-two settlers were killed on the upper Yadkin. The sheriff of Rowan County was besieged in his own cabin. A group of travelers bound for Augusta was set upon by a hundred mounted Cherokees and when the slaughter was over fifty whites were dead and others, including children, were found wandering in the woods, scalped but still alive.

Meanwhile, in the darkened frontier cabins, people slept lightly, if at all, listening through the night for a messenger's tap at the window, the unspoken warning of Indians approaching. At such a signal, those who lived in the vicinity of a frontier fort went at once to take refuge there. Others joined neighbors, barricading themselves in the largest cabin. A vivid recollection of such a night was set down years afterward by a young pioneer, Joseph Doddridge:

The whole family were instantly in motion: my father seized his gun and being myself the oldest of the children, I had to take my share of the burthens to be carried to the fort. There was no possibility of getting a horse in the night. Besides the little children, we caught up what articles of clothing and provisions we could get hold of in the dark, for we durst not light a candle or even stir the fire. All this was done with the utmost despatch and the silence of death; the greatest care was taken not to awaken the youngest child; to the rest it was enough to say *Indian*, and not a whimper was heard afterward.

The Boones "forted up" more than once in those dark days. They went to Fort Dobbs, some miles to the west, a substantial enclosure of oak logs garrisoned by Captain Hugh Waddell and a company of forty-six militiamen. Daniel, having seen his wife and babies safely inside, would then march off with the rangers to patrol the mountains west of Salisbury in defense of the farther settlements. But the refugees at Fort Dobbs had to remain inside, sometimes for weeks at a time, frightened, cramped, irritable, unable to tend crops or even venture beyond sight of the stockade.

In February 1760, Fort Dobbs itself was attacked by a strong force of Cherokees, and though they were beaten off by the rangers, Rebecca had had enough. She was pregnant a third time and persuaded Daniel that they had to leave the Yadkin until the Indian wars ended. Many, including Sarah and Squire and their younger children, had already gone. In the spring, Daniel packed his family and belongings into a two-horse wagon and rode off toward Virginia. His younger brother Edward, called Ned, and his sister Elizabeth and her husband, William Grant, went with them. They followed the northeast line of the Blue Ridge more than two hundred miles to Culpeper, a tobacco-growing community not far from Fredericksburg, the market town on the Rappahannock River, and there they settled.

Boone tried hard to live the earnest life of a townsman. He would not plant tobacco, but hired out as a wagoner to carry it to Fredericksburg for others, thirty-five miles away. But there was much about Virginia society—cautious, correct, privileged—that rubbed against his rough frontier egalitarianism, and he felt sometimes ill-used. He once told the story of a planter who had sent a slave to help him haul tobacco to market and provided a poor piece of bull's neck as sustenance for the two on the journey. When Boone saw it, he directed the black to throw it on the ground, then he began stomping on it.

"What are you doing?" asked the man.

"Oh, nothing particularly," replied Boone gravely. "I thought it looked plaguey tough and I was only trying to see if I could possibly make it tender."

The slave duly reported this strange behavior to his master, who understood Boone's message and thereafter furnished better fare. But the affront to Boone's plebeian spirit was not soon forgotten.

It was in this period that he made the acquaintance of George Washington who had recently married and was often in Fredericksburg seeing to his wife's property and the business of his own nearby estate at Mount Vernon. One can envision the young backwoodsman hesitantly approaching the tall, distinguished planter, not three years older but already a notable figure of the Virginia colony; Boone introducing himself as having ridden in two campaigns under the Colonel's command, and Washington responding with the well-contained warmth that was the best he could manage, even among social equals. Obviously they would never be friends, but their paths were to cross.

Boone did some target shooting with friends that year and thereby earned a bit of extra money. But there could be little hunting for game was as scarce as tobacco was plentiful. It became plain to all who knew him, and especially to Rebecca, that he must soon be off. He waited until Susannah was born in November; he arranged with his brother Ned to look after his family's well-being. Then he made his goodbyes and set out to the west, traveling this time farther than he had ever gone before, crossing the Blue Ridge Mountains and on into Tennessee.

At some time during the journey he took up with an old slave named Burrell who had once grazed cattle on the far side of the Blue Ridge and knew the country. From a base in an abandoned cabin, they hunted and explored the hills of eastern Tennessee, Boone feeling like a man long imprisoned and let free at last. When Burrell turned back he went on alone, along the Watauga River to the Holston, then back and down a tributary that became known as Boone's Creek. A solitary figure in the surrounding silent barrens, he wore a long hunting shirt of deerskin and a beaver hat—he hated the coonskin cap with its long bushy tail worn by most men and never put one on. From a belt around his waist hung a powder horn, bullet pouch, scalping knife and tomahawk. At night he tied his moccasins to his rifle; should he be surprised by Indians and forced to run, he had only one thing to grab. But he was not attacked. He was alone on the land, a tangled, stony wilderness scoured by rampaging streams and "desolate as the day God made it." It was useless for farming and too open for hunting, but it was the land a man would have to cross to reach Kentucky, and now he had seen it with his own eyes.

Returning to Culpeper by way of the Yadkin valley, he learned that the southern colonies were mounting a last effort against the Cherokees, and that Hugh Waddell was mustering five companies. He hurried home to sell his skins and provide for Rebecca and the children, and was back in the Yadkin in time to join up.

This was the end for the Cherokees. One militia column spent the better part of the summer systematically destroying their villages, burning fourteen hundred acres of corn and driving five thousand braves, with their women and children, into the hills. Meanwhile a northern attack force drove straight through the wilderness to the Long Island on the Holston and broke the back of the Cherokee resistance.

Boone was among those present when the Cherokees came to the council fire and, on November 19, 1760, agreed to a lasting peace. He had learned some priceless lessons, that if you must fight Indians the way to do it was to strike through the forests as the Indians themselves did, suddenly and hard, and never to announce your presence until you were ready to attack.

When his term of service ended he did some more wandering, this time with James Norman, a Culpeper neighbor, and Nathaniel Gist, a comrade-in-arms. They hunted and trapped all winter, roving through a great horseshoe of mountains that curved from the northwestern corner of North Carolina through Tennessee and back to Virginia. At night they talked of the lands beyond the mountains, and especially of Kentucky, where Nathaniel's father, Christopher Gist, had looked on the riches of game and soil, and the things Boone saw in the firelight lit his eyes and fired his fantasies.

In the spring he returned to Sugartree Creek to see to the cabin and to plant a crop. In autumn he harvested it, then spurning a chance to set off on another winter hunt, he started for Virginia with James Norman, intent on bringing Rebecca and the children back. It had been twenty months since he had last seen his family and with peace returned to the Yadkin at last, he looked forward to rescuing them from the sterile, stiff-necked East and reestablishing his home hard by the frontier. He would farm some, very well, but at least he would be close to the good hunting and to that unexplored, unclaimed country that kindled his dreams.

When he reached Culpeper there was a new baby in Rebecca's house.

Whose was it? Daniel asked, his world falling toward ruin.

"She is your brother Ned's," Rebecca replied. Her face was drawn with anxiety but her voice was steady and unafraid. She said that she had been so long alone, that the other men had returned from the Cherokee War but Daniel had not. She couldn't even be sure whether he was alive. And Ned had come to comfort her and he had looked so much like her Daniel—and so it had happened.

No one can know what thoughts went through Daniel Boone's mind, what dark impulses tore at him in the next silent moments. Then he asked the baby's name.

Jemima Boone, she told him, head high.

"Well," he said eventually, "if the name's the same it's all the same." And they began packing to return to North Carolina and no more was ever said about it between them, not ever. Daniel loved Jemima as his own, and she went where he went, even after she was married and had children of her own, to Boonesborough and Missouri, and he lived out his last years in her house.

III

O My Dear Honeys, Heaven
Is a Kentucky of a Place

That winter, the abandoned, weed-grown cabins along the Yadkin came alive again. The Boones came back, Daniel and Rebecca, Sarah, Squire and all their kin. There were crackling fires on hearths that had long been cold, and children played in the dooryards and the men went to work clearing away the wild growth in their deserted fields.

But the Indian wars had lasted a long time and the frontier still flared with unrest, the fragile social order tearing apart. Now in every border settlement there were those without heart for the slogging, sweaty work of pioneering; and in the troubled times their baser instincts prevailed. Along the Yadkin, even after the war was over, there were some who continued their "vicious habits and became pests to society." Bands of desperadoes, hidden away in strongholds in the hills, raided farms and robbed storekeepers. Local government, chaotic and sometimes itself corrupt, seemed incapable of protecting the settlers from even the most outrageous crimes. Two men kidnapped the daughter of a farm family and the father was forced to appeal to his neighbors for help; Daniel Boone led the group that rescued her. Not long after a man named Cornelius Howard, a respected member of the community, was found to be in league with a ring of freebooters that had been preying on the settlers for two years. A neighbor had chanced on a treasure of stolen tools and farm implements in his barn.

Boone was badly shaken. Howard was married to Rebecca's sister Mary; he himself had been hunting with the man! But when an angry crowd came together for the purpose of hanging Howard from his own rafter, Boone persuaded them otherwise. They would make the culprit lead them to the gang's hideout, he said; perhaps they could recover more of their lost property. Soon Boone was bound into the hills at the head of a party of seventy, Howard unhappily showing the way. At the cleverly masked hideout, more than twenty miles from the settlements, they surprised the thieves and quickly overpowered them. They found heaps of farm equipment, dry goods, log chains and household articles; in a nearby meadow were dozens of rustled horses and cattle.

The ringleader's wife, a tornado of a woman named Owens, turned violent with rage when she realized that it was Howard who had given them away. She went for a concealed pistol and would have killed him on the spot if someone hadn't wrenched it away from her. She cursed and called Howard a Judas, vowing vengeance.

All the gang members were taken to prison in Salisbury and soon condemned to the gallows. But Howard, who had helped the settlers break the ring, and Mrs. Owens, who was, after all, a woman, were eventually freed. And one day while "Judas" Howard, as he came to be known, was leading his horse across a stream, he was shot dead from the bordering woods. No one ever doubted who dispatched him.

The time of trouble dragged on. There were other gangs and, even worse, there were magistrates whose notions of justice were plastic enough to accommodate the worst criminal if sufficient money changed hands. Unscrupulous sheriffs and land agents oppressed the unlettered back-woodsmen with claims that their deeds were flawed. Greedy justices imposed exorbitant fees: one dollar to record a deed; fifteen dollars for a marriage license. In the circumstances, many a respected Yadkin family was founded by a couple that simply took each other for better or for worse and let it go at that.

In time, agitated bands of citizens calling themselves Regulators took matters into their own hands. They began by pursuing horse thieves and looters and trying them in improvised courts, whipping some, hanging others. Goaded by the corruption of the statutory government, heady with a sudden sense of their collective power, they invaded county courthouses, beating unpopular attorneys and judges, establishing themselves as the law. For nearly a decade the turmoil of the Regulation haunted the border country, threatening civil war, pitting friend against friend and family against family. Not until 1771, when government forces crushed the insurgents in a pitched battle, was the Regulator movement broken.

But it was not dead. Some of the spirit that had driven these frontier farmers to defy the constituted authority—a sense of independence, a longing for personal liberty and a free soil—smoldered on. They had committed sometimes grievous excesses in the name of that liberty, but insisted they had been pushed to it by the tyranny of the King's magistrates. And when they rose again to join in the colonial revolt against the King himself, there would be those who remembered with bitterness that Daniel Boone had taken no part in the Regulation.

For one thing, the whole affair began to smack of politics, about which he knew little and cared less. Again and again during that dark time, he packed his gear and set out for some wilderness to hunt. But for another thing, he had come into the debt of one Regulation victim, Richard Henderson, a lawyer and circuit judge who had been driven from his bench by a mob, and his home and crops burned in the night. Boone considered Henderson his friend and the incident appalled him.

It was an odd friendship. Henderson was one of the most prominent attorneys in the North Carolina colony when they met. A striking man, not yet thirty, his force of manner and dashing oratorical gifts had won him eminence at the bar and a lucrative practice. His family had been members of the Virginia gentry; he was married to the daughter of an Irish lord. How did he come to know a scratch-farming backwoodsman like Daniel Boone? They had met through old Squire Boone, a justice of the Rowan County court. And though Daniel often was unable to pay even his legal fees, Henderson took a liking to the young woodsman and time after time defended him in court against suits for bad debts.

Averse to wagoning, indifferent to farming, Boone had turned more to hunting and trapping. Sometimes he returned with a wealth of hides and furs, but sometimes he returned with nothing at all, having for weeks followed a river or a ridgeline for the pure joy of seeing where it led. At other times Indian bands robbed him of his catch, horses, traps and weapons. And it all cost money—seven dollars for a rifle, three or four times that much for a good horse. There was never any doubt in his mind that he would pay back his creditors—the *next* winter's hunt would surely do it—but he probably could not have changed his wandering ways even if he were convinced that they would someday put him in debtor's prison.

Meanwhile Henderson good-naturedly remarked that Boone "had the honor of having more suits entered against him for debt than any other man of his day, chiefly small debts of five pounds and under contracted for powder and shot." To help, he once had Boone's name added to the list of those appointed to lay out a wagon road, "the best and nearest, from the Shallow Ford upon the Yadkin River to the Town of Salisbury."

But the friendship wasn't all one-sided. Henderson's legal circuit brought him to Salisbury often and he liked to sit in Steele's Tavern and listen to the lean hunter tell of his journeys into the wilds, the sharp blue eyes in the weathered face bright with memory of the marvels he'd beheld—the lush lands and the boundless hunting grounds on the far side of the dark green mountains—an empire whose edges he had barely touched.

Richard Henderson was a man with powerful imagination and a keen sense for life's possibilities. Every day brought more ships to America and every ship brought more immigrants. They pressed other settlers westward; they themselves pushed closer to the great mountain barrier. And Richard Henderson knew that nothing would long keep men from crossing those mountains to fill up the rich and open land beyond. Kentucky especially—of which Boone spoke with longing—seemed a natural extension of Virginia's vague western borders. Those who could establish title to that land would control its settlement and surely profit handsomely. A bold man could even think of establishing a proprietary colony there, in the manner of Penn or Lord Calvert.

He was aware, of course, that a Royal Proclamation of 1763 had specifically reserved the western lands to the Indians; but he also knew that not a merchant or speculator in Virginia believed this would long keep anyone out. George Washington expressed the prevailing view. "I can never look upon that proclamation in any other light," he wrote to his land agent, "(but I say this between ourselves) than as a temporary expedient to quiet the minds of the Indians. Those seeking good lands in the West," he added, "must find and claim them without delay."

Now Henderson came to the same conclusion. The epic idea, sparked by a restless debtor in a backwoods hamlet, took on life. The lawyer organized a land company to investigate the possibilities for speculation and colonization and hired Daniel Boone as confidential scout and surveyor. Boone was to report on lands he covered on his long hunting trips and seek out others that seemed especially fertile and advantageously located. And of course his purpose was to be kept secret in order not to either stimulate the interest of rival speculators or rouse the Indians, who were not unaware of the white man's ambitions in the West.

Boone's secret could not be kept long however. Despite his caution, it became common knowledge that he was working for Henderson. The matter of land acquisitions was much in the air and seeing the two often together, aware of their separate yet reciprocal interests, reasonable men could only ask what else they would have in common. At least once, in 1764, Boone conceded the relationship. Encountering some hunters he knew who were just returning from a foray into Kentucky, he told them he "wished to be informed of the geography and locography of these woods, saying that he was employed to explore them by Henderson & Co."

And so Boone and Henderson, two wholly different men with contrary passions—the one with a hunger to find a new land and roam it freely; the other to rule it—were bound together. The one thing they shared, a lust for Kentucky, would shape the westward expansion and transform a nation.

Around this time, Boone began taking his eldest son, James, then seven years old, hunting with him. He enjoyed the company, and of course it was time to see to the boy's larger education. There was much to teach him, for a good hunter was not merely a tracker of game—he was a naturalist, an explorer, a gunsmith. He had to know what the sunset foretold and the smell of the wind. He took his directions from the sun and the stars, and if they were clouded over he could find the north by feeling for the mossy side of a tree. He had to know where medicinal plants grew, how to repair his rifle and use a tomahawk and skinning knife. He had to learn the ways of the animals and birds, and especially to distinguish between their true call and the clever imitation of an Indian lying in wait.

All these things Boone taught his son in the long hunting seasons that ran from October to March. He taught him to stalk game before dawn or in earliest morning when the dew deadened the sound of footsteps on fallen leaves; and how to move upwind toward a browsing deer, standing motionless whenever it raised its head, stealing closer when it bent to browse again, as close as a hundred yards, the maximum range of a Pennsylvania rifle.

As always his graphic way with words made the most lasting impressions. "Wisdom comes by facing the wind," he told the boy. "Fools let it carry them." Once, when he seemed to be lagging and James urged him to hurry, he said, "Hurry? Why don't you know that a man will overrun a lot more than he'll ever overtake?" And soon pulled the boy off the trail to show him bear droppings and, nearby, the winter den.

Sometimes, in an open camp, they would be overtaken by a blizzard. Then the father would heap the fire high and, buttoning the boy into his buckskin coat, pulling the blankets over their heads, feet to the warming blaze, they would sleep the storm away. James showed every sign of taking on his father's matchless woodsmanship and there developed a particular closeness between them.

But Boone was not content. He continued to be plagued by his debts and the harassment of land agents and tax collectors. The thing that ran in the Boone blood—the urge to move on—pressed him to leave the troubled Yadkin. As early as 1764 he tried to persuade Henderson to finance an expedition to Kentucky. The magic land was there, he *knew* it was; there, beyond the mountains, was the place to found the new colony. Boone would take some good men and he would find it, and then they would all be rich. But Henderson wasn't ready. It was too soon to defy the royal proclamation. Such a trip would cost a great deal of money and without some legal authority, it might all go to waste.

That year Boone was involved in an unpleasant incident. A sickly woman named Tate, a neighbor to Rebecca's father, was in danger of losing her small wheat crop because her husband was off on a hunt and there was no one to do the threshing. When Boone heard this, he went to the Tate place and made short work of the job. But just as he was finished the husband appeared and, covering his guilt that another had had to do his work, accused Boone of an improper interest in his wife. Boone replied that he felt sorry for Tate because being a fool and an ingrate was more of a burden than any man should have to bear. That led to blows, and though Boone thoroughly thrashed the other, the episode further oppressed him.

Rowan County was changing, as had Exeter and Culpeper. "Civilization" was again catching up with the frontier, and Boone hated it. A lesser breed of men seemed to be coming to dominance, men who brought slaves to the settlements, not only to work their fields but to sell to one another. Men whose notion of tracking game was the fire hunt. Dozens of them, firebrand in one hand, rifle in the other, would form a circle a mile across, then close in, driving every living thing deeper into a trap from which no animal, no matter how small, was allowed to escape. It was an effective though cruel way to get meat, but to Boone, who believed that the sanctity of wild things required a man to pit his woodland skills against them, it was contemptible. When someone told him that a fire hunter had accidentally been killed by the crossfire of another, he expressed no sympathy and was taken for "a cold cuss."

Soon after he moved his family sixty-five miles northwestward into the Brushy Mountains near the upper Yadkin. Within a year he moved twice more, settling finally above the mouth of Beaver Creek, a few miles from Wilkesboro. Here he was in wilder country, closer to the mountains he loved to roam. But still he remained restless and dissatisfied. In January 1765, old Squire, aged sixty-nine, died and was laid to rest on Burying Ground Ridge near Mocksville. Later that year, his brother Squire married Jane Van Cleve. Things were happening; the years passed and the world was moving on, but he remained standing still. He was nearly thirty-one years old and his dreams of finding a new land and a new life were still locked in his heart. If only Henderson would make a decision. If only something would happen.

Then, in the late summer of 1765, a party of five old militia friends from Culpeper, among them Major John Field and William Hill, sought him out. They were on their way to Florida where the recently installed British governor was offering one hundred acres to each Protestant immigrant. The distance was five hundred miles or more, and how would he like to join them?

The answer was yes, swiftly given, not only from Boone, but from his newlywed brother Squire, just turned twenty-one, and from John Stewart, who had recently married their youngest sister, Hannah. Daniel promised Rebecca, whom he called "my little girl," that he would be home in time for Christmas dinner, and early on an August morning, the eight men mounted up and rode off to the south seeking, at the very least, high adventure.

Boone's record book shows that they stayed overnight in the border settlements along their route through the Carolinas. Then following the Altamaha River southeastward through Georgia, with the water high and game scarce, they plodded through endless swamps, often forced to lead the horses mile after weary mile, and were perpetually at war with swarms of stinging, biting, buzzing insects, the likes of which they'd never seen. Nor had they ever seen such a land—if land it was—forever wet underfoot and hung with thick wet curtains of moss, echoing with the raucous cries of alien and invisible wild creatures, but not a speck of game to shoot at. Once John Stewart became separated from the group and passed two days in that dank and trackless morass before they finally found him, half-starved and sick with fever.

They were all suffering hunger and exhaustion when sheer chance brought them stumbling into a Seminole Indian camp. For a tense moment the Indians stared at these haggard apparitions and their fate was clearly in the balance. Then Boone dug a looking glass out of his pack and presented it to a young girl in the suspicious circle around them and they were accepted. The Seminoles fed and sheltered them, treated their bites and sores, and when they had rested a few days, supplied them with venison and honey for the next leg of their journey.

They pushed on. Reaching St. Augustine, they struck westward exploring the St. John's River and finally reaching Pensacola, on the Gulf of Mexico. For a time Boone was intrigued. Pensacola, settled by the Spaniards more than two hundred years before, was a warm and drowsy little town, a world apart from the raw, bustly, acquisitive frontier settlements he'd known. It was pleasant to look out on the open sea, to watch the pelicans fishing and squadrons of cranes flying overhead. There were orange trees everywhere and grapevines ten inches thick, and it seemed as though a man could feed his family without ever leaving his dooryard.

Just before they left, someone offered to sell him a house and town lot and he said, "Done!" The others watched in astonishment as he signed a promissory note and put down the last of his money to seal the bargain. He set off barely able to contain his excitement at the prospect of breaking the news to Rebecca that their days of wandering were over. But as they plunged deeper into the swampland his enthusiasm began to fade. Where would he hunt? On one side were these cursed swamps, and on the other the sea. And what was there worth shooting? Pelicans? Alligators? That was hardly his idea of game.

Boone's initial enthusiasm was typical of his innocence; a blind eye to pitfalls and sharp practices and sometimes reality. In the wilderness, he moved with the absolute confidence of a man who knows all the hazards and has taken all the precautions. In the towns and settlements he remained forever a greenhorn, victimized, scorned, bypassed, and consequently doomed to spend nearly all his life poor and in debt.

Approaching the upper Yadkin in late December, Boone stopped to hunt, and on the morning of December 25, deliberately slowed his pace so that he could walk in the door at dinnertime, just as he had promised. There were joyous greetings, then the bountiful Christmas meal, and only at its end did he tell Rebecca about the house in Pensacola. He also told her that the land was probably too sandy for even a kitchen garden, and that of course they might never have a chance to see their friends and families again, it being such a terrible distance; so that when Rebecca said she wasn't at all sure she wanted to move to Pensacola he said she was probably right, and that was that.

Now he knew all the alternatives—north, east and south—at first hand, and the West pulled him more strongly than ever. It was fixed in his mind that he would find a passage through the mountain chain and reach Kentucky. He was unmoved by the danger. He had confidence in his ability to deal with the Indians. Once, hunting alone in Tennessee, he woke in the night and found himself staring into the firelit faces of a Cherokee band. This was not the first time, nor would it be the last, when Boone had to talk his way out of trouble.

"Ah, Wide Mouth," said the Cherokee leader who had recognized him, "have I got you now?"

Boone smiled and said he was happy to see his red brothers. Had they eaten? He had meat—the hunting was good over on the Holston. And what news did they have? Whatever the news, it did not keep him long in the vicinity once the Cherokees had partaken of his venison and left his camp.

He continued hunting, exploring, wandering. From the Brushy Mountains he struck out again and again into the Blue Ridge and the southern Appalachians, crossing the rivers and ridges between, going farther and farther and coming to know the country as no one ever had. Those who hunted with him said he never forgot any place he had ever been. But he did not consider that region the West; it was not Kentucky.

He had only a few hunting companions, preferring solitude to the roistering abandon of most men who reacted, mile by mile, to the distance they put between themselves and their wives. But while most men of the frontier were as much farmers as hunters—their meager acreage required little attention and hunting was their sport and livelihood—only a bare handful, like Boone, was willing to be gone from civilization and family for years at a time. These few men came to be known as the Long Hunters. It was they who first saw the unknown streams and mountain gaps, the salt licks, buffalo trails, valleys and rich meadows far beyond the settlements. They gave these places the names we use today, and they eventually enheartened their more prudent neighbors to settle the far country. Hardly any came to possess the great open reaches of land they found but they left their mark on it, and their poignant tree carvings are a record of their triumphs and disasters, an assertion of their presence in the overwhelming emptiness. In Washington County, Tennessee: "D. Boone cilled A. Bar on tree In the Year 1760." And another time, encouraging his comrades to push on to a fresh-running stream: "Come on boys here's good water." A group from the Holston settlements, robbed by Indians after months in the wilds, left a cry of desolation on a barkless poplar: "2300 Deer Skins Lost. Ruination By God."

One of the most remarkable westward journeys of the Long Hunters was made by Benjamin Cutbirth, John Stewart and two others of the Yadkin valley, all younger than Boone, in the summer of 1767. They crossed the Appalachians and explored all that unknown country between the mountains and the Mississippi River. English traders had for fifty years been plying the lower Mississippi and its southerly approaches, but so far as is known those adventurers were the first white men ever to cross the mountain barrier and reach the great river overland. They hunted all that winter and in spring rafted down to New Orleans where they sold their peltry, bear bacon, venison hams and tallow for "quite a respectable property."

Meanwhile, Boone spent an unhappy summer castigating himself for not having gone with Cutbirth and the others, and eventually came to believe that they hadn't asked him (they had) because at thirty-four he was too old for their company. Sometimes he went to militia musters at Wilkesboro. He was allowed to participate in the competitive shooting only if he accepted a handicap. It didn't matter. Holding his rifle with one hand, he outshot the best of the local marksmen. That would cheer him for a while—the prize was usually several quarters of beef—but he felt every day hurrying by, and he was still waiting.

With the first snap of autumn, he abruptly decided that he, too, would cross the Appalachians, determined that this time he would reach Kentucky. With two of his Florida companions, Squire and William Hill, he crossed the Blue Ridge and the valleys of the Holston and Clinch rivers, breaking through to the far side of the Cumberland Mountains by following the Levisa Fork a hundred miles north to the headwaters of the Big Sandy. "The streams are the guides which God set for the stranger in the wilderness," wrote historian Hubert H. Bancroft. From its westerly course, Boone concluded that this stream, the Big Sandy, must flow into the Ohio, passageway to the Kentucky heartland. The fact is that he was right, but the three turned north too soon and found themselves landlocked on the rugged Cumberland plateau. Still they pushed on through the lonely land, under the enormous empty sky, following a buffalo trace along a westerly fork of the Sandy. Here, as Boone put it, they were "ketched in a snow storm" and decided to make closed quarters for the winter.

It turned out to be a profitable encampment. Great droves of buffalo came to lick at a nearby salt spring, as did deer and an occasional bear not yet fat enough to den for the winter, and the hunters barely had to leave their log shelter to bring down all the meat they needed and to collect mounting stacks of pelts and skins. In the long evenings they passed the time talking about the spirit world that Hill, a cheerfully impulsive sort, felt sure really existed. He proposed a pact with Boone that whoever died first would return in spirit and let the other know he was there. As it happened, Hill died within the year and though Boone grieved for the loss of a good and cheerful hunting companion, he couldn't resist telling the story of the pact they made on the Big Sandy, grinning as he ended, "I never have heard from him, though."

When spring opened the land, the three debated whether or not to go on. The country was rough and forbidding, ridged with laurel-covered hills that made progress difficult, and in the end they chose to return to North Carolina. They did not know that they were already in Kentucky, on the western slopes of the Appalachians, and that a journey of only two more days would have brought them into the fat, storied bluegrass they lusted for.

Boone had not been home many months when there came knocking at his door the old comrade-in-arms, John Findley, who had first fired his dreams of Kentucky. Thirteen years had passed since they marched west with Braddock, and Boone, then a lad of twenty-one, had listened eagerly to the old trader's campfire tales of that earthly paradise.

The years had not treated Findley well. He had wandered the Northwest trying to build a stake for a second venture into Kentucky, once signing on with a trading fleet bound down the Mississippi. With his usual bad luck, his vessel foundered and had to be lightened, and he and his goods were put ashore in the remote Illinois country. Now, leading three old horses, he was peddling needles, ribbons and such odd trinkets as might appeal to the frontier housewives. He said that someone in Wilkesboro had told him Boone lived nearby, and that he had merely stopped by to say hello to an old friend. But it seems clear that he had come south, a long way from his usual haunts, and sought out Boone's cabin not by chance alone.

Soon his horses were stabled and he was fed. Then he was sitting at the hearth, once more spinning out the yarns of Kentucky that fired Boone's imagination—endless tracts of fertile, well-watered land, unclaimed, untouched; herds of buffalo so thick that, passing, they made the ground tremble; and deer and elk and beaver beyond counting; and at the Falls of the Ohio such a profusion of waterfowl that a man could eat duck or goose whenever he chose.

Boone invited Findley to spend the winter and they would talk some more. So by day the peddler led his tired horses from one household to another, trying to earn a few dollars by offering his wares to farm families mostly too poor to buy; and by night he talked. Boone sent for his brother Squire and their brother-in-law John Stewart and night after night Findley entranced them with his memories of Kentucky's meadowlands and canebrakes and teeming game. Stewart, who had crossed the Ohio to reach the Mississippi with Cutbirth not two years before, added tales of his own epic adventure. Daniel and Squire told of their frustration on the Big Sandy the previous winter when they were forced back so close to their goal.

Findley said that there was a better route, that it went further to the west, following the Warrior's Path through what the Indians called Ouasioto, a gap in the Cumberland range. He allowed that he was no woodsman, just an itinerant peddler, and that he knew it to be a long and dangerous journey. But if he had a small party of hunters led by someone as experienced as Daniel Boone, he was absolutely sure he could show them the way. And after only a season or two they would return with a wealth of furs and skins.

Someone asked him about the Indians and he shrugged. The Indians would not be happy to see a hunting party on the far side of the mountains, but Kentucky was a big place and with caution and a bit of luck their presence need never be known. Then he leaned toward them and said what he had come all that way to say—that he was nearing fifty years of age and didn't want to die without seeing Kentucky again. This was his last chance. And looking from one to the other, he asked if they would go with him.

The answers came speedily enough—they would—and Boone passed a jug of whiskey to commemorate the decision. To him, John Findley suddenly represented the face of destiny, the turning point in his life, the solution to all the nagging pressures and discontent that increasingly darkened his days. He was now in debt for several hundred dollars— thanks to Judge Henderson's intercession several of Rowan County's most prominent citizens had advanced him substantial sums—and he was, at that very moment, under summons to appear at the March term of the court at Salisbury.

After the first flush of enthusiasm, money was much on all of their minds. How would they finance such an expedition? None among them had the cash to pay for the horses and equipment they would need. Boone thought he had the answer. Thus, when Richard Henderson arrived at court for the new term on March 5, Daniel Boone, John Stewart and John Findley were waiting for him. Quickly Boone spoke his piece. He was prepared to lead a party of skilled woodsmen into Kentucky now, among them a man who had already been there. They would explore this richest of all the open domains in the West and they would find for Henderson and his land company the territory they sought for colonization. In return he needed two things: enough money to pay their costs, and a continuation of the lawsuits against him.

It happened that Boone's proposal had come at a turning in Henderson's own affairs. Western land speculation had never been long out of his mind, although his preparations had been slow and cautious. But only a few months before, by treaty signed at Hard Labor, South Carolina, the Crown had acknowledged Cherokee ownership of the Kentucky heartland. Now Henderson was faced with the necessity of negotiating with the Indians for land he once hoped to gain by royal grant. Others would have the same idea. And meanwhile, treaty be damned, hunters and squatters kept pushing into the back country. The time had come for him to make a move and Boone soon had his answer. Henderson's land company advanced money for the expedition and his law firm went to court to assure that the expedition leader would not be detained by legal encumbrance. Some years later, Thomas Hart, a partner in the land company, wrote:

> I have known Boone in times of old, when poverty and distress had him fast by the hand; and in these wretched circumstances, I have ever found him of a noble and generous soul, despising everything mean. . . . A person so just and upright could have become involved in such financial difficulty only through a certain naive indifference to the forms of law.

It can be assumed that some such equally generous testimonial, perhaps by Hart himself, was offered when the suit against Boone was heard on March 19, 1769. In any event, the case was continued and the three woodsmen sped back to the Yadkin in high excitement.

The early spring was given over to plans and preparations. It was agreed that young Squire would stay behind to look after the three households until the corn crop was laid by; then, following the route carefully set down by Findley and Boone, he would join the group with fresh supplies before winter came. Thereafter, Daniel's James, now eleven, would have to keep meat on the family table.

As Boone and his companions would be fully occupied hunting and exploring, they hired three neighboring farmers, William Cooley, Joseph Holden and James Mooney, to keep the camp and skin out the game the hunters brought in. Suddenly, after the long winter daydreams, the realities of preparation made the time speed by. Equipment was collected, rifles repaired and cleaned, bullets and powder packed and tomahawks honed. And on a bright and cheerful morning in mid-spring, the six adventurers assembled at Boone's cabin and climbed up on their horses. Strapped behind each saddle was a blanket and bearskin and a small store of provisions. The packhorses carried traps, extra rifles, camp kettles and tools for casting bullets. In their own minds, they were off on an adventure, a long hunt. There is small chance that they recognized the real significance of their expedition—that they had set off to open a continent.

Others, however, would assume the grand goals for them. The first would be a Pennsylvania schoolmaster named John Filson, with a penchant for inflated English, who a generation later brought Boone to world fame by writing his "autobiography." These are the unlikely words with which he has Boone begin:

> It was on the first of May, in the year 1769, that I resigned my domestic happiness . . . and left my family and peaceable habitation on the Yadkin River, in North Carolina, to wander through the wilderness of America in quest of Kentucky.

As though he had been made to do it, an act of penance! And yet there *was* a certain inevitability to the moment—all of Boone's life had led up to it; from that moment, the still-unborn nation was irrevocably set on the path westward.

Within twenty-five years, an irresistible surge of settlers would cross the mountains and sweep over the valleys and rich meadowlands, a brave and restless people in quest of new homes, new lands, new liberties, and Boone would be in their vanguard. He was not the first—not the first to reach Kentucky, nor first to explore or settle it—but he knew the land and likeliest routes as no one else did, and trusting his name and cool self-possession, men followed him. His life would come to symbolize the western movement.

By 1790, there would be 70,000 people in Kentucky and Boone's fame and the speculator's trumpetings had endowed it with a mythical shape in the eyes of the new nation's other 4 million inhabitants. A common story of the time told of a Baptist preacher, returned to his earthly congregation from a heavenly visit. Casting about for the most graphic way to describe the glories of the hereafter, he cried out, "O my dear honeys, heaven is a Kentucky of a place."

A goodly group of Boones, Bryans and Van Cleves gathered that morning, May 1, to watch the little procession leave. Some of the men joked about the high times the six would have in the West, but when they tried to engage Squire in their raillery he turned away from them. The two wives, Rebecca Boone and young Hannah Stewart, stood close together in the middle of the road, silent, waving and watching closely until the bobbing figures disappeared in the trees ahead. Of the two, one would hear nothing of her husband for a year nor see him again for two, and the other would never see hers again.

The Iroquois called the country *Ken-ta-ke*, which in their language meant great meadow. It was not given that any should journey easily to its heart, so unyielding was the land around, and the Indians took this as a sign that the Great Father had reserved its bounty for them alone. Boone and his men, ranging westward across the valleys formed by the headwaters of the Tennessee River—the Watauga, the Holston, the Clinch—could only hope that God would go with them.

In the beginning they traveled through country that both Boone and Stewart knew well. They found the gaps in the dark timbered mountains and came down into Powell's valley. But when they left the settlement at Martin's Station, the white man's last outpost, they moved into the unknown. It was a region of steep spiny ridges and rivers howling in the rocky gorges below, of woodlands so thick that dead trees never fell but leaned forever in each other's arms. And the only way through was the Warrior's Path.

Trodden by generations of Cherokees bound north in search of their Shawnee enemy, the secret trail had more recently served as an attack route to the frontier settlements. Having found it, the six hunters pushed ahead acutely aware that they could ride into an ambush around the very next turning. On through the thickets they went, splashing over the streams, until they came to a long valley with an insurmountable mountain wall rising steeply on the right. Then, suddenly, there was a break in that sheer face of white rock, a deep saddle only some three hundred feet above the valley floor, and the trail rose up and crossed between the dark mountains and led down in such a gentle decline that Boone and his companions did not even have to dismount. They had found Ouasioto, the Cumberland Gap, as Findley had said they would.

There were some whoops and hurrahs from the rejuvenated explorers, but they did not stop. A fair wind rustled the freshly leafed trees and encouraged them to push on through the rugged terrain. At dusk they ate and slept, and at first light moved north again. Sometimes they made an open camp and hunted for hides and meat for the pot. But not until June 7 did they make a permanent encampment.

They were now well out of the mountains and into the central levels of Kentucky. On a fork of the Kentucky River that is still called Station Camp Creek, they unpacked their gear and set about putting up a log shelter. Only a short distance from the Warrior's Path, it was not an ideal site for a base camp. But the weather had turned wet and the men hankered for shelter and rest. As they had seen no sign of Indians, Boone made no objection. He was eager to strike off and see more of this fabled land, unencumbered by camp-keepers and packhorses.

Day after day now he set out in a new direction, sometimes alone, sometimes with Findley and Stewart. He never missed an opportunity to climb the loftier hills, to view the country and measure it. He was to remember a particular summer day when he scaled to the top of a rise eight hundred feet above the Kentucky River and gazed out over the bluegrass uplands that stretched away to the north and west and vanished in a darkening blue haze. This was his moment and he stood a long time, savoring it. He knew the land below to be rich as it was lovely to look at, covered with loam like black velvet and teeming with elk, deer, beaver and buffalo, and just looking at it he felt himself "as mighty as Boaz of old."

The main business of that summer and fall was hunting. Deerskins were in prime condition and the hunters paired off, usually Boone and Stewart, Findley and one of the camp-keepers, and went off in opposite directions, making temporary camps as they moved farther from their base. But Station Camp Creek remained headquarters, and there, day by day, their stack of deerskins mounted. The two camp-keepers who remained behind built tall scaffolds to keep the bales of skins secure from bears and wolves. They then busied themselves scraping and curing the fresh skins brought in by the hunters, and preparing a supply of meat for the winter either by smoking it or cutting it into jerk.

Boone was a happy man. He had found a new land to rove; he had some good companions to hunt with; and the deerskins would put money in all their pockets. They had a variety of meats laid by for the cold weather ahead—venison, buffalo rump steaks, bear bacon, elk and turkeys—and a store of bear oil and buffalo tallow for cooking. Before many weeks passed, Squire would be along with more traps and a fresh supply of salt and ammunition, and with news of his loved ones. Though his younger brother would be traveling three hundred miles or more through dangerous and utterly alien country, Boone never doubted that they would find each other.

The autumn days did not pass without incident. Once, hunting alone, and "thinking to have a good breakfast," Boone brought down a buffalo at the edge of a milling herd. Breakfast was late that morning: his shot stampeded the pack and three hundred massive, maddened beasts came charging in his direction. Only by leaping behind a tree and jabbing at them with his rifle barrel as they thundered by did he save himself. Another time he and Stewart were trapped in an open meadow by a stampeding buffalo herd a mile across. Stewart turned to run, but Boone grabbed his shirt and pulled him to the ground. There was no outrunning that charging drove; they had one shot and he was going to take it. With what must have seemed maddening coolness to Stewart, Boone examined his flint and priming, put his rifle to his shoulder and—waiting, waiting—squeezed the trigger when the lead bull was barely twenty feet in front of them. The rifle report went unheard in the thunder of pounding hooves, but the bull dropped its head and its legs buckled and it tumbled to the ground, dead, directly in front of them. They dove into the shelter of that mountain of beef and bone, and the storm swept past as the herd shied and broke around them.

It all made good campfire talk. But on December 22, as biographer Filson has Boone say: "The time of our sorrow was now arrived, and the scene fully opened." Toward the end of that day, Boone and Stewart were returning to camp along a buffalo trace when, with no warning, they suddenly found themselves surrounded by a strong party of Shawnee horsemen, rifles raised. Boone, composed, smiling, was at his friendliest: had his red brothers been hunting? Had they had good luck? He could show them a place where. . . . He was abruptly cut off by the Shawnee leader, who called himself Captain Will. The white men were to lead him to their hunting camps, all of them, and there were to be no tricks.

Boone remained calm. He had his own plan. He would take the Indians first to a small encampment where he had left Cooley to skin out some game. Cooley would surely hear the approach of such a large party and swiftly make off to Station Camp to warn the others. They would have ample time to load up the main supply of skins and get them and the horses to safety while Boone and Stewart were leading the Shawnee on a round of the outlying camps. The Indians would find a small stack of skins at each, and this would satisfy them, but the bulk of the hunters' catch, the result of half a year's hard effort, would be saved.

And so it went until the Shawnee and their two prisoners rode into Station Camp. Findley and the camp-keepers were gone, all right, fled in terror, but everything else remained—the horses, the stores, the skins still neatly baled on the scaffolds. Captain Will broke into a broad grin as his braves began gathering it all up, but Boone could not believe his eyes. Years afterward he told his son Nathan that a man had to choose a hunting partner as carefully as he chose a wife, and there is little doubt that he was thinking of that bitter moment at Station Camp Creek when he saw everything he had worked all these months to accumulate, and his supplies and equipment as well, fall into the hands of the Indians.

Captain Will was hugely satisfied and had no desire to harm his prisoners. A day or so later he turned Boone and Stewart loose, even furnishing them with a small rifle and enough powder and shot to provide for themselves on the way home. But home they were to go, Captain Will sternly told them. Game was the Indians' cattle. "Now brothers, go back to your homes and stay there. Don't come here any more, for this is the Indians' hunting ground, and all the animals, skins and furs are ours. If you are so foolish as to venture here again, you may be sure the wasps and yellow-jackets will sting you severely."

No doubt the Indians felt that they had been most forbearing with the white intruders—two white scalps were not, after all, an inconsiderable trophy. But as Boone and Stewart saw it, they had been robbed and soon they swung back on the Shawnee trail and began tracking them north. It is not that they were unmoved by Captain Will's warning: that night Boone had a nightmare in which he was attacked by a swarm of yellow jackets and he named the place where they'd slept Dreaming Creek, and so it is still known. But they did not hold with the Shawnee's moral values—wild game was nobody's cattle but free to whoever brought it down. More to the point, they were in a rage at having lost everything on which they'd risked so much—their time, their hopes, their very lives—and they were bound to have a try at recovering some horses. Then at least they could send back to the Yadkin for fresh supplies.

Two nights later, while the Indians slept, they crept into the encampment, freed five horses and galloped off. They rode hard all night, pausing at daybreak only to give the horses water and rest. They hadn't even had time to congratulate each other; Boone had just stretched his weary bones on the grass and Stewart was kneeling to tighten his moccasin lace when, with a sudden hammer of hooves, the Shawnee pursuit party rode up over a hill and was on them.

Captain Will was still in high good humor. He chided Boone and Stewart for turning into horse thieves and, tying horse bells around their necks, forced the two men to prance up and down, the bells clanging and the Indians howling with glee. It was an indignity Boone did not forget, but in later years he laughed about it, too.

As the white men refused to be reasonable, said Captain Will, he would have to take them along; perhaps when he and his brothers had crossed the Ohio River and were safe in their own Scioto country, he would let them go. For a week the two chafed over every mile put between themselves and their comrades, and all the miles yet to come. Then one evening when the Indians were making camp alongside a giant canebrake, Boone touched Stewart's arm. His eyes indicated a stack of rifles lying on the ground, carelessly left unguarded. A moment later each had seized one and was racing for the tangled cane.

The Shawnee's first thought was to guard the horses. Only then did they surround the canebrake, waiting for Boone and Stewart to come stealing out. Stewart was ready to try, but Boone cautioned him to stay where he was. "They won't come in here—not even a Shawnee could find a man in a canebrake. And before long they'll give up and leave, watch." So they stayed hidden in the dense thickets and by the following afternoon the Indians tired of waiting and rode on.

The two hunters cautiously emerged. There was no longer any hope of pursuit; the Indians would be across the Ohio River before they could catch up. So they headed for Station Camp at full speed, covering the ground in little more than twenty-four hours. But when they reached it no one was there and the campfires were cold.

When Cooley had come bursting into Station Camp with the news that Boone and Stewart had been taken prisoner by the Indians, his panic seized the other two camp-keepers and they were immediately driven by the same thought: to save their scalps. Despite Findley's entreaties that they help him salvage the deerskins, they declared that they valued their own hides more than any deer's and were going home. Then they plunged into the woods and Findley, aware that he would not last long alone, had no choice but to follow.

They made their way southward until, shortly after the new year, they encountered Squire Boone and a companion, a young man named Alexander Neely. They had brought horses and provisions, traps, rifles— everything the hunters now needed so desperately. It was a remarkable exploit for only two men, but to Squire Boone it seemed in vain. He was distraught to learn that his brother and brother-in-law had been taken captive, especially as the camp-keepers put the worst possible face on it. Still, he tried hard to persuade the others to go on with him. Surely they owed it to Boone and Stewart to try to find them, or at least what had happened to them. And now, with fresh supplies, they needn't go home empty-handed.

The camp-keepers remained adamant; the argument continued as they pitched a camp on the spot where they had met. Then, as they were preparing to eat, there was a rustle of brush, two gaunt figures striding toward them, Squire diving for his rifle. But there was no need for alarm—it was Daniel Boone and John Stewart.

There were loud shouts of greeting, much back-clapping, the dangers of the wilderness forgotten in the heady moment. There were also sheepish attempts at explanations by the three camp-keepers and an easy willing-ness to forgive and forget by Boone. What was done was done; now they had everything they needed for a new start. But Cooley, Holden and Mooney had had enough; they were determined to return to North Carolina. And Findley, ailing, feeling his age, said he'd best show them the way.

So the old trader made his way back to Pennsylvania. But he could not outrun his bad luck. He reached home to learn that his wife had died. Somehow he managed to fit himself out for another trading trip but never got started. Then a letter from Philadelphia, published in a London newspaper in 1772, reported that the Senecas had lately murdered a whole family on Buffalo Creek "and robbed John Findley of above five hundred pounds worth of goods." A year later he died.

The four remaining hunters established a new camp on the north bank of the Kentucky, near the mouth of the Red River. Deer grew thin and scruffy in winter and their skins were then valueless, but the trapping season had begun and they set off, sometimes in pairs, often alone, to bring back thick pelts of beaver and otter that, as Boone later said, were "to recruit his shattered circumstances; discharge the debts he had contracted . . . and [enable him to] shortly return under better auspices, to settle the newly-discovered country." They built a small canoe, enabling them to set traps far up and down the Kentucky and along the smaller streams that fed it.

But more trouble was in store. Late in January, after a period of heavy rainfall, Stewart paddled across the surging Kentucky and strode off into the woods. No one was alarmed when he did not return that night—each of them had spent days alone in distant camps—but when a week passed and he still had not appeared Boone crossed the subsiding Kentucky and started out on his track. He would say later that after these long months together, after the hazards they had shared, he had come to love Stewart as though he were a true brother, and that there wasn't a man alive he trusted more. Stewart was then twenty-six years old and the father of four children, one of whom he had never seen.

Boone did not find him. In time he found his camp with cold embers and the initials, J.S., cut into a nearby tree, but no more. His fate remained a mystery for five years. Then Boone, leading a party of axmen in the blazing of the Wilderness Road, came across a skeleton in a hollow sycamore tree near the Rockcastle River. The arm had been broken by a bullet wound and nearby lay Stewart's powder horn. Holding it in his hand, thinking back to that winter day in 1770, Boone understood at last what had happened. Taken unawares and shot by Indians, Stewart had been forced to flee without his rifle. Unable to cross back over the swollen Kentucky, he had made for the settlements, traveling miles to this forsaken spot where, wounded, his strength spent, he had dragged himself into the shelter of the hollow tree and there had died, first victim in the war for Kentucky.

Alexander Neely was undone by Stewart's disappearance. He was not the hunter the Boones were and did not have the woodsman's stoic strength. He packed his gear and started back for North Carolina. Now the two brothers were alone. Neither gave a thought to returning; they had work to do. They moved to a new camp and, as Filson put it, "prepared a little cottage to shelter us from the Winter storms." They tended their traplines, ate mainly from their provisions with an occasional beaver tail for variety, and were content. Even in Filson's account, the genuine feelings of Boone the natural man, free of society's tensions, free of concern for anything but his own and his brother's safety, shine through the bombast:

> Thus situated, many hundred miles from our families in the howling wilderness, I believe few would have equally enjoyed the happiness we experienced. I often observed to my brother, You see how little nature requires to be satisfied. Felicity, the companion of content, is rather found in our own breasts than in the enjoyment of external things: And I firmly believe it requires but a little philosophy to make a man happy in whatsoever state he is.

By spring, they had cached a good supply of furs. But as stores and ammunition were running low, it was decided that Squire would go back to the Yadkin. There he could sell the catch, see to their families and the most pressing of Daniel's debts, and return in a few months with fresh supplies. On May 1, exactly a year after Boone had set off on his great adventure, they loaded the horses, shook hands, and Squire Boone and his little caravan vanished in the greening trees.

Boone was now absolutely alone in the wilderness, "without bread, salt or sugar, without company of my fellow-creatures, or even a horse or dog." Why did he stay? The trapping season was over, and he hadn't enough powder and shot to hunt for anything more than fresh meat. Why, then, hadn't he gone back with Squire?

Because he had come to explore as well as to hunt and trap. Because he had made a commitment to Richard Henderson and only by fulfilling it would he be able "to recruit his shattered circumstances." Had he meant only to find a new home for himself and a few Yadkin neighbors he could well have settled on any of the verdant stretches between the Rockcastle and the Kentucky rivers. But he felt that his fate was tied to Henderson's. There could be a new colony in this new land, and Boone, as its discoverer, would own a vast tract there, and debts and the endless demeaning pressures of the settlements would be behind him forever.

And so he set out to explore the land and came to know it better than any other white man ever had. He ranged up the Kentucky, pausing, near Otter Creek, at a place where a long meadow reached to the water's edge and giant sycamores threw their shade over a hundred acres; where, as he sat watching, a drove of buffalo came to lick at a salt spring. Cattle could thrive here; hogs could fatten on acorns and beechnuts. And there were plenty of salt licks, needed to cure hides and preserve meat. He decided that this was the place for Henderson's first settlement.

He moved on, up the Licking River, then north to the Ohio, and followed it west all the way to its falls, studying the plains and waterways, locking away in memory the rise and fall of the land and the groves of trees and springs of cool water. For safety, he slept in the canebrakes and kept moving, rarely making camp in the same place. "A certain sense of insecurity heightened his enjoyment," wrote Draper. "He pursues no old paths, but reconnoitering the country gathers a new horizon with every sunrise."

The Indians seemed aware of his presence, but they never quite caught up with him. Sometimes the "Whoo! Whoo!" of an owl in the night, so slightly off key that only the canniest woodsman would recognize it for an Indian signal, sent him gliding deeper into the cane. At least once the Shawnee found his camp, but it was so like one of their own that they sketched a map in the sand as an invitation for him to join them. He did not accept.

Another time, so the story goes, they finally did have him cornered. He had been exploring a promontory high above the Dick's River when a solid line of Captain Will's braves materialized behind him to cut off his retreat. Ahead was a cliff, sheering away to river and rocks a hundred feet below. As the Shawnee closed in, tomahawks raised, war whoops shattering the wilderness serenity, Boone concluded that he had only one chance and took it. Gathering breath, he went racing for the land's edge and threw himself hurtling into space. The Indians, convinced that that was the end of Boone, came running up—to catch a last glimpse of him clambering down through the branches of a lofty sugar maple that reached up to within a death-defying leap of where they stood. Scrambling and sliding, Boone made his way to the bottom and walked safely off while, above, the Indians gaped into the foliage where he had vanished, his legend among them blooming.

There is another tale of Boone in this period, that he spied a lone Indian fishing from a fallen log and, as a precaution, shot him dead. But it is so at variance with logic and what we know of Boone's character that it is best laid to rest. To shoot an Indian where there might be fifty more within earshot would be less a matter of self-defense than an overture to disaster, an act no woodsman of Boone's experience would even consider. Nor was it the sort of thing Boone would do. He never killed wantonly.

There is, in fact, Boone's own account of an encounter with a helpless Indian on this first sojourn in Kentucky. He was an old brave, too sick to travel and so left by his tribe to die by the side of the trail. Boone comforted him, then went back some distance to where he had killed a deer and brought the old warrior a supply of meat before traveling on. It is hard to credit such an act of compassion to a man who would shoot another defenseless Indian in the back.

Boone was at peace. He ate venison and wild turkey, berries, nuts and fruit. He listened to the quiet of the woods, feeling himself at one with nature, chanting out sometimes in spontaneous response to the long melancholy howl of the wolves at evening. Once, in the Green River country, a party of Long Hunters heard a high, keening cry in the forest. Warily they closed on it, rifles ready. It was Daniel Boone, alone in the wilderness, stretched out on a deerskin, and singing out his joy to the summer sky.

They went on and he was alone again. He was alone until July 27 when Squire returned and, by prearrangement, the two brothers met at Station Camp Creek, each one having covered hundreds of miles through strange and hostile country. Squire brought good news: Daniel had a third son, born two days before Christmas, and Rebecca had named him Daniel Morgan.

With a fresh supply of provisions, the two resumed their hunting in the limestone regions along the Kentucky River, carving their initials into the walls of caves where they slept. Once a wolf raided their camp and made off with Daniel's felt hat. He shot it down easily enough, then discovered its pups in a nearby lair. He and Squire tried to tame and raise them, but they soon ran off. Long afterward, telling a grandson of the incident, Boone noted that no matter what a man might do, a wolf remained a wolf.

In the fall of the year, Squire again went back to the Yadkin with a pack train of deerskins, returning in December with traps, supplies and extra horses. They spent the winter gathering a rich yield of furs, the most valuable harvest of pelts they had yet collected. At last, Boone reasoned, they had enough to pay off all the debts and provide for a permanent return to Kentucky. In March 1771, they loaded up the bales of peltry and started home. Boone was now filled with the deepest emotions. He yearned for his wife and children. He was elated with the success of the mission and with his prospects. He had explored Kentucky, "a second paradise," and at last had the wherewithal to make part of it his. But in early April, having passed through the Cumberland Gap, only a few days' travel from the settlements, the brothers were set upon by an Indian band and robbed of everything they had. After two years of privation and danger, Boone returned to the Yadkin poorer than when he had set out.

KENTUCKY

IV

A Dark and Bloody Ground

For a time after his return Boone was in black despair. But brooding ran contrary to his nature. He had, after all, seen Kentucky and despite all hazards returned alive and well. That was no small thing. And he was with his family again, a good wife and seven healthy children, a considerable asset on the frontier. The older boys, James and Israel, were turning into skilled woodsmen, both of an age where they could help provide for the table. As for Rebecca, she had held the family together and thriving for two years, tending the crops and keeping the cabin. Waiting faithfully for his return, she had greeted him with a fervent embrace and not the nagging reproach that would have fallen on the heads of other men he knew.

And his hopes for Kentucky still lived. His zealous report to Judge Henderson had had a marked effect. He had excited in his mind "the spirit of an enterprise which in point of magnitude and peril has never been paralleled in America."

But still Henderson did not move. He busied himself applying to judicial authorities in England to gain some semblance of legal sanction for the purchase of Indian lands. Also, he now held an appointment as associate justice on North Carolina's highest court and would not be free of official obligations for two years. He urged Boone to be patient and in evidence of his sincerity engaged him as a confidential agent to journey out among the Cherokee villages and diplomatically test the chiefs' interest in selling the trans-Allegheny region to the Henderson land company.

For the next two years Boone roamed the West. He moved his family to the Watauga Valley in Tennessee so they could be closer to him, but he was seldom home. He sought out the Cherokee encampments and walked in, cheerful, self-assured, chatting with the braves and chieftains, sometimes hunting with them—taking care never to outdo them—and then turning the talk to Kentucky and whether they might consider selling their claim to it. He became convinced that they would sell if paid enough and conveyed this information to Henderson. No response.

He returned to Kentucky at least twice, once venturing so far west along the Cumberland River that he met a party of French hunters who had just crossed the Mississippi bound east. Another time he went back to his old cave haunts with Benjamin Cutbirth, adding another set of initials and a new year—1773. On his return from this journey, Boone stopped in the Clinch Valley in a settlement called Castle's Woods and made the acquaintance of a hardy frontiersman, Captain William Russell. Russell, who had served with honor in the French and Indian War and pioneered the Clinch settlements, was much taken with Boone's ardent accounts of Kentucky. One's enthusiasm fed the other's, and as the talk went on they suddenly agreed that they would lead a party of settlers into Kentucky before the year was out.

Boone was rejuvenated by this decision—to hell with Henderson and his legalisms! Defeated Regulators and discontented farmers were already moving toward Kentucky, no matter what laws the royal governors made, and he did not mean to be left behind. He went directly to the Yadkin and sold his farm and everything he owned that was not easily portable.

Wherever he journeyed, Boone could always recruit willing followers simply by announcing his departure. In this case, five families from the lower Yadkin immediately agreed to go and a contingent of Rebecca's relatives, perhaps forty men from various settlements, arranged to meet him in Powell's Valley in westernmost Virginia. Meanwhile Captain Russell was rallying his own people in Castle's Woods.

It has long been a tradition that the irresistible attraction of a new and open land set these brave spirits, and those who followed, on the path westward. But it is also true that Boone and the others who set out that early autumn day to settle a strange new country were as much pushed as pulled. A few men, like Richard Henderson, saw the western land as a wellspring of great wealth and power. Most, though, yearned for it as an escape from crushing debt and the pernicious quitrent system that meant a man was never quit of paying rent even after he had bought his land and no matter how hard he worked. For them this far country promised an end to rapacious tax-gatherers and crown-sanctioned extortionists, freedom from the laws of a tidewater aristocracy that showed little understanding and less compassion for the poor border inhabitants. These were the grievances that made the West increasingly appealing and sent the frontiersmen of the 1770s into Kentucky. As for Boone, provocations only fed his desire to move on, to claim land of his own, to go where no one had ever been. Against that overwhelming longing, he was blind to danger and the fact that settlement in the West had been expressly forbidden. He would pay the price.

On September 26, 1773, the Boones and five other Yadkin families moved out from the old family cabin on Bear Creek, accompanied half the first day by a group of neighboring relatives. Among these was Sarah Boone, Daniel's mother, now seventy-three years old. A member of the party recalled that:

> . . . when a halt was called for the separation they threw their arms around each other's necks and tears flowed freely from all eyes. Even Daniel, brave and manly, was seen to lift the lapels of his pouch to dry his eyes whilst his dear old mother held him around his neck weeping bitterly. Daniel was devoted to her and she loved him above all her children.
>
> Boone ordered his men to fire a salute and they moved forward whilst the neighbors returned in silence to their homes.

They crossed into Virginia, then traveled northwestward twenty-five miles to Castle's Woods, among the farthest of the outpost settlements. Here they were united with Captain Russell's group, about thirty strong, including some experienced woodsmen. One was an old friend, Michael Stoner, who spoke with a pronounced German accent, having grown up in Pennsylvania Dutch country. Another was David Gass, one of the early Clinch settlers.

Now they turned west, crossing the Clinch and Powell mountains. In Powell's Valley they met the Bryan party and divided themselves into three detachments. Boone was up front with the main body—the Bryans, the Yadkin families and the baggage. Next came the livestock, tended by James Boone and Captain Russell's oldest son, Henry, both around sixteen, and two younger boys, James and Richard Mendenhall; also with this center group were two hired hands, Isaac Crabtree and a man remembered only as Drake, and the Russells' two slaves, Adam and Charles. Russell himself brought up the rear with David Gass and a few others.

And so they moved westward, fewer than a hundred souls in the enormous wilderness, strung out in a ragged single file, miles between the first and the last. There was no road, only a trace too narrow for wagons. There were a few small carts pulled by bulls that carried butter churns, the larger kettles and some household goods. Whatever other meager possessions each family brought had to be packed on the horses, leaving room for the women and younger children to ride. The rest walked. On the horn of Rebecca's saddle she had slung a deerskin satchel; it contained all her family's clothing.

The way ran counter to the ridgelines, a steep and densely overgrown region where the dark woodlands pressed in on the trail from both sides. But they pushed steadily forward. By nightfall on October 9, they reached Wallen's Ridge in westernmost Virginia and expected to cross through Cumberland Gap the following day. The three groups pitched their camps some distance apart, the boys in the center along a small creek where the cattle could drink. They built a fire, ate supper and spread out their blankets. Wolves howled somewhere in the darkness and the Mendenhall brothers, unaccustomed to the night sounds of the forest, huddled closer to the fire. Isaac Crabtree laughed at their fears. When they got to Kentucky, he teased, they would hear buffalo bellowing from the treetops. Finally the little camp was still.

The Indians came just as the sun rose, a small band of painted Shawnee. They stood motionless, fixed as the forest itself, waiting for the sharpening light to outline their victims. There was no warning, no sound except the whir of the flying arrows and the muffled thump when they struck. Drake and the Mendenhall youths were killed in the first volley, and James Boone and Henry Russell shot through the hips so that neither could move. Then the Indians sprang on the camp with their terrifying war cries. The cattle broke and ran. Isaac Crabtree, scrambling awake, was hit in the back but plunged into the woods and managed to get away. Of the two slaves, Charles was quickly caught and his head split open with a tomahawk, but Adam, leaping over the stream bank and crawling to cover under a pile of driftwood, became history's horrified witness to the savagery that followed.

Among the attackers was a huge, broad-cheeked brave who had sometimes visited the Boone cabin. Adam heard young James call him by name—Big Jim—and plead for his life. Soon, though, he was pleading for a merciful death. He got neither. The Indians tore out James Boone's and

Henry Russell's fingernails; they gashed their faces bloody with their knives and gouged at their bodies, taking care not to inflict a fatal wound. The palms of the two boys were shredded in endless futile attempts to turn aside the slashing blades. Finally the work was done. The screaming stopped and the boys died. The Indians took their scalps and as much booty as they could carry. They left a war club by the bodies, an act of bravado and challenge.

Adam crept from his hiding place and stood trembling over the ghastly spectacle. Then he staggered off in search of Captain Russell, but was so undone that he wandered the woods for days before he was found. Crabtree had better luck; he reached the Russell party within hours and gave them the grim news. Russell rushed forward and fell weeping to his knees, overcome by the sight of the tormented bodies. Someone else had to order the graves dug.

A runner was dispatched to notify Boone. The column came to a halt, Boone directing the people to shelter and posting sentinels in case the Shawnee struck again. When he rode back to the scene of the massacre he carried a precious linen sheet, sent by Rebecca, to keep the earth from her son's body. Boone wrapped the two murdered boys together, the eldest sons of the Boones and the Russells, and laid them in a single grave. Then the grave was filled, the dirt pounded down hard, and heavy rocks laid on top to protect the bodies from wolves.

Only Boone wanted to go on. He had given up or sold everything he owned and staked it all on this attempt to settle Kentucky. The others refused. Their livestock was scattered and their courage sapped—it had been a terrible mistake to try penetrating this hostile country. And so the brave expedition ended at the massacre site, by the newly made graves, and the caravan started slowly back. Daniel and Rebecca Boone had nothing in North Carolina to go back to. When David Gass offered them the use of a cabin on his property in Castle's Wood, they accepted. In the spring of the following year, Boone returned alone to James' grave. He found that the wolves had dug part way into it and, after assuring himself that the bodies had not been molested, he began carefully filling it in again.

Perhaps this hour of secret mourning at Wallen's Ridge serves to epitomize the untallied mortal cost of the westward expansion. Beyond the battle, beyond the epic drama in which a simple, semiliterate people force back the frontier with the doggedness of pine roots cracking granite so they can grow, beyond the mixture of blood and politics that fused the wilderness to the new nation—beyond all that is this moment at Wallen's Ridge: a father sitting by the grave of his firstborn, a boy just turning into a man, who has been tortured to death.

The father sits there a long time, a lonely figure in deerskin dyed black, the blue eyes clouded by defeat and staring down at the fresh earth where the wolves, during the winter months when they are ravenous with hunger, have been pawing; a father slowly filling in the grave where his dreams and his son lay buried.

> James was a good son [Boone later wrote], and I looked forward to a long and useful life for him, but it is not to be. . . . Sometimes I feel like a leaf carried on a stream. It may whirl about and turn and twist, but it is always carried forward.

A storm broke and Boone took shelter in the trees. When it passed, he made camp and lay awake watching the clearing sky. Not far off he heard a movement, a certain rustle in the brush. For a time the woods were silent, but when he heard the movement next, it was closer. He had lived too long in the wilds not to recognize the approach of Indians, but as he later said, he was in the grip of such a profound depression, "the worst melancholy of my life," that for a terrible moment he did not move. Perhaps he would let his life end in the same place his son's had. But the instinct for self-preservation finally stirred him. As long as he lived he could try again; anything—even Kentucky!—was possible. And slipping to where his horse was hobbled, holding the bell silent, he swung up into the saddle and galloped away in the night.

Somber echoes of the murders reverberated along the southwestern border. Red men and white men had killed each other before, but the special ferocity of this attack, the fact that two of the victims were the sons of well-known frontiersmen, put the news "in everyone's mouth." Eventually, two Shawnee chieftains who participated in the raid were caught and executed.

The Indians had grievances of their own. Isaac Crabtree, Captain Russell's hired man, took his personal revenge by walking up to a group of innocent Cherokees watching a horse race at Watauga settlement and shooting one dead. When the governor offered a reward for his arrest, he was told that it would be easier to find two hundred men to protect Crabtree than to get ten to bring him in. A border brigand, Daniel

Greathouse, slaughtered the family of a prominent Mingo, Chief Logan, plying them with liquor until they were helpless and murdering, among others, Logan's brother and a pregnant sister-in-law. After he had scalped the men, Greathouse cut the unborn child from its mother's body and impaled it on a stake.

The western tribes had cause for bitterness as well. That same spring James Harrod led a force of thirty-one men three hundred miles beyond the farthest outpost, well west of the Kentucky River, and on land specifically designated by solemn treaty as belonging to the Indians, was busily establishing a white settlement. Meanwhile, a large party of surveyors had also crossed into Kentucky and was blazing trees and marking off tracts of land, making it plain that legions of settlers would follow. The whack of the white man's ax and the crack of his rifle were heard by the Indians as a death knell, foretelling their ultimate doom.

Finally they buried their own differences to unite against the threat. Mingo and Shawnee carried the war pipe from village to village and runners were sent off to rouse the farther tribes. Then the remote settlements were attacked; the Shawnee established a blockade on the Ohio River.

This last news particularly alarmed Colonel William Preston. He was a militia commander and chief surveyor of Fincastle County, that vast and barely defined western sweep of Virginia that comprised Kentucky and parts of present day Ohio, Indiana and Illinois. It was he who had sent the surveyors into Kentucky and now, with the war fires blazing, he feared for their lives. On June 20, 1774, he wrote to Captain William Russell, Boone's comrade on the fateful attempt to settle Kentucky and now commander of the Clinch Valley militia, to send "two faithful woodsmen" to find the scattered surveyors and conduct them back to the settlements. Less than a week later Russell replied, "I have engaged to start Immediately, on the occasion, two of the best Hands I could think of, Danl. Boone and Michl. Stoner." On July 13, he wrote again:

> I am in hopes, that in two or three weeks from this time Mr. Boone will produce the gentlemen surveyors here, as I can't believe they are all killed. Boone has instructions to take different routes till he comes to the Falls of Ohio, and if no discovery there, to return home through Cumberland Gap . . . if they are alive, it is indisputable but Boone must find them.

By the time the letter arrived, the Indians had already struck. On July

8, a group of settlers, staking out land a few miles north of Harrod's new town, called Harrodsburg, were set upon by twenty Shawnee warriors, and two whites were killed. The next day Harrod gathered the rest of his company and made for the settlements. Two parties of Preston's surveyors, working not far from Harrodsburg, returned there on July 24 to find the place abandoned. Nailed to a tree at the river landing was a chilling message: "Alarmed by finding some people killed we are gone down this way."

They, too, started back and eventually returned home safely. But the largest group of surveyors, nine men under Hancock Taylor, was farther away and had no warning of the imminent danger. On July 27, paddling down the Kentucky, they were fired on from the bank. One man was killed outright, and Taylor, hit twice, died a few days later. Leaderless, frightened away from the river, the surviving seven began wandering the forbidding forest with no clear idea of where they were or what to do.

Meanwhile, Boone and Stoner, having set out from Castle's Woods on June 27, crossed the mountains and made for the Kentucky River along the North Fork. They exercised extreme caution, seeking out hidden ravines in which to build their small fires, then sitting back to back as they ate. Afterward they obliterated every trace of the camp before slipping into the woods to sleep.

When they reached Harrodsburg it was ominously deserted, and this hastened them on to the Falls of the Ohio. Still without sign of the surveyors they started back by a different route, searching the land for miles on both sides of the Kentucky. They were a well-matched pair, Stoner with his stolid, stubborn courage, and Boone, who knew the land and kept seeking out the ridges and streams that would lead them into its most sequestered reaches. And somehow, deep in that trackless country, they finally came upon the seven lost men of Taylor's party. On August 26, having traveled some eight hundred miles through the wilderness in sixty-one days, Boone and Stoner led the last of the surveyors back to the Clinch settlements.

The bloody little thrusts and counterthrusts and the single pitched battle that, together, history came to know as Lord Dunmore's War was now raging on both sides of the mountain barrier. It is aptly named. Lord Dunmore, royal governor of Virginia, by his incredible insensitivity to

Indian grievances and by endless provocations in furtherance of his own land speculations, created the war. It was not without consequence; the training and battle experience the colonials received under Lord Dunmore in 1774 would help them drive him out of Virginia in 1776.

Within days of his return with the surveyors, Boone was commissioned a lieutenant in the Virginia militia and assigned to the defense of the Clinch. Indian raids had terrorized the valley and many families feared to leave the forts to tend crops. Others fled east, and Major Arthur Campbell, ranking officer in the district, said in one report, "Since I began this letter I am mortified with the sight of another family flying by."

Boone was given command of Moore's Fort, largest in the Clinch chain. Soon the people at Blackmore's Fort, twenty miles down the river, petitioned to have him promoted to captain with responsibility for their safety as well. This was done, and Russell's Fort added to his charge too—a total of three forts and fifty-six militiamen.

He seems to have been the boldest commander on the Clinch, calling out his men when neighboring forts were attacked and ranging into the wilds to fight frequent skirmishes on the Indians' home ground. "Mr. Boone is very diligent at Castle's Woods," wrote Campbell to Colonel Preston, "and keeps up good order."

But Boone's men were not Boone. Once, riding to the relief of Blackmore's Fort, they left seven horses outside. By morning the Indians had stolen six. Another time, despite his orders, three men left the fort to check a pigeon trap several hundred yards away. The Indians fired from the cover of the woods, killing one. Boone and the entire company rushed out to beat the woods until dark, finding nothing. But when they returned to carry the dead man into the fort there was a war club by the body.

The fact is that they were garrison soldiers, bored through the long dreary days when nothing happened and less than ready when it did. At Moore's Fort, discipline often fell to pieces when Boone rode off to make the rounds of his command. During the warm September days the men liked to lie in the grass outside the stockade, their rifles carelessly laid by, even to play ball and swim in a nearby pond. Rebecca, who had brought her children and forted up with some twenty other families, especially resented this. Apart from the obvious danger, she felt it an affront to Daniel's leadership. On one such day, she and several of the other women loaded their guns with a light charge, the way the Indians did, and went to the far side of the fort where they fired rapidly. Then they raced to the gates and slammed them shut. The men outside panicked and ran in every direction, several of them diving fully clothed into the pond. Afterward, when they realized Rebecca's trick, they were so furious that some wanted to whip her, but she stared them down.

Lord Dunmore's War ended with a battle at Point Pleasant in what is now West Virginia, where the Kanawha River flows into the Ohio. Here, early on the morning of October 10, a strong force of Shawnee under Chief Cornstalk attacked an encampment of eleven hundred colonials. The fiercest combat that would ever be fought between Indians and white men east of the Mississippi raged all day, with heavy losses on both sides. But the colonials held their ground and in the evening Cornstalk called the other chiefs together. "What will you do now?" he asked. Their answer was silence. "Let us kill all our women and children and go and fight until we die," he said. Still there was silence. Then Cornstalk rose, struck his tomahawk into a post and said, "I'll go and make peace."

The end of the war emboldened Richard Henderson. The Indians had been subdued and he finally held in his hand some moot legal opinion that bolstered his courage to defy the royal governors. The judicial authority he relied on had impeccable credentials: he was the King's own Lord Chancellor. The trouble was that his ruling holding that royal assent was not required in respect to lands that might "be acquired by treaty or Grant from any of the Indian princes or Governments," applied to the Indians of India and not to those of North America.

Henderson didn't care. He sensed a tide running in his favor and was even prepared to flout the Crown if he had to—something colonials had been doing with increasing frequency. He recently had heard how in Boston a band of hotheads had heaved a cargo of tea into the harbor in protest against the duty. Some radicals even talked of revolution. It would all come to nothing, of course, but meanwhile the King and his minions would be too occupied to take more than passing notice of his little enterprise in Kentucky.

Henderson now made some specific plans. He and his partners proposed to buy 20 million acres of land from the Cherokees, nearly all of present Kentucky and Tennessee, and establish there a fourteenth colony with themselves as proprietors. In recognition of the snares and dangers ahead, they bound themselves together not only to furnish needed expenses and share the rewards equally, but also "to support each other with our lives and fortunes."

Boone, summoned once more, made a final exploratory trip to Kentucky, then spent the next five months among the Cherokees, detailing Henderson's offer and emphasizing that he sought to buy, not steal, their land. He told them the treaty was to be signed at Sycamore Shoals on the Watauga in March and urged the chiefs to attend.

Meanwhile, a series of handbills and newspaper advertisements boldly proclaimed the company's "Proposals for the encouragement of settling the Lands purchased by Messrs. Richard Henderson and Co.," followed by a list of blandishments: fifty soldiers were to be raised for the "protection of the settlers of the country"; every man growing a crop of corn and pledging himself to defend his community against Indian attacks could buy up to five hundred acres of land for only five pounds; land was also promised to those who established mills, ironworks and salt factories.

The reaction was swift and sharp, thunder following lightning. Governor Dunmore denounced the private purchase of land from the Indians by "one Richard Henderson and other disorderly persons, his associates." Governor Josiah Martin of North Carolina was even more choleric, referring to Henderson and his partners as an "infamous Company of Land Pyrates," whose invitation to "many Debtors, and other persons in desperate circumstances to desert this Province would result in the great injury of creditors." And a North Carolina official wrote in amazement to a mutual friend: "Pray, is Dick Henderson out of his head?"

Henderson ignored them all. The enterprise was going well. It was the greatest sensation North Carolina had known since the Regulators were put down. Early in the new year the undertaking was given a new name, the Transylvania Company, and soon after the proprietors dispatched six wagons full of clothing, tools, trinkets and firearms to the ancient Cherokee treaty grounds at Sycamore Shoals. There they were stored in huts placed so the arriving Indians could not avoid seeing them. Their value was set at eight thousand pounds sterling; another two thousand pounds was to be paid in cash.

By the first days of March, Henderson and his associates and Daniel Boone were on the scene. Soon the lodges of the Cherokees covered the little valley. Aging chiefs and impetuous young warriors, squaws with their papooses—twelve hundred in all from the far-flung bands—crowded in among the sycamores. They were fed by dozens of Watauga families hired by Henderson to scour the terrain for beef, venison, turkeys and corn to keep the guests in good humor. Everything was provided but rum; the rum would wait until the treaty was signed.

At first all went well. Henderson opened the treaty making by formally inquiring whether the land he proposed to buy was, in fact, owned by the Cherokees. Attakullaculla, leader of the nation for more than fifty years, replied that it was. Then the great proposal was put forward: in exchange for all the goods in the six cabins, the Transylvania Company would buy from the Cherokee Nation that land that was watered by the Cumberland and the Kentucky, east to the mountain barrier. Boone had carefully drawn out the boundaries and the chiefs crowded around to look.

Attakullaculla, who had once crossed the ocean and dined with the King but who was now wizened and bent, rose to speak for the Cherokees. Claiming the confidence of his people, supporting the good faith of the white brothers, and particularly of Colonel Henderson—whom in less formal moments he called Carolina Dick—he expressed himself in favor of the sale. Other chiefs endorsed the proposal. It seemed only a matter of signing the treaty and breaking out the rum.

Then the son of Attakullaculla, Dragging Canoe, asked to be heard, his words recorded by the chief interpreter:

> The whites have passed the mountains and settled upon Cherokee lands, and now wish a treaty. When the whites are unable to point out any further retreat for the miserable Cherokees, they will proclaim the extinction of the whole race. . . . Such treaties may be all right for men too old to hunt or fight. As for me, I have my young warriors about me. We will have our lands.

There was a moment of stunned silence, then the assembly was thrown into tumult. Heated arguments erupted on all sides. Henderson, appalled at the breakdown of his carefully orchestrated negotiation, hastily suspended the sitting and called the chiefs to a feast.

Later that night, the official interpreters and the half-breeds who assisted them scurried between the white men's quarters and the Indian lodges. But Daniel Boone, who needed no interpreter and spent hours in earnest talk with Dragging Canoe, was the one who saved the treaty. It was as Dragging Canoe had told it, Boone said. The white man was moving across the mountains and would not be stopped, for his numbers were great and kept growing. But the Cherokees did not require the western land; they still had a place to live and hunt. Would it not be better, then, to sell Kentucky to a friend like Richard Henderson rather than risk losing everything in battle with an enemy?

Next day the mood of the council was once more calm. The Treaty of Sycamore Shoals was described by the interpreters and accepted without objection. The Transylvania Company had won what it came for, an empire of ninety thousand square miles, for the colonial equivalent of fifty thousand dollars.

But Henderson was not quite finished. He had yet more goods and firearms that his red brothers had not seen, and there was yet land between Kentucky and the place where they stood. "I do not love to walk over the land of my brothers," he said, "and want to buy from them a road to Kaintucke."

Again Dragging Canoe rose in angry objection. "Why do you always ask more?" he demanded. But again Henderson prevailed, gaining as right of way a wide strip of land from the Watauga country to the Cumberland Gap, where his newly acquired realm began. Defeated, Dragging Canoe cried out, "We give you from this place!" as he pounded his foot on the earth where he stood and flung his arms out toward the mountains.

Afterward the unhappy young chieftain took Boone's hand and drew him to one side. The Cherokees had given their brothers a fine country, he said, and would not harm them there, though others might. Then he pointed westward and said that there was a dark cloud hovering over the land of Kentucky, and that those who went to settle it would find that the ground was dark, too, dark and bloody.

It took days to set down both the Great Grant and the Path Deed, as the agreements came to be known, and to translate them so they could be read aloud in both tongues. The signing was done on March 17, 1775. A great feast was then set up under the trees and, finally, the rum passed and the treasure of goods distributed. They spread only thinly. One warrior, given a shirt as his portion, gaped at it in disappointment and said that he could kill more deer in one day on the land sold than it cost to buy such a shirt.

By that time Boone was long gone from Sycamore Shoals. As soon as the treaty was assured, he had hurried off to the Holston where some of the best woodsmen in the country were waiting for him. They were going to cut a road to Kentucky for the settlers.

History touched the place called Boonesborough in 1775 and, in a single generation, passed it by. Not for a century and a half has there been anything left of its thirty-odd cabins and the parallelogram of random stockade meant to protect the inhabitants from the wilderness. The small grassy plain on the Kentucky River on which it stood became part of a state park, easily reached via either of two superhighways. In 1974, the

Kentucky Parks Department completed a handsome reconstruction of the old fort.

But one wonders how many of those who come here on a summer day to escape the systemized shuffle of life in the late twentieth century are aware that this meadow was once an outpost of civilization, the end of the Wilderness Road? How many have noticed the small stone memorial inscribed with the names of those who lived here two hundred years ago? The stone has weathered badly; the names are hard to read: Boone, Callaway, Hays, King, Stoner, Tates.

Other men had crossed this land earlier, traders and hunters, but these are the names of those who first brought their wives and children to a home in Kentucky and, on this spot, some died defending them. They had advanced the line of settlement by hundreds of miles, and then, defying the wilderness, the Indians and the British army, they stayed. And so this handful saved the West for the United States.

On a warm March morning in 1775, thirty of them waited for Boone at a three-mile spit in the Holston River called the Long Island. They had been recruited by him to cut the road into Kentucky and now marked time until he brought word that the treaty making was done. Boone's younger brother Squire was among them, lately taken with the rugged Christian faith of the southern uplands and turned occasional Baptist preacher, but ready as ever to march when Daniel rolled the drumbeat of adventure. Among them, too, were two warm friends from the Clinch whose woodland skills Boone knew well, Michael Stoner and David Gass; his hunting companion, Benjamin Cutbirth; a new son-in-law, William Hays, married to his eldest daughter, Susannah, just days before the assembly on the Holston; and a neighbor from the Yadkin days, Richard Callaway. Callaway was a good ten years older than Boone, with experience in the French and Indian War and a colonel's commission in the Bedford County (Virginia) militia. There is reason to believe that he was not entirely happy to take orders from the younger man, and certainly Boone's prominence in the days ahead heightened his resentment. Callaway brought with him a slave woman to cook, the only female in the party. All these men Boone had chosen personally. He was equally pleased with a North Carolina contingent of eight sent by Henderson. They were commanded by Captain William Twetty, a rugged giant of a man accompanied by a black manservant and a fierce little bulldog. Among them was a romantic youth named Felix Walker who would one day write a vivid account of the historic journey.

Each of the road cutters was to receive the sum of ten pounds, ten shillings, "for work making roads to Cantucke," around fifty-three dollars. That was then enough to buy more than four hundred acres in the bluegrass country. Boone, as the leader, had been promised two thousand acres.

He arrived at the Holston on March 9 and the following morning they loaded the packhorses and started forward. They were bound for Otter Creek, near that bend in the Kentucky River, 250 mountain and wilderness miles away, where five years before Boone had sat alone and envisioned a settlement among the giant sycamores. He did not wait for word that the treaty with the Cherokee had actually been signed. If all went well, Henderson would soon follow with the settlers; if it did not—well, they were thirty and well armed. Having dreamed the dream for so long and come so close, Boone was resolved not to be turned back by anything short of an overwhelming catastrophe.

Walker wrote:

> we put off from the Long Island, marked out our track with our hatchets . . . killed a fine bear on our way, camped all night and had an excellent supper. Perhaps no adventurers ever felt so cheerful and elated; every heart abounded in anticipating the new things we would see (and) under the influence of these impressions we went our way rejoicing . . . taking our leave of the civilized world.

All the daylight hours they swung their axes at trees and the sinewy canes, counting their advance not in miles but yards, but leaving behind a clear and passable track in the wilderness. At Moccasin Gap, gateway to the rugged Clinch Mountains, they found the Warrior's Path and followed its meanderings in a westerly direction. Now the work was easier, for they had only to widen the way and carry off dead logs.

They forded the Clinch and crossed Powell Mountain, coming soon to Martin's Station where Captain Joseph Martin, driven off once by hostile Indians, was trying a second time to establish a settlement. The trailblazers took on some supplies, then pushed ahead through the valley. They followed the long white wall of the Cumberland Mountains for twenty-five miles, the way ahead open, but the surrounding country cut by ravines and hidden by thickets, and every man among them half-braced for a war whoop.

But there was no ambush, no sign of Indians. They reached Cumberland Gap without incident and crossed over, the mountains rising starkly a thousand feet above their heads. Down to the Cumberland River the trail had been pounded smooth by generations of migrating buffalo, but beyond, across the broken hills overgrown with scrubby trees and down through the bogs studded with immense canebrakes, the Wilderness Road was aptly named. Beginning here, mile after endless punishing mile, they cut brush and cane and vines thick as a man's thigh; they felled trees and filled sinkholes; they lifted fallen timbers off the path, then trudged back and dragged them forward to bridge streams and the seemingly bottomless swamps in their way.

Boone was in his element. With an uncanny feeling for the topography of the land around, he found the best fords and the lowest passes. When, in the middle of a blind forest, he said they would turn north, no man questioned him. When he promised that they would soon be out of the morass and look down on the broad and open bluegrass country, they hacked wearily, hopefully, away. He was confident and clearly in command. He had come to believe that his years as a hemmed-in farmer were only a testing time; his true calling, in the Bible's words, was to make a way in the wilderness. And now, at last, he had come together with his special destiny.

By March 22, they had cut their way through the worst of the canebrakes and, as Felix Walker put it, "We began to discover the pleasing and rapturous appearance of the plains of Kentucky." At Big Hill they left the mountains behind and came down into a rich, rolling clover meadow, green hills in the distance, some turkeys strutting past. "It appeared that nature had spread a feast for all that lives," wrote the exuberant Walker. When they camped in the wooded hills at Taylors Fork on the evening of the 24th, they were barely fifteen miles from their destination at Otter Creek. Heartened but bone weary, the men slept heavily.

About half an hour before daybreak they were dashed awake by the boom of rifle fire. Almost at once the Shawnee were in their camp, tomahawks held high as they closed for the kill. The road cutters bounded to their feet and raced wildly for the woods. Remarkably, nearly all of them made it, some half-naked, others without their rifles. Squire Boone who had grabbed a shirt, mistaking it for his shot pouch in the dark, went crawling about trying to borrow ammunition. Felix Walker, shot in the hip, dragged himself off to hide behind some bushes. But Captain Twetty's slave was dead, and Twetty himself had been shot in both knees and could not rise. He would surely have been scalped on the spot, for two braves were almost on him. But his little bulldog charged them, snapping at their ankles until by the time they managed to tomahawk it, Boone and his men were firing on them from the woods and the raiders withdrew.

Boone posted guards and took stock of the situation. One man was missing. A few horses had been stolen, but the camp supplies and baggage were intact. Since Walker and Twetty were too badly hurt to travel, the others built a small log barricade and carried them inside. Here Boone tended them as well as he could, but Twetty's wounds festered and he failed rapidly. He died during the third night, as a late spring snow fell, and in the morning they buried him alongside his slave.

That same day Colonel Callaway's black woman, gathering firewood in the forest, came back to camp shrieking, "Indians! Indians!" The men snatched up their rifles, Boone calling out orders: they were to take a stand behind the trees; they were not to run until they saw him fall. An agonizing moment passed as they crouched in their places, waiting for the worst. Then a cry from the forest—"Don't shoot!"—and the missing road cutter, having hidden three days in fear that the Indians had slaughtered them all, walked back into the camp.

The road cutters soon learned that they were not the only white men in the wilderness, nor the only ones to be attacked by the Shawnee. Hunters, sent by Boone to scout the terrain and bring in some meat for the pot, returned with a stunned and shivering boy whose party, he told them, was bound overland to Harrodsburg, where Captain James Harrod had just reestablished his old settlement. Their campfire made a good target for the Shawnee. The boy had seen two men hit, and though the others scattered, he thought the Indians would have no trouble tracking them through the fresh snow. He himself had escaped by running barefoot up an icy stream.

Boone went at once to the other campsite, taking Squire with him, "and found two men killed and sculped." Suddenly there were those in his party who, as Walker said, were cast into "a deep gloom of melancholy." If the Shawnee were determined to drive the whites out of the country, how could they, a bare handful, resist them? That day a few apologetically collected their gear and started back.

Meanwhile Boone sent a scout to instruct all hunters and settlers in the vicinity of Harrodsburg to meet him at the mouth of Otter Creek that they might all stand together against the Indians. On April 1, when there was still no word from Henderson, he dispatched a memorable letter to him:

Dear Colonel:

After my compliments to you I shall acquaint you of our misfortune. On

March 25 a party of Indians fired on my Company about half an hour before day and killed Mr. Twetty and his negro and wounded Mr. Walker very deeply, but I hope he will recover. . . . My advise to you, Sir, is to come or send [help] as soon as possible. Your company is desired greatly, for the people are very uneasy, but are willing to stay and venture their lives with you, and now is the time to flusterate [the Indians'] intentions and keep the country, whilst we are in it. If we give way to them now, it will ever be the case. This day we start from the battle ground, for the mouth of Otter Creek, where we shall immediately erect a Fort.

I am, Sir, Your most obedient
Omble Sarvent

DANIEL BOONE

The letter reached Henderson on April 7 as he camped in heavy snow within sight of Cumberland Gap. It was the latest blow in a whole series of misadventures that had plagued his company from the time they set forth from Sycamore Shoals three weeks before. He headed a powerful force of nearly fifty men, mounted and armed, as well as a number of slaves; forty well-loaded packhorses, a herd of cattle, and a train of wagons filled with ammunition, seed corn "and a varied store of articles of prime necessity at an isolated location." Two of his partners, Nathaniel Hart and John Luttrell, rode with the column. But almost from the first day, overly venturesome scouts got lost and horses wandered off. They were so ineptly led that on the very doorstep of a hunter's paradise they resorted to slaughtering cattle for food. Though Boone warned against the use of wagons, Henderson had persisted; now, mile by mile, the trail had to be widened to accommodate them and, crossing the stony Clinch highlands, the wagons had to be taken apart and carried over piece by piece along with all their contents. Arriving at Martin's Station on March 30, Henderson was dismayed to find that there was no possibility of taking the wagons any further along the narrow, rock-bound trail. Five days were now lost building sheds for them, storing much of the powder, and reloading the packhorses with essential supplies.

Faith in Henderson's command of the enterprise shriveled. His partners were particularly unsettled as they saw the shrewd, incisive courtroom lawyer buffeted and often bewildered by this wilderness world. As historian Thomas D. Clark wrote, "Once beyond the great commercial pageant at Sycamore Shoals, Henderson never again demonstrated first-rate leadership of his colony."

Meanwhile, other bands of adventurers, having heard that Kentucky was to be opened to settlement and anxious to claim the best land, rushed past Henderson. This was galling enough to the proprietor—it was, after all, *his* land now. But even worse was the spectacle of these same people flying back, eyes still glazed with the terror of what they had seen or imagined. The Indian attacks were real enough: Earlier on the very day Boone's letter arrived Henderson had word "from Mr. Luttrell's camp that five persons were killed on the road to Cantuckee, by Indians."

Henderson pushed on in Boone's track, crossing over Cumberland Gap, trying to counter the demoralizing fear that ran through his camp like a contagion. In the next several days he counted nearly a hundred people streaming back—frightened squatters, those who had deserted Boone, and his own men. Nor could he prevail on more than a few to continue on with him. But even that was not the worst of his worries. Recounting those critical days for those of the proprietors who remained behind, he confessed that the entire venture then rested with Daniel Boone:

> With me, it was beyond a doubt, that our right, in effect, depended on Boone's maintaining his ground. . . . it is impossible to make the picture worse. Every group of travelers we saw, or strange bells which were heard in front, was a fresh alarm; afraid to look or inquire, lest Captain Boone or his company was amongst them, or some disastrous account of their defeat.

It was a particular irony. Before, Henderson had seen Boone in only one dimension—Boone the debtor and supplicant, Boone the simple backwoodsman, his prowess in the wilds conceded, but of little importance in the security of the settlements. Now, here, Boone alone stood between Henderson and financial ruin, perhaps death. It may be that at last he saw Boone full size.

The snow turned to rain. As the column inched forward through the mire, Henderson decided that it was absolutely essential to get a message to Boone, to reassure him that reinforcements and provisions were on the way. William Cocke, the wagonmaster, volunteered to carry this word forward, but asked that a second man accompany him, as the way was long and plainly dangerous.

No one else stepped forward. Tears in his eyes, facing disaster, Henderson offered ten thousand acres to Cocke and to any man who rode with him, but there were no volunteers. Finally Cocke agreed to go alone, and on the morning of April 10, a dark, forbidding day, he galloped away into the rain. He carried a "good Queen Ann's musket, a tomahawk and no small quantity of jerked beef"—and Henderson's deepest apprehension.

Ahead of him lay 130 miles of Shawnee-swarming wilderness, every grove of trees a possible ambuscade.

Henderson could have proceeded with a tranquil mind. Boone had never thought to turn back, though still more of his men defected. Even as Cocke rode forward on his perilous mission, the road cutters were at Otter Creek, building temporary shelters and marking off lots at the place they promptly named Fort Boone. They had moved on from "the battle ground" and toward the evening of April 1, they reached the site Boone had chosen for the capital of the new colony, the open plain on the south bank of the Kentucky River. The West was unlocked.

The Wilderness Road, a crudely cut trail barely wide enough for an oxcart, became the pioneer's highway, a highroad to America's future. And for the next twenty years, the settlement founded and forted where the Wilderness Road ended would shield the restless men who brought their families to settle Kentucky, and would provide a blessed stopping place and supply depot for those moving on to the lands beyond.

For the weary road cutters, the long journey was over. After the weeks of worry and toil, after the long days of danger and the shattering moments of death, they had reached the promised land—and it was all Boone had foretold. As his little party came in sight of the peaceful grassland, a buffalo herd of two hundred or more crowded around the salt lick near the mouth of Otter Creek, raised their heads at the alien smells and sounds and lumbered away across the river. The land sloped in a thick green turf toward the westward flowing Kentucky. There were two strong-running springs and, nearby, a stand of immense sycamore trees. Even as some of the men unloaded the horses, others, with the eternal land hunger of the frontiersman, were pacing off lots.

All their thoughts were on the land and on the wealth of skins they could take from the deer and buffalo that roved so close. When the two-acre parcels adjacent to the "fort" had been distributed, the men ranged farther out to study the terrain with an eye to future claims. In spite of Boone's urging, they made no move to see to their mutual security. Not even the death of another of their number, shot by a roaming band of Indians, stirred them. The camp remained unfortified and only half-watched, an indulgence that would plague the new settlement.

Cocke rode in on April 17, to mutual thanksgiving, and Boone immediately sent Stoner and three men with a string of packhorses to lend assistance to Henderson's caravan. They made contact the following day.

Henderson wrote in his journal: "Camped that night in the eye of the rich land. Stoner brought us excellent beef in plenty." Two days later they marched into Fort Boone and were saluted by the fire of twenty-five rifles, "all that was then at Fort." Henderson reported to the Transylvania Company proprietors:

> Captain Boone related the history of his adventures, and came in for his share of applause; here it was that the whole load, as it were, dropped off my shoulders . . . and though we had nothing here to refresh ourselves with, but cold water and lean buffalo beef, without bread, it certainly was the most joyous banquet I ever saw.

It was an auspicious time for new beginnings. April 20 was Henderson's fortieth birthday. The day before, in Massachusetts, British soldiers marching to seize a colonial military depot were met at Lexington by a ragtag militia calling themselves minutemen; the British opened fire, killing eight, and marched on. But at Concord, more minutemen appeared, materializing from behind rocks, trees and fences, and they cut the redcoat force to shreds and drove it back to Boston. It was the opening battle of the American Revolution.

On the same day, a Virginia judge, shown a judgment for debt against Daniel Boone with the notation that he possessed "no goods," issued a warrant for his arrest. Across the back of it someone soon wrote, "Gone to Kentucky."

V

The Fourteenth Colony

Lord Dunsmore, who now had troubles of his own, took time to prophesy a bad end for the restive colonies. In a somber letter to the Earl of Dartmouth, he wrote:

> The established Authority is insufficient to restrain the Americans. They acquire no attachment to place: But wandering about seems engrafted in their Nature; and it is a weakness incident to it that they should for ever imagine the Lands further off are still better than those upon which they are already settled.

He was not entirely mistaken but, as usual, had misread the character of the Americans. They moved on not because wandering was engrafted in their nature, but because they sought the open land that had brought their fathers to this new world. A good piece of ground they could clear and farm had come to represent not money alone but a certain standing, a dignity they had not found in the older settlements, a proper place for their children. It ran bone deep, this impulse, like some new and innate human drive.

Did they see themselves as America's pioneers, charting the way west for civilization? It's unlikely. Most had their own grievances against "civilization" and were glad to leave it behind. As a group they were proud, stubborn and cantankerous—traits that might not endear them to eastern neighbors but in the wilderness would help them stand off Indian raids, accidents, natural disasters and recurrent plagues of smallpox and malaria. And so they set off, at first the men alone, with a rifle, a horse, a few head of cattle, and perhaps a sack of seed corn and one of salt.

They followed Boone's Wilderness Road and soon began to trickle into the Transylvania colony. They had traveled a long way. When Henderson showed them the available lots and explained his proprietorship like a good salesman, they went to work building cabins. The promising look of the land and Henderson's easy eloquence momentarily allayed any misgivings they may have felt that this self-assured aristocrat should be imposing the terms of their settlement.

But there were other pioneers already encamped in the Transylvania domain with whom Henderson would have to deal differently. James Harrod, a swarthy, strapping frontiersman with rough manners and a bulldog determination had not been frightened off by the Indians and was unlikely to be intimidated by the Transylvania Company. Returning to Harrodsburg with a band of young adventurers, he soon had started a second settlement at Boiling Springs, fifty miles to the west. He was already raising corn. Benjamin Logan, who traveled partway with Henderson on Boone's road, had turned off and established himself at St. Asaph, some thirty miles south of Harrodsburg.

And one day there walked into camp a stalwart young man named John Floyd posing still another problem. Floyd, leader of a thirty-man surveying party, wanted to know if Henderson would make them a grant of land on reasonable terms; otherwise they meant to cross to the north side of the Kentucky and settle beyond Transylvania's boundaries. Floyd did not need to say that in that case they would be taking their thirty-one rifles with them and that the defense of the Transylvania colony would no longer concern them.

But this was the sort of problem Henderson could handle—the give and take of negotiation between reasonable men, the conception of a legal compact to protect his interests. He wanted no difficulty with Logan and the tempestuous Harrod, and so agreed that they were to stay where they were. As for Floyd, whom the judge credited with "an honest, open countenance, and no small share of good sense," he and his men were given leave to settle "in a compact body for mutual defense" on any lands not already spoken for. In return, the three had only to agree to abide by the preeminent authority of the Transylvania Company.

On May 8, 1775, he ordered the four settlements to hold elections for members of a "House of Delegates of the Colony of Transylvania," and these men to assemble at Boonesborough on May 23 for the purpose of providing the new colony with a government and necessary laws. When Logan and Harrod accepted, they implicitly recognized the proprietorship of the Transylvania partners—all Henderson really wanted. It was also in this document summoning the convention together that the names Transylvania and—in recognition of Boone's transcendent service—Boonesborough, its capital, were first formally used.

The original cluster of cabins generously called Fort Boone did not satisfy Henderson. The day after his arrival, he noted in his journal that it was not large enough to accommodate his people, and that the road cutters, first on the scene, had claimed the best adjacent lands. He "was at some loss how to proceed." Finally, he decided to build a second fort about three hundred yards up the river, "the only commodious place near or where we could be of service to Boone's men or *vice versa.*"

After some days spent clearing and felling trees for the cabin walls, the new fort was finally begun on April 26. Noted William Calk, a Virginian who kept a peppery diary, "We Begin Building us a house & a plaise of Defence to keep the indians off." But the work went slowly. The men crowded into the company store to claim supplies against the wages due them, then went swarming out over the terrain marking off land. Henderson fumed and pleaded but could not persuade them to first finish seeing to their mutual shelter and safety. Everyone with a compass and a chain became a surveyor, laying out lots within the two-mile town site, then going farther out to choose larger tracts that they could claim by planting a corn crop and promising to pay the proprietors a quitrent of two shillings for each hundred acres.

Still there was grumbling. "The western waters," as Henderson caustically put it, "having, as yet, produced no visible alteration with respect to morals or Christian charity amongst us." There had been endless fussing about the surveys and the choice of town lots. When it was decided to allocate them by public lottery, Calk, with rustic pungency, wrote, "We all view our loots and Some Don't like them." Finally, on April 25, a second lottery was held, "at the end of which everybody seemed well satisfied."

More trouble to come was foreshadowed in a rankling discord between Henderson and his partners. Nathaniel Hart, having coldly told Henderson that he supposed his choice of a site for the new fort would serve, refused to have anything to do with it. He went beyond the town's boundaries to select his own land and reported to John Luttrell, another partner, "that he would have nothing to say to the Fort, things were managed in such a manner." Luttrell also settled outside the fort, but left two of his people behind to work.

"Cannot guess the reason of his discontent," Henderson wrote of Hart. Then, as his own anger mounted, he unburdened himself to the proprietors in North Carolina: "Should any successful [attack] be made on us, Captain Hart, I suppose, will be able to render sufficient reasons to the surviving company for withdrawing from our camp, and refusing to join in building a fort for our mutual defence."

The reasons, it now seems safe to say, were grounded in Hart's and Luttrell's contempt for Henderson's leadership. His audacity had gotten them as far as Sycamore Shoals, but his limitations had grown more apparent every day since. He knew nothing of the wilderness; it had been Boone who found this place, Boone who led them to it. Yet here was Henderson, who had spent his adult life in courtrooms and taverns, presuming to chart the destiny of the new settlement and to direct the day-by-day affairs of a hundred or more trail-toughened woodsmen—he who could not get them even to stand a regular watch or complete the defenses! Hart, a tough-minded businessman, thought this dangerous foolishness. Nor was he happy about Henderson's increasingly regular habit of retiring to his quarters with his problems and a jug of whiskey, not to emerge until the following day, red-eyed and woeful.

It was mid-June before Boonesborough took shape, a rectangle enclosing about an acre of ground, one long wall parallel to the river fifty feet away. There were blockhouses at the four corners, the one to the northwest and its adjacent cabins occupied by Henderson. Twenty-six cabins in all made up the fort, with three others inside; in one of these, Squire Boone set up a gunsmith shop. From a distance it appeared a formidable garrison. But the fact is that there were gaps between the cabins that Henderson could not persuade the men to enclose with stockade, and two gates, planned for the center of each long wall, remained unbuilt.

There were daily difficulties. Neighbors quarreled, horses strayed, hunters got lost. But the most pressing problem was an alarming shortage of food. The store of bread was exhausted and there would be no corn crop until August. Those provident enough to have planted a vegetable garden guarded the seedlings well. As for meat, there turned out to be symbolic significance in the buffalo herd frightened off by the road cutters when they first arrived; never again were buffalo seen in the vicinity, and soon they had all retreated to the far side of the Ohio. So wasteful were the hunters, killing five or six buffalo and not taking half a horse-load from all, that they quickly drove the game deep into the wilds, then had to range twenty, even thirty miles from the fort in search of meat, sometimes not returning for a week. As early as May 17, Henderson was writing gloomily:

> Hunters not returned. No meat but fat bear. Almost starved. Drank a little coffee & trust to luck for dinner. Am just going out to our little plant patches in hopes the greens will bear cropping.

Hunger and hardships notwithstanding, preparations went forward for the convention of the Transylvania settlements. In elections held May 20, six delegates were chosen to represent Boonesborough, among them Daniel and Squire Boone, and four each for Harrodsburg, Boiling Springs and Logan's Station at St. Asaph. These twelve rode in on May 23.

As there was no place within the fort suitable for their purpose, the delegates chose a spectacular elm tree for the temporary site of the Transylvania legislature. Beneath the branches, said to reach out so far that a hundred people could seat themselves in its shade, they met in solemn assembly the following day. Henderson greeted them with a full and florid declamation:

> You, perhaps, are placing the corner stone of an edifice, the height and magnificence of whose superstructure is now in the womb of futurity. . . . I have not the least doubt, gentlemen, but that your conduct in this convention will manifest the honest and laudable intentions of the present adventurers, whilst a conscious blush confounds the willful calumniators and officious detractors of our infant, and as yet, little community.

He said that "all power is originally in the people," but the fact is that the people of the Transylvania colony had very little power under the authoritarian government he imposed. The delegates could enact legislation, but the proprietors reserved the right to veto it, and they alone would appoint judges and "all other civil and military officers." Their right to an annual and eternal quitrent of two shillings from every landholder was written into the constitution. It was not a great amount, but it was a mark of vassalage.

The convention enacted nine laws, providing, among other things, for the punishment of criminals and a ban on "profane swearing and Sabbath breaking." The most significant piece of legislation was Daniel Boone's bill to conserve game. After little more than a month "in the eye of the rich land," the men had gone hungry because trigger-mad hunters had driven off the deer, buffalo and bears; without some regulation, they would stay hungry. Boone's bill set limits for each hunter and forbade the waste of meat. All his life he had opposed the wanton slaughter of game, and at Boonesborough he did something about it.

The convention ended with the medieval rite of seisin, the conveyance of a piece of turf to Richard Henderson, symbolizing his full and final possession of the colony. That soaring, sun-filled day was the high-water mark of his life.

It all seemed a fair beginning. The men were flushed with high hopes and a momentary security in their land titles. But Henderson had badly underestimated the character of these pioneers he sought to rule. Headstrong, free-thinking spirits like Boone, Harrod and Floyd had not turned their backs on the restraints of the East to risk everything for the privilege of becoming the docile subjects of a feudal barony in the West. "In Kentucky," they said, "one man's trigger finger is as good as another's." And so the end of Transylvania was written into that beginning. Henderson was to be thwarted less by outside pressures than by the ultimate disaffection of his own people, whom he privately called "that set of rascals." A few months later, his proprietorship threatened from within and without, he went back to North Carolina to meet with his partners; it was the end of his influence at Boonesborough. Real leadership of the colony fell to Daniel Boone and that June he went east to fetch Rebecca. He took with him a party of men and packhorses to bring back the supplies stored at Martin's Station when the wagons were abandoned.

Since spring, the Continental Congress had been sitting in Philadelphia, directing the colonies' patchwork resistance to British efforts to enforce control by the power of arms, and debating whether a peaceful resolution of their differences with the Crown was possible now that blood had been shed. George Washington, named to command the ragged Continental army that had just been defeated at Bunker Hill, was still insisting that he "abhorred independence," and Thomas Jefferson hoped for "the most permanent harmony with Great Britain." But to a lowborn visionary named Thomas Paine, only lately arrived in America, the colonials' course was clear: "A greater absurdity cannot be conceived of than three millions of people running to their seacoast every time a ship arrives from London, to know what portion of liberty they might enjoy."

The Transylvania proprietors were caught with one foot in each camp. Uncertain which side would prevail, they tried to offend neither, petitioning in the same remarkable letter for both the rebels' recognition and the royal "regard and protection." Addressing himself to the Continental Congress, Henderson reaffirmed the partners' allegiance to the King, pledged their lives in his support and "flattered themselves" that the new colony, "without any expense to the Crown, will be acceptable to His Most Gracious Majesty." In the next paragraph, he took it all back:

> If the United Colonies are reduced, or will submit tamely to be slaves, Transylvania will have reason to fear. . . . Having their hearts warmed with the same noble spirit that animates the United Colonies, and moved with indignation at the late Ministerial and Parliamentary usurpation, it is the earnest wish of the Proprietors of Transylvania to be considered as brethren, engaged in the same great cause of liberty . . . therefore, the Memorialists hope and earnestly request that the infant Colony of Transylvania may be added to the number of the United Colonies.

The answer was no. The company's ambiguity did not help their cause, but the real difficulty was that the Continental Congress, beset and divided, had no desire to take on any additional problems. John Adams noted that "The proprietors have no grant from the crown, nor any from any colony, are within the limits of Virginia (and) charged with Utopian Schemes." Their imposition of quitrents, he added, was a form of vassalage hardly consistent with the republican aspirations of the thirteen colonies. When Jefferson advised the partners to go back to the Virginia convention and seek its approval, Henderson's high-flown dream for the Transylvania colony was doomed.

Meanwhile, Boone, unaware of these maneuverings, was back on the Clinch. Rebecca was pregnant and carrying beyond her time. When the child was finally born, a boy named William, he was sickly and lived only a short while. The parents grieved until they had buried him, then turned to face the next day. Grief was a luxury few could afford on the frontier— every day claimed its due. There were preparations to be made for the trip west. At long last Daniel Boone was taking his family to Kentucky.

They did not go alone. As always, there were good men willing to throw in their lot with Boone and, meeting up with the work detail at Martin's Station, they made an impressive party—"twenty-one guns," cattle, hogs, dogs and a string of packhorses loaded with ammunition and provisions. They marched into Boonesborough on the afternoon of September 8, a heartening sight to the men who had bravely remained behind. But none of those, nor any of the newcomers, ever demonstrated greater faith in the little settlement than had Boone. He alone had brought his family, and Rebecca and young Jemima were, in his own words, "the first white women that ever stood on the banks of the Kentucke river." Although the Transylvania Company was to become a footnote to history, the return of Boone with his family assured the continuing life of Boonesborough.

The journey had taken nearly two months, a long and tedious time for Rebecca. The fort, when she first saw it from the hills flanking the long meadowland, was a welcome sight. From the distance it must have seemed to her little different from others she had lived in. Closer, the differences became painfully clear. There were still only a handful of cabins, many unfinished and open to weather and the curiosity of passersby. There was no privacy, no well, no stockade, no fortifications. Outside, the straggly cornfields lay within easy rifle range of the wooded bluff across the river. Not that that mattered for now: Every stalk had already been picked clean.

And they were three hundred miles deep in the wilderness, and the next nearest place of human habitation, Harrodsburg, they told Rebecca, was, "not nearly so advanced as Boonesborough." She had lived on the frontier all her life, but always within a day's ride of a town, a store, a doctor, a militia troop. There were none of those amenities here. There was only what they had brought and would build, and no one to fall back on but each other. And accepting it all, this remarkable woman went to work settling her family into the cabin her husband had built in the hollow down from the fort. It had never occurred to Boone that she might do otherwise.

In Henderson's continuing absence, he gradually assumed effective control of the fort, sending out scouts to patrol the country and search for Indian signs, and pressing for completion of the stockade. As summer passed and crops were harvested in the East, Boonesborough had a surge of newcomers. Among them was Simon Kenton, a strapping youth, only twenty, but already well known in Kentucky as a daring Indian fighter and woodsman. Boone promptly appointed him a scout and sent him off on patrol. By the end of September, Squire and Richard Callaway, who had also gone east for their families, returned, as did a company of Bryans. With the presence of Jemima Boone, a comely thirteen, the Callaway daughters, and other recently arrived young women, a sudden spate of shaving and haircutting overtook the men.

There were other indications that Boonesborough was settling into a community. The Boones gave up their cabin in the hollow and moved up to the "big fort." Soap kettles and clotheslines appeared, as did an occasional looking glass; the whir of a spinning wheel could be heard in the soft autumn afternoons. A man named William Pogue, remembered as "an ingenious contriver," was soon turning out cups, washtubs and churns, and offering them for sale. There was even a soothsayer, a shrewish sprite of a woman who professed the ability to read a man's character by looking into his eyes. Whether she could or couldn't, her judgment seemed decisive. "If she found a man to be a coward," notes the company ledger, "he stood a poor chance to get his washing or mending done."

As with any community, there were dissensions. Virginians were jealous of the preponderant numbers and consequent influence of the North Carolinians, who, in turn, resented the steady influx of "outsiders." One man's cow fattened in another man's pasture; and *she* hadn't yet returned the salt she'd borrowed two weeks before. But it was land that led to most of the disputes—land they all dreamed of by night, and land they sought, claimed and quarreled about by day. They scrambled over each other's survey chains and inevitably overlapped each other's boundary lines, and more than once Boone had to intervene to avert bloodshed.

But even the worst of these clashes was forgotten and the settlers stood shoulder to shoulder in the most galling grievance of all—the Transylvania Company. Those who came in Henderson's party or immediately behind had accepted his proprietary government without fully understanding it; all they'd known for certain was that the company claimed to own Kentucky, and that only Henderson could dispense any part of it. But now they were here! They had staked out their land and cleared it, built cabins and planted corn. They were willing to pay the brutal physical price of conquering the soil, but not to be bound again into a lifetime of quitrent serfdom. The revolutionary winds, sweeping westward over the mountains, stirred their longing to be their own men, to be free.

Henderson and his partners tried to soothe their anger with words, but when the proprietors claimed seventy thousand acres of choicest bluegrass for themselves and raised the price of land for everyone else, the settlements passed from dissent to mutiny. James Harrod, in one of his most thunderous rages, addressed a petition to the Virginia assembly "imploring" that Harrodsburg and Boiling Springs be taken under its protection. The spirit of revolt spread to Boonesborough and a second petition was sent off, this one sparing no detail of the people's ire: it was remembered that Hart and Luttrell had taken for themselves land meant for the town; Henderson held all the most convenient acreage "whilst some of your petitioners have been under the necessity of clearing ground at the risk of our lives"; he had even "had the fence that was made by the people broke" for use around his own gardens.

Boone took no part in all this. He was tugged by conflicting loyalties—his natural sympathies with the people but unable to turn his back on Richard Henderson, to whom his hopes, if not his fortunes, had been tied for fifteen years. In any event, he must have sensed the inevitability of the outcome. Without the people's allegiance, the only thing Henderson really owned was the paper his deeds were written on, and he could not claim the people's allegiance if they were unwilling to give it.

In the end, an aggressive young Virginian named George Rogers Clark, who was beginning to make a name for himself in the West, took the settlers' case directly to the Virginia legislature. On December 7, 1776—by which time Virginia had declared herself a free state, independent of Great Britain and with sovereignty over all the lands she had ever held—the assembly created the County of Kentucky and incorporated it into the Virginia Commonwealth, and two years later pronounced the Transylvania purchase void.

Eventually, Henderson and Company was voted a consolation grant of two hundred thousand acres on the grounds that the proprietors had "incurred a heavy expence and have had great trouble and risques." In 1779, Henderson took his dreams to western Tennessee, promoting a colonization of the area around what became Nashville. But as the Boonesborough store ledger had tartly put it, "he had habits of intemperance," and he died soon after at the age of fifty. Boone was given nothing and, in fact, lost the two thousand acres he was to have earned for cutting the Wilderness Road.

By the time news of Transylvania's dissolution reached Boonesborough, it was among the least of Boone's worries. In the winter of 1775, scouts had begun reporting Indian signs in the vicinity. But things had been quiet for so long that no one paid any heed to these warnings or took any precautions.

They should have. North of the Ohio River, word had finally reached the Shawnee tribes that the white man had come to Kentucky to stay. The

Indians intended otherwise. At the very least they would exact a bitter price. In full fury, the Shawnee made ready to take the warpath. Toward the end of the year they persuaded some renegade Cherokees to join the battle, among them a chief named Hanging Maw who had known Boone in the Watauga country. Hanging Maw counseled caution. No brave he ever knew was the equal of Boone, he said, calling him Wide Mouth, in the Cherokee way. His brothers must proceed with great care.

Two days before Christmas, Colonel Arthur Campbell, a North Carolina militiaman, and two youths named McQuinney and Sanders left Boonesborough and crossed the Kentucky looking for good bottomland. Although Campbell, at least, should have known better, none carried a rifle. They were seen separating, Campbell disappearing upstream and the boys climbing a hill into the forest. Then a shot was heard and a cry for help from the hill. Campbell came scuttling back to the landing. He had seen "a couple of Indians," he shouted out to Boone and the other men hurrying across the river. But the rescuers saw nothing and the search continued. Finally, three days after Christmas, they found McQuinney's body. He had been murdered and scalped and left in a cornfield three miles from the fort. They never found Sanders at all.

The result was panic, a flurry of long-delayed work on the fortifications, some timid souls packing to leave. There were reports that the British were goading the Indians to war. Rumors of attacks on the outer settlements sped the exodus. As a militia commander, Colonel William Russell, who, with Boone, had lost a son in the bloody first attempt to settle Kentucky, warned the settlers to give up and return to safety before it was too late. By July 1776, barely two hundred people remained of the five hundred who had made the long westward trek.

But those who were still in Kentucky were there to stay. In the first place, said Boone, it was unseemly for a man with a family to run. When someone asked him about the second place, he replied, "There is no second place, nor any other place—Kentucky is my home."

The doughty John Floyd wrote, "I want to return as much as any man can do; but when I think of the deplorable condition a few helpless families are likely to be in, I conclude to sell my life as dearly as I can in their defense." His words were to prove sadly prophetic.

The time of trouble had barely begun. The British had indeed come to realize that the Indians could be a formidable and ferocious ally in their war to put down the American insurrection. And Kentucky was the back door to the rebellious colonies. Without the thin line of settlers' stations in the wilderness, the isolated border posts in western Virginia and the Carolinas stood naked to attack. And beyond lay the undefended colonial towns and cities. For the next six years, the British assiduously courted the Indians, paying for their allegiance in weapons and trade goods, and endlessly inflaming them against the backwoods settlers who had robbed them of their land and game. At Detroit, the British lieutenant governor, Colonel Henry Hamilton, became particularly adept at inciting Shawnee raids and sieges against the Kentucky outposts. He offered a bounty for American scalps and was scornfully referred to in the settlements as "The Hair Buyer."

It was all an epic misjudgment of British statecraft, and perhaps fatal to their chances of winning the Revolution. The fact is that they could have won all of Kentucky to their side with little more effort and less cost than it took to woo the Indians. A war for independence was an outlandish concept in the far-off settlements; the Indian danger was real. Most emigrants felt no special affinity for the colonies they had recently abandoned; some even sided with the British and, as the fighting spread across the seaboard and partisan passion was inflamed, many declared Tories fled North Carolina seeking a haven in remote Kentucky, among them a number of Rebecca's relatives. In any case, the settlers almost surely would have allied themselves with any government that recognized their land claims and promised to protect them against the Indians.

But the British were blind to this alluring possibility. Instead, they persisted in their campaign to win Kentucky by terror—the last battle of the Revolution would be fought at Blue Licks, north of Boonesborough— and so assured the settlers' ultimate allegiance to the newly created United States of America.

At Boonesborough that summer of 1776, provisions were scarce and ammunition running low. But apart from Callaway, a chronic worrier, few among the hardy pioneers brooded about the danger in the new land. Though scouts ranging out across the country reported fresh Indian signs nearly every day, there had been no attacks since December. A few of the people had even built cabins on the far side of the river. Meanwhile, the corn grew, apple and peach trees had been planted and the most recent arrivals brought goodly flocks of poultry. The firm beginnings of a colony had been made.

Sunday afternoon, July 14, seemed to hold everything the people had come seeking in Kentucky—a clear and tranquil sky, and the full rich sun to nourish the eager land. Jemima Boone, sixteen-year-old Betsey Callaway and her younger sister Fanny were canoeing on the river just below the town. Jemima had cut the bottom of her foot on a sharp stubble of cane and was trailing it in the cool water while the other girls paddled. They were clearly Boonesborough's prize beauties, Betsey already engaged to marry Samuel Henderson, younger brother of the judge, and Jemima and Fanny, though only fourteen, with serious suitors of their own.

There was some talk of picking wildflowers on the far shore, but Jemima, looking at the dense cane and the dark forested hills behind, said she thought they had better not. But the canoe was already close to shore and the current nosed them into a gravel bank. Before they could make a move, the cane rustled and quivered and then suddenly exploded in a swarm of shaved heads and painted faces. Ruddy arms snatched at the boat and lunged in at them.

"Indians!" Fanny Callaway shrieked.

She tried to beat them off with her paddle but it broke. All three, wild with terror, screamed until strong hands were clamped over their mouths and they were dragged through the shoals, kicking and splashing up a shower of water. Under cover of the cane, the Indians flaunted knives and tomahawks. Speaking English, they demanded silence, one of them grabbing a fistful of Betsey Callaway's hair in menacing emphasis. Then the captives were rushed up into the dark hills. The canoe, the only one at the settlement, was left beached on the far bank.

There were five of them, three Shawnee and two Cherokees, and they were led by Hanging Maw; one of the Shawnee was the son of Chief Black Fish. They had come to spy out the Boonesborough defenses, but female prisoners were a particular prize and when these all but fell into their hands, Hanging Maw was willing to waive his own counsel of caution. Three young squaws would be a handsome trophy to parade through the Shawnee villages across the Ohio.

By the time they reached the high ground, Jemima Boone had collected her wits. She threw herself down and said they could kill her, but she could not go another step in bare feet, and held up her cane wound for emphasis. Hanging Maw, in high good humor, produced a pair of moccasins for her. Then, as the three girls gasped with shame, he cut their toe-length dresses off at the knee to free them "for a long journey—and we walk fast." He told them to wrap the bottoms around their legs so they would not be scratched by underbrush.

Jemima now recognized the Cherokee chief. Playing for time,

innocently twisting her heels into the ground so the evidence of their presence would be plain, she told him that she remembered his visiting her father, Daniel Boone, when they had lived on the Watauga.

"You Boone's girl?" Hanging Maw asked, astonished.

"Yes."

"And they, too?"

"Yes," she lied. Then she pleaded with him to let them all go.

Hanging Maw shook his head and grinning, said, "Well, we do pretty good for old Wide Mouth this time."

But it was clear that his elation was tempered with concern: Wide Mouth would not be long starting after them. The Indians peremptorily yanked the girls to their feet and scurried off along the ridgeline, where there was little vegetation to betray their passage. Coming down out of the hills, Hanging Maw sought out thick canebrakes to travel through and divided the party to leave confusing, crisscrossing trails. At the brooks and creeks they left no trail at all, walking hundreds of yards upstream or down before striking out overland again, always working their way northward, toward the Ohio.

But Jemima and the Callaway girls, born to the frontier, knew a few tricks too. They kept dropping shreds of skirt behind for those who were sure to follow, and when the Indians caught them at this, they broke twigs until their hands blistered. Betsey, who wore high heels, made certain they left a distinct imprint in the soft earth before Hanging Maw, noticing, knocked them off with his tomahawk. With her injured foot as excuse, Jemima delayed their progress by periodically falling to the ground with "pain." In all, they were about as submissive to Hanging Maw and his braves as a wounded bear.

By nightfall the raiders had covered only eight miles and had to make a cold camp close to the Warrior's Path, fearing that a fire might be seen by pursuers. They ate dried buffalo tongue, offering to share it with their captives, who found it all but unpalatable. But in accordance with fundamental tenets of both the Cherokees and Shawnee, the girls were not molested, an unlikely forbearance had the captors been white. Before the Indians stretched out on the bare ground to sleep, they tied each girl, sitting, to a tree; except for fragments of nightmare-torn dozing, the three were awake all night long. With the first light of dawn, Hanging Maw hurried them off.

At midday they came upon a pony the Indians had found earlier and left tied for their return. Now, hoping to gain some speed, they put Jemima up on its back. Pretending she knew nothing about horses, she managed to slide off at every hill. In fact, she knew a great deal: when the way was level, she tickled the pony's flank, causing it to rear, and off she would tumble. Exasperated, one of the braves tried mounting to show her how to ride properly, whereupon the now thoroughly vexed pony turned and bit his arm. Finally they abandoned it altogether.

But thereafter the Indians pressed relentlessly ahead, their tempers frayed, and threatened death if the girls continued to delay. Sometimes they hauled them along by the wrists so that it was impossible for them to leave signs of their passing. Mainly they followed the Warrior's Path, but often broke off into nearby buffalo traces or crossed the open country when it could better cover their trail. They did not stop until dark and then, again, ate hard smoked meat in a dark camp. But the next day, still moving swiftly northward, they paused to kill a buffalo and cut out the juicy hump. Soon after, they stopped to cook it. Hanging Maw's confidence had returned. He and his braves had now put more than forty miles between themselves and Boonesborough and were just below the Licking River, only another day's march from the Ohio and the safety of the Scioto country.

Sensing the Indians' self-assurance, the girls' spirits sank. Until now they had kept up their hopes with the certainty that at any moment their fathers would appear with a pursuit party and save them. But they had been kidnapped on Sunday and now it was Tuesday, and soon they would be beyond rescue. Hungry, footsore, utterly spent, suddenly they could see only a lifetime of concubinage in some faraway Indian village—or worse—and they wept bitterly. Betsey Callaway held Fanny and Jemima to her, but could not comfort them.

On the Sunday afternoon of the girls' disappearance, Flanders Callaway, cousin to Betsey and Fanny and an ardent aspirant for Jemima's hand, walked down to the river landing to meet their canoe. When he saw it aground on the north bank, when there was no response to his repeated calls, he raced back to the fort and gave the alarm.

No one doubted what had happened, and confusion and bedlam caught hold of the settlers. Betsey's sweetheart, Samuel Henderson, only half-finished shaving, dropped his razor and snatching up his rifle, raced for the river. Others followed, but they could only mill around on the bank, for there was no way to cross. Every one of them wore their Sunday clothes, blousy breeches that would be torn to shreds in the brambles.

Daniel Boone was enjoying a peaceful Sunday afternoon nap. Awakened by Rebecca with the bad news, he dashed down to the river without even bothering about his moccasins. But he quickly established a sense of order. Picking lithe young David Gass out of the highly agitated throng, he sent him swimming across the river to retrieve the canoe, without which they were helpless. The other men were to cover Gass with their rifles in case there were Indians still lurking on the opposite shore. When Richard Callaway and some mounted men rode up, Boone dispatched them to a river ford about a mile downstream; he would meet them on the far bank.

He crossed in the canoe with John Floyd, young Henderson and three others. The kidnappers' trail was easy enough to find, but by this time the sun was less than an hour high. Callaway and his party wanted to ride directly after them, but Boone persuaded them otherwise. The Indians could be overtaken, he assured them. The real difficulty would be to steal up on them and rescue the girls before the alarm was given; the clatter of ten approaching horses could only guarantee that the girls would be tomahawked. The horsemen, he said, should ride north to cut off the Indians' retreat at the Lower Blue Licks, where they would have to cross the Licking River.

While Callaway led his party off, irritated again at having to do Boone's bidding, the men on foot plunged into the deeply shadowed hills. But they had barely gone five miles before darkness overtook them and they were forced to make camp for the night. When someone remarked that Boone was still barefoot, he sat down to consider their situation and realized that none of them was prepared for a wilderness pursuit or the battle to come. They had no food, little ammunition and wore clothing fit for Sabbath services under a warm sun.

For the second time that day he singled out David Gass. "How are you feeling after your swim?" he asked.

"Cold."

"Well, here is a worthy way to keep warm," he said, and hurried him back to the fort for the needed supplies. Before morning, that brave young man had returned with powder and lead, a supply of jerk, proper breeches and deerskin shirts for each man—and Daniel Boone's moccasins. They started out as soon as they could see the trail.

For a time, the telltale signs left by the captives led the pursuers along at full speed. But beyond the first night's camp, the Indians had split up going through a canebrake and left not one trail but five. Although the

Kentuckians eventually found the true one, they lost nearly an hour checking each of the diversions.

Boone decided to change tactics. He was convinced the warriors were taking their prizes back to the Shawnee villages along the Scioto and now proposed abandoning the trail altogether and pursuing a straight course in that direction. But some of the others, who knew only enough about Indian ways to be taken in by them, wondered aloud how they could ever hope to rescue the girls if they didn't follow the trail. To which Boone dryly remarked that there were no special rewards for finding cold trails and abandoned camps, "unless you set a store by having some Shawnee bucks beholden to you." The important thing was to close the distance. In a day or so, when the Indians were closer to home, they would grow less cautious; the pursuit party would not only pick up their trail again, but would have a better chance of taking them by surprise.

There were no more arguments and the men moved silently and speedily north. They crossed the Indians' trail more than once, recognizing Betsey Callaway's heel prints or finding shreds of clothing and a littering of broken twigs, but neither stopped nor deviated from their course. By dark, they had covered nearly thirty miles and as they slumped to the ground, suddenly hearing the mysterious night sounds of the forest, even the doubters sensed the closeness of their quarry and knew that the next day would bring a battle.

Tuesday's dawn had barely risen before they resumed the chase, Boone in the lead. He said there was a fork of the Licking River not far ahead and "supposed" they would find the place where the Indians had crossed. They reached the fork around 10:00 A.M.: on the bank directly in front of them there were fresh moccasin tracks; the water was still muddy. Now, Boone said, they would follow the trail.

It led them back to the Warrior's Path, then intermittently left it, as though the Indians had reminded themselves to safeguard against Wide Mouth's pursuit. But now it was too late. Like a predatory animal, Wide Mouth had patiently tracked his prey into a corner and paid no attention to its last futile efforts to get away. Soon he came on the slaughtered buffalo. Ahead, he told his men, there would be water. The trail would disappear again, but only because the Indians would have taken a final precaution before making camp to prepare their meal. They would find them in that camp, he said.

Just before noon a little creek crossed their path, swallowing the trail. But wading downstream, they smelled smoke, then saw muddy tracks marching up the north bank. Boone halted his men in the water and gave final instructions in an urgent whisper; they would separate into two groups and close in with absolute caution; no one was to fire until he did, and then they were to pour in a full volley and charge the camp. If anyone blundered, if they gave themselves away too soon, the survivors would stay to bury at least three dead girls.

Stealthy as Indians themselves, the white men now crept up on a patch of cane, Boone and John Floyd the leading riflemen approaching from the upstream side. They caught sight of the camp at a range of thirty yards and stopped. They saw the girls, Betsey sitting against a tree and the other two with their heads in her lap. The Indians were well dispersed, one preparing the buffalo hump for the fire, another gathering wood. The sentry was lighting his pipe. With a start, Boone recognized the Cherokee carrying a kettle down to the stream as Hanging Maw.

At that moment, someone fired prematurely, missing. Instantly all five Indians wheeled toward the captives, but Boone and Floyd had already put their rifles to their shoulders. As they squeezed off their shots and the crashing din echoed in the forest, the sentry, Black Fish's son, pitched headlong into the fire. Somehow, he managed to rise and stagger off. The brave spitting the buffalo clutched his breast, which spurted blood as he ran, bent and stumbling, into the deep cane.

Jemima had jumped to her feet. "That's Daddy!" she sang out.

More rifles roared and the other three Indians broke for the canebrake. As Betsey leaped up, one flung his tomahawk at her and it buried itself in the tree trunk against which, an instant before, her head had been resting. Nor was her peril ended. As the whites, howling war whoops, charged the camp, one of them mistook her for an Indian—her cotton leggings now soiled to the color of deerskin, her hair bound up and her skin darkened by exposure—and would have brained her with his rifle butt had not Boone grabbed his upraised arm. "For God's sake, man, don't kill her now!" he cried. "We've come all this way to save her!" A moment later, Samuel Henderson clutched the sobbing girl in his arms.

There was no pursuit. Boone, joyfully holding Jemima, had won what he'd come for and now wanted only to get the exhausted girls home to their mothers. Besides, he did not believe that the Indians could escape Callaway's company at the Licking River ford. But next day, when the horsemen caught up with Boone and his men, Callaway lamely reported that he had seen the tracks of the retreating Indians and decided to return to Boonesborough. Boone did not ask the obvious question—how the fleeing Indians, without arms or even moccasins and with at least two wounded, managed to slip through Callaway's hands—but others did. And Callaway, though relieved to have his daughters safe, was moodily aware that all Boonesborough would soon know that Boone had succeeded and he had failed.

Eventually, Boone was to learn from Black Fish himself that both wounded braves had died before reaching the Licking. Hanging Maw, whose reputation for sagacity among the Shawnee evaporated with the kidnapping fiasco, returned to the Cherokee villages and earnestly tried to repair his standing with the whites. His squaw, at least, must have assumed he succeeded: after his death, she petitioned the United States Congress for a pension!

Meanwhile, Boonesborough celebrated the girls' safe return, and the story of their dramatic rescue was told and retold in all the settlements. Within the month, Betsey and Samuel Henderson were married by Squire Boone. It was the first wedding in Kentucky and properly celebrated with dancing and "the first home-grown watermelons, of which the whole station was proud." Flanders Callaway and John Holder, the other eager swains, took their participation in the rescue as reason enough to press their own suits, even suggesting a triple wedding. But they would have to contain themselves for another year, until Jemima and Fanny were fifteen. At that, Colonel Callaway was not overjoyed to have his nephew marrying into the Boone family.

A few days after the wedding, a returning settler brought to Boonesborough a Virginia newspaper with some stunning tidings: on July 4, the Continental Congress had signed a proclamation declaring that henceforth the thirteen colonies were free and independent of Great Britain. The newcomer read the text of the Declaration of Independence, as it was called, to the assembled garrison. Some let loose loud cheers and war whoops, but others sullenly walked back to their cabins. There were those at Boonesborough, the Bryans among them, who regarded their oath of fealty to the King as sacred and thought the revolutionary fervor dangerous tomfoolery besides. They would have a difficult time in days to come, and would create difficulties as well.

But the fact is that the news was only a passing sensation that summer. The settlers, rebels and loyalists both, were more concerned with the matter of survival for the kidnapping had turned out to be only the Indians' opening thrust, an omen of trouble and terror yet to come. During the absence of the rescuers, who were nearly all the able-bodied men at the fort, raiders had burned Nathaniel Hart's cabin and destroyed five hundred young apple trees that had been transported across hundreds of miles of wilderness. Shawnee warriors haunted the woods around the settlements. Hunters disappeared. On Christmas Day, a war party attacked a Harrodsburg company on its way to get desperately needed ammunition, then besieged McClelland's Station, north of the Kentucky River. They were beaten off, but the isolated settlers, afraid they could not survive a second attack, retreated to a temporary haven at Boonesborough on the last day of 1776.

The Indians had dug up the hatchet. The harrowing Year of the Three Sevens was about to begin.

VI

Boonesborough: The Battle Joined

In the beginning, the Indians contented themselves with "secret mischief." Small raiding parties roamed the woods or lurked outside the settlements waiting for the chance to steal a horse or take the scalp of an unwary cattle herder. They would hurl a firebrand into a cabin at Harrodsburg, vanish, and without warning appear again at Boonesborough to ambush a hunter. One day they ran to the very gates of a fort to snatch an infant from its mother's arms and dash its brains out against a tree; another day, they were satisfied to lay in hiding until they could steal away with a red cloak that someone had hung out to air. As sinister as the toll they took was this terrifying unpredictability.

The white man's hand could be ruthless, too. Many a warrior's scalp was shamelessly carried back to the settlements, and at Harrodsburg they fed Indian bodies to the dogs because they believed it would make them fierce. Mainly these things were done to bolster the settlers' own courage. Before long, though, seven settlements were abandoned, leaving only Logan's Station, Harrodsburg and Boonesborough. In all Kentucky there were not 150 fit riflemen. Late in February, a Harrodsburg committee sent a plea for help to Virginia's Governor Patrick Henry:

> We are surrounded with Enemies on every side; every day increases their numbers. To retreat from the place where our all is centered would be little preferable to death. Yet our Fort is already filled with widows and orphans and their necessities call on us daily for supplies . . . the apprehension of an invasion in the Ensuing spring fills our minds with a thousand fears.

But the best Virginia could do was to legitimatize some actions the Kentuckians had already taken on their own: a fixed period of military service was mandated for every able-bodied man; and Daniel Boone, James Harrod and Benjamin Logan were given captains' commissions in the Virginia militia and appointed commanders of their respective forts.

At Boonesborough, where Boone had begun strengthening the fortifications the very day he returned with the kidnapped girls, two tall blockhouses were completed in March and all the cabins finally palisaded. He kept two permanent scouts, Simon Kenton and Thomas Brooks, reconnoitering the north side of the Kentucky River all the way to the Ohio so that there might be some warning of any large Indian force. His remaining twenty-eight "guns" were divided into two platoons, one standing guard while the other plowed and planted; then they changed over.

Still, that month two men working in a nearby field were shot dead by the Shawnee. A few days later Boone himself was jumped by an Indian as he tracked a bear along a nearby creek. The brave's tomahawk diverted by Boone's ever-present beaver hat, the two fell into punishing hand-to-hand combat, rolling on the muddy bank and falling down to the stream. There Boone came up with his knees straddling the Indian's head and kept it pressed under the water until every flailing and quiver had stopped. The stream is still known as Drowning Creek.

But the trouble was that few of the other settlers had Boone's strength or wilderness cunning. One of them heard a turkey cackle and went into the woods after it. He did not return. Hearing this, Boone knew he was down to twenty-seven guns. The tempting gobble was heard again, and this time Boone went, slipping into the woods and concealing himself in the hollow of a tree. Soon enough the "turkey," a war-painted Shawnee, went stealing past him gobbling away. "Hey!" Boone called. As the startled Indian spun, tomahawk raised, Boone shot him through the heart. Nearby he found the dead settler; he had already been scalped.

The scarcity of fresh meat grew critical. In pursuit of game, a lone rifleman now had to slip out of the fort in darkness and ride fast and far, shooting from the saddle and butchering his kill while hanging on to the bridle, for there were Indians everywhere in the woods. Loading only what he could carry on a single horse, the hunter would make for home, galloping across the dangerous open ground around the fort at full speed. As the warm weather came on and salt stocks dwindled, it was impossible to store an edible supply of meat.

The situation was equally grim at the other settlements. One man was chased to the very gates of Harrodsburg, only to have them slammed shut in his face, the Shawnee so close that the people did not dare open up. He threw himself behind a stump and lay curled and cowering while bullets plunked all around and the settlers did their best to protect him with a covering fire. Finally someone thought to dig a hole under the stockade and they pulled him in.

Terror was the Indians' most telling weapon. An old pioneer named Barney Stagner had taken it on himself to care for the fort spring, about a half mile away; he was under the delusion that the Indians would not harm him because he was so close to death anyway. But one day his body was found by the spring with the head cut off, and thereafter the children went about in constant fear of encountering the headless ghost of Barney Stagner.

Squire Boone, who had taken his family to Harrodsburg, was attacked within sight of the fort, a glancing tomahawk cleaving open the side of his face. Armed with his short sword, he ran it through the Indian who, incredibly, fought on. Wet with blood, the wounded men grappled until, at last, the Indian died, breaking the sword at the hilt as he fell. Squire was left with a lifelong scar—and two weeks later was shot from the cover of the woods, suffering a broken rib.

Simon Kenton had returned to Boonesborough early in spring to report to Boone and have a brief rest. He was a remarkable man, well over six feet tall and, at twenty-two, already judged among the best of Kentucky's wilderness scouts. The story is told of how Boone once closed on someone in the forest and froze in place, just far enough away to take the other for an Indian. For hours the two men slipped from tree to tree, trying for a shot, but both taking such expert advantage of the cover that no shot was possible. Toward dusk Boone was ready to congratulate his matchless adversary, Indian or not, and called a greeting. Out of the brush stepped Simon Kenton.

His presence at Boonesborough on the morning of April 24 was providential. The cows gave the first hint of trouble; they stood shuffling at the open gates and refused to go out to pasture. Sometimes that was a sign of Indians, sometimes plain bovine stubbornness. Boone sent two men down toward the river to investigate; they were also to bring back some firewood. Kenton stood at the gate covering them.

They were returning, arms loaded, when a battery of shots from the woods dropped one, Daniel Goodman. He began crawling toward the fort; the other let his logs fall and raced for the gate. Now six Indians burst from the woods and ran Goodman down, tomahawking him as he tried desperately to get to his feet. Kenton charged, firing as he ran, and killed the lead Indian. The other five Indians took to their heels when Boone and ten more riflemen came running through the gate. The whites chased after them, thinking that this was just another Shawnee hit-and-run raid.

It was a bad miscalculation, and they would pay heavily. For this time Black Fish had struck in force, and his opening feint had worked well. While Boone and his men ran past Goodman's body, sixty yards from the gate, fifty Indians broke from the woods behind them and rushed to cut off their retreat.

"Back to the fort!" Boone called out, and, as the stunned men wheeled about, "Boys, we'll have to fight for it—sell your lives dear!"

He spoke not of their danger alone; beyond those open gates, only a bare handful of riflemen was left to defend the women and children. His men fired a single volley and, with no time to reload, charged into the melee of painted bodies, swinging their rifles like clubs. In time, there was a scatter of supporting fire from the fort.

But the Shawnee still had full charges in their rifles and one, firing from behind a stump, hit Boone in the leg, shattering his anklebone. A warrior was instantly astride the fallen man, tomahawk swinging back, when Kenton—of whom it was said that he could reload on the run—shot him through the chest. Still another Indian jumped on Boone, grabbing a shock of his hair to raise the scalp. But by this time Kenton had rushed up and smashed the painted head with his rifle stock. Dropping the rifle, he swung Boone up into his arms and began running toward the fort, dodging, kicking, but always shielding the wounded man with his own great bulk. The other men tried to protect them; some were dragging casualties, too. And so, yard by yard, they fought their way back. At the last moment, when Kenton was staggering under his burden, Jemima Boone, watching white-faced from the gate, sprinted out and lent him a welcome arm of support over the final stretch. Then the last man was in and the gates were swung closed after them.

Boone, carried to his cabin, demanded a battle report at once. It was grim: one killed, seven wounded. Next the commander turned weakly to Kenton. "Well, Simon," he said, "you behaved like a man today. You are a fine fellow." Finally he let Rebecca see to his wound.

The Shawnee stayed only until nightfall. Their trick had failed and they were not prepared to mount a siege. But a month later they came again, firing on the fort from daybreak until long after dark. And early on July 4 they struck with an even stronger force, burning out the little collection of cabins in the hollow once known as Fort Boone. For two days they pressed the attack, killing one man and destroying all the crops that were not under the very walls of the fort. On the morning of the sixth they were gone and the parched livestock could be let down to the river. Boone, who had lain abed for a month and walked with a stick for another, had been in full command throughout.

Now, even more perilous than the shortage of food, the ammunition supply was nearly exhausted. There were those already talking of throwing themselves on the mercy of the people at Harrodsburg or Logan's Station when someone remembered the existence of some brimstone and saltpeter, brought in with Henderson's original stores. It was quickly uncovered in a corner of the magazine, and while the women melted their pewter plates for bullets, Boone ordered charcoal made. Then he and a few old frontiersmen who knew the art of powder-making produced enough to tide them over for a few weeks more.

Next came the matter of fresh water, until then supplied by an outside spring or when they were under attack and shut up in the fort, by some catch barrels. Facing up to the danger of a protracted siege, Boone ordered a well dug. But it was tedious work and little progress was made.

Later that summer help came. One morning forty mounted men rode majestically across the meadow, ranks open so that Shawnee spies mistook them for two hundred. To the beleaguered, rejoicing settlers, they seemed a thousand. They were mainly volunteers from the Yadkin, commanded by Major William Bailey Smith of the Virginia militia. The fort was further cheered by the appearance of the first American flag to be seen west of the mountains, and soon the red, white and blue with its thirteen stars was flying over the blockhouse. Smith's men and the other militia troops that came over the next months had all signed short-term enlistments, however, and were soon gone. But while they stayed the fort was secure and the people free to tend their crops.

In late autumn they heard that Cornstalk, chief of all the Shawnee, and his son had been brutally shot down by American soldiers at Fort Randolph, though they came under a flag of truce. This was not good news; Cornstalk had tried to be a friend to the whites, and his murder could only further inflame his people. The last good news the Kentucky pioneers had that hard year of 1777 was the return of Benjamin Logan from the Holston with as much powder and lead as four packhorses could carry.

Not knowing worse was to come, the people were glad to see the last of the Year of the Three Sevens and swore they would never forget it. From beginning to end, they had had no rest or peace of mind; nothing could be done in a normal way, not hunting, not planting or cultivating crops. If the Indians weren't murdering, they were stealing. Two hundred horses were spirited away that year, so that hunters sometimes had to carry meat home on their shoulders.

Josiah Collins, who reached Boonesborough early in 1778, said, "We found a poor distressed, ½ naked, ½ starved, people; daily surrounded by the savage." Daniel Trabue, another newcomer, wrote in his diary, "The people in the fort was remarkably kind to us with what they had, but I thought it was hard times, no bread, no vegetables, no fruit of any kinds and no ardent spirits."

On top of it all, the winter was the most severe anyone could remember. And again there was no salt.

Early in January, Boone led a company of salt makers on the long cold ride to Blue Licks, forty miles north on the Licking River. They were thirty strong, men from each of the three forts; a string of packhorses carried their heavy iron kettles. They were to alternate month-long shifts with a relief party until a year's supply of salt had been made and sent back to the settlements.

Unable to cure hides or preserve game, faced day after day with a dreary diet of turnips and cornmeal mush and only an occasional slim ration of flavorless venison, the settlers grumbled about the lack of salt and worried over the sickness it threatened. With salt, they could be warmly dressed in deerskin jackets and adequately fed on cured meats; without it, the bitter winter would take a heavy toll. And so the salt-making expedition had been organized, now, while the Indians were likely wintering in their Scioto villages and a troop of eastern militia was on hand in case a few stray warriors ventured south of the Ohio.

The work went well. All day fires blazed under a dozen huge kettles filled from the salt spring, boiling and steaming away to leave a crust of precious white crystals. It took ten kettles of water to make a bushel of salt, and all day the men were busy fetching water and chopping wood to keep the fires high. By the time they began expecting the relief party, three hundred bushels of salt were stored for transport and three men with loaded packhorses had already been sent back to the settlements.

Boone regularly kept at least two scouts out. On the morning of February 7, he sent his new son-in-law, Flanders Callaway, and Thomas Brooks off to the east while he himself rode west to reconnoiter the country and bring back some meat for the men. He made a looping circle of nearly ten miles, pausing only to slaughter a buffalo and load the meat on his horse. He was returning on foot along the river when the sky darkened and he was overtaken by a blizzard. Leading the horse through a veil of slashing snow, he suddenly realized that he was not alone in the desolation. Four Indians were loping after him, not thirty paces behind.

He thought first to cut the meat from his horse and ride off, but buffalo grease had frozen his knife fast in its sheath. Then he abandoned the horse and began to run. He heard shots and knew the Indians were giving him fair warning—no one could miss at that range, except intentionally. What could he do? Turn and kill one? He would never get a chance to reload. Try to outrun them? They could follow his tracks in the snow all the way back to the Kentucky River. He broke into a walk, then stopped and leaned his rifle against a tree, stepping away from it in the sign of surrender. His gloating captors were Shawnee, which he had anticipated, but an hour later he was in their camp and that was a stunning shock.

Around a long fire sat more than a hundred armed and painted warriors—a full-fledged war party. It was obviously equipped and directed by the British army, and with many whites among them, it was strong enough to annihilate the salt makers and go on to overwhelm the Kentucky settlements. For Boonesborough, mainstay of the wilderness defense line, was in fact helpless without the salt makers' thirty rifles and those of the relief party, now on its way to Blue Licks. And once these warriors had tasted blood at Boonesborough, nothing could stop them from continuing on to Harrodsburg and Logan's Station and crushing both.

These dark thoughts churned through Boone's mind, but his face betrayed no anxiety. Indeed, he seemed glad to be among old friends. The Indians knew him at once. One rose and made a speech praising his hunting skill, and many came up to shake the hand of their celebrated captive. Boone recognized Captain Will, who had taken him prisoner during his first exploration of Kentucky. "Howdy, Captain Will," he said cheerfully. "You steal my horses, remember? You put a bell around my neck. But then I run away, right?"

Captain Will laughed with glee and clapped the smiling white man on the back. "Boone, you not run away this time," he said.

A chief approached, a strong, stocky brave past middle years. By the black man at his side, an escaped slave named Pompey who had joined the Shawnee as an interpreter, Boone knew that he was in the presence of the mighty Black Fish. If the war chief himself had assumed command of this foray, real trouble, indeed, was promised for the settlers.

They shook hands. Black Fish asked where the men at the salt licks had come from and Boone told him. The chief nodded thoughtfully and said, "Tomorrow we will kill them. Then we will capture your fort."

Boone knew that the Indians could do this, and that if the women and children were not massacred on the spot, few would survive a winter march to the far side of the Ohio. But in a calm voice he said only that the great Cornstalk would not have taken the warpath just because the British paid him to do it. Black Fish replied angrily. His warriors were not painted for the British, but to avenge Cornstalk's death.

> When the Red Coats came to us and offered us much paint and many guns to fight the Long Knives, we refused. But our great chief Cornstalk went to the fort of the Long Knives to talk peace with them. Then the Long Knives murdered him and his son, although they came in peace and without arms. The spirit of chief Cornstalk calls out from his grave to us to take revenge for these murders, and we will do it.

Now Boone understood why the Shawnee were on the march in winter. Choosing his words with care, he said that the Long Knives who had killed Cornstalk were full of treachery and had dishonored all the whites. But they were not of Boone's tribe; the Kentuckians wanted only to live in peace with their Shawnee brothers. He sensed that Black Fish was taking to him—as most Indians did—and that if he kept talking he might at least save the defenseless settlers at Boonesborough.

"We will kill them anyway," Black Fish said, but less vehemently.

Boone shrugged. "Perhaps, but many Shawnee will fall, too. There are thirty good riflemen at the licks, and twice that number at the fort." His manner was so open and artless that the lie came out as convincing as the truth.

"Cornstalk will not rest until we take revenge."

"He will rest if you take prisoners. And the Red Coat governor in

Detroit will pay you twenty pounds for each one." Boone sat on a rock and the war chief, intrigued, squatted by his side. Boone said that he himself would lead the Shawnee to the licks and surrender his men if Black Fish gave his word that they would not have to run the gauntlet. In the summer, when it was warm and the militia was gone, they could return together and take all who remained at the fort back north with them on horses. They would go willingly then if he told them to, Boone said, and would either live with the Shawnee as their adopted children, or place themselves under the Red Coats' protection at Detroit. But they would fight a battle before they would make a long winter journey with their women and children.

Black Fish rose. It was a fair bargain, he said, and thrust out his hand to seal it. But when they had shaken he said that if there was fighting at the licks, Boone would be first to die.

They started early the next day and in three hours had reached the low hills surrounding Blue Licks. The snow was still falling and the Shawnee, silent and unseen, encircled the salt-makers' camp. Then Black Fish sent Boone out to parley. Two warriors walked a few paces behind, rifles trained on his back. The first whites to notice thought the three scouts had returned together. Then they saw the Indians' raised rifles and went for their own.

"Don't fire or we will all be massacred!" Boone called out. "You are surrounded!" He kept walking toward them, still talking. He said they had no choice except to surrender, but that the Indians had promised to treat them well and would not force them to run the gauntlet. They were to stack their arms; if anyone resisted, all would be killed.

The stunned salt makers watched the unlikely trio close on their camp. Then, beyond, they saw the ring of Shawnee moving toward them from the hills. Bewildered, heartsick, the men stacked their rifles and, at the Indians' command, sat down. Boone was relieved to see that Thomas Brooks and young Callaway were not among them: at least the fort would have quick word of what happened.

Now a group of rash young braves stepped forward and demanded that the white men be put to death in spite of the assurances just given them. All but Boone. Boone would be taken to Boonesborough and made to surrender the people there.

The salt makers did not understand these chilling words, but Boone did. Appalled, he turned to Black Fish, but the war chief ruled that a council must be held. Those who favored putting the prisoners to death

would be heard, and those favoring mercy. Then they would pass the war
club and abide by the decision.

Hours passed while the deliberations dragged on, Pompey sitting next
to Boone to help with the translation. But Boone understood more than
enough Shawnee to know that the vote would be extremely close. He was
in a further agony lest the long-expected relief company now come
marching innocently into camp. But at the last, asking for the right to be
heard, he seemed entirely self-possessed as he rose to contend for the lives
of his twenty-seven men. He spoke in English, Pompey translating, and for
the first time the unhappy Kentuckians realized that they might be dead
before the day was out. One of them, Joseph Jackson, later wrote down
Boone's moving defense.

> Brothers! . . . You have got all my young men. To kill them, as has been
> suggested, would displease the Great Spirit, and you could not expect success,
> either in hunting or at war. But if you spare them, they will make you fine
> warriors and excellent hunters to kill game for your squaws and children.
> These young men have done you no harm. They are engaged in a peaceful
> occupation, and unresistingly surrendered upon my word that such a course
> was the only safe one for them; and I consented to their surrender on the
> express condition that they should be made prisoners of war and treated well.
> I now appeal both to your honor and your humanity: spare them and the
> Great Spirit will smile upon you.

Then the war club was passed, to be hammered to the ground by
those who wanted the salt makers to die, and handed over by those who
would let them live. Black Fish, having apparently already decided that he
would take Boone for his adopted son, allowed him to vote. The final count
was fifty-nine for death, sixty-one for life, and when no one noticed, Black
Fish and Boone exchanged secret smiles.

But now the British agents pressed the Indians to march on
Boonesborough at once and force its surrender. Surely, given their
formidable numbers, and with the salt makers held captive, they could
make short work of the remaining defenders. But Boone again warned of
the fort's strength, and Black Fish had had enough. The Indians had
already won a great victory, he said. Not since the white man came to
Kentucky had the Shawnee taken so many prisoners. They could return to
their villages in triumph; Cornstalk had been avenged.

Later, Governor Hamilton in Detroit would complain bitterly that
"the Savages could not be prevailed on to attempt the Fort, which by

means of their prisoners might have been easily done with success." But the Indians, gleefully scattering the three hundred bushels of salt over the snow and collecting their spoils of kettles, rifles and horses, were content as they herded the Kentuckians into a file and started north.

Late in the afternoon, Callaway and Brooks returned to a deserted camp. Realizing what had happened, they rode at full speed for Boonesborough.

The snow had stopped. Dispirited, with little to say even to each other, the white men trudged through a silent wilderness carrying the Indians' booty, the bare white woods stretching endlessly ahead, a cold wind knifing through buckskin and flesh to chill their bones. Only Boone walked unburdened. A brave had tried to make him carry one of the kettles, but Boone said he would not. When the angered brave thrust it at him, Boone knocked it to the ground and then sent the Indian sprawling after it. The Indian rose with drawn tomahawk, but Black Fish intervened. Boone would carry nothing, he said. He seemed amused.

The Kentuckians puzzled over this. Why was their leader so privileged? It was true that he had saved the fort, but some—dreading the imprisonment ahead, the long and perhaps permanent separation from their families—wondered if he'd really had to surrender them to do it. Nor were all the Shawnee pleased to see Black Fish side with the white man. But doubters on both sides were soon to be appeased.

Right after they made camp at dusk that first day, a group of braves began tramping down the snow to make a long clearing. Boone recognized its purpose at once and reminded Black Fish of their agreement: his men were not to be made to run the gauntlet. Black Fish nodded. He said he had no such intention for Boone's men. But Boone himself—well, he would surely remember that the promise was never extended to him. He smiled. His warriors were waiting, he said.

Boone gaped. He had no argument. He had protected his men but failed to exempt himself and was now to be held to the letter of the agreement. At that he was being honored: most prisoners were forced to run the gauntlet of an entire village—women, children and old people, as well as warriors, all lined up in a double row ready to beat the unfortunates with fists, switches, branches, stones and tomahawk pipes as they fled, staggered and finally crawled through the lines. An Indian once explained it as his people's way of saying, "Howdy." It was a favorite diversion in the villages, though the weaker among the white captives were often beaten to death. As Black Fish walked with him to the forming columns, Boone said he was gratified to be allowed to run through the war party only. "We will see which can hit hard and which hit like children."

Suddenly lowering his head, he rushed between the lines. Fists and tomahawk pipes pummeled him, but he kept his footing and danced from side to side, either too close or too far from the flailing warriors to be hurt by the full force of their blows. When one stepped directly in front of him, both arms up to strike, he bent even lower and charged, butting the stupefied brave full in the stomach and sending him crashing and sliding through the snow. The Indians rocked with laughter and, a moment later, when Boone had cleared the gauntlet, they gathered around to shake his hand and congratulate him. Again he had risen in their esteem. Black Fish was pleased.

True to his promise, the chief treated the whites well, but they suffered from the stinging cold, especially as they had to be tied at night. Boone did his best to keep their spirits up, sitting with them at the evening fires and chatting as though they were only on a long winter hunt. His wit did not fail him, even when the suspicious ones deplored his friendship with the Indians. "Well," he said once, "any time a man has a tomahawk to my scalp, I'd a sight rather he be a friend than an enemy."

One man, without socks, declared that his feet were bound to freeze. "No they won't," Boone said. "Even potatoes wouldn't freeze with that much dirt on them." And grinning, tossed over a pair of his own socks.

When another man, bemoaning his fate, cried out, "Lord, Thou has eternally played hell with me!" Boone responded, "Look here, only death is eternal. Give the good Lord another chance." And they all had a bit of a laugh.

And so the days and nights passed. By mid-February they had crossed the Ohio in a large boat stored by the Indians and started for the northern reaches of the Little Miami River. They were bound for Little Chillicothe, largest of the Shawnee villages. On February 18, when they already could see the council house and the smoke of the wigwams, the Indians stopped to paint their own faces, then made a proud and imposing entry, the long line of prisoners and booty strung out for three hundred yards.

All the people turned out to greet their warriors. They were exultant; no one could remember such a great Shawnee victory, not since the defeat of the Long Knife Braddock at the Forks of the Ohio twenty years before. And when the people clamored for a gauntlet, Black Fish did not deny it. In spite of Boone's protest, the rest of his men now had to run the ranks of everyone in the village. Afterward there was a great war dance and those among the whites who had best withstood the journey and the gauntlet were adopted into the tribe. An exception was Andrew Johnson, who did nothing right; but as he was barely five feet tall and entranced them all with his dim-witted clowning, Captain Will chose Johnson to be his adopted son. The rest, termed "no-goods," were to be taken to Detroit and sold to the British.

This party set forth on March 10, ten prisoners and forty warriors and squaws. Boone was among them, not because Black Fish had any intention of parting with him, but to display for the Red Coats of George III evidence of the Shawnee's prowess in battle, a war prize of the greatest importance. And, indeed, the Red Coat chief at Detroit, Lieutenant Governor Henry Hamilton, was duly impressed. Like everyone else west of the mountains—American, British or Indian—Hamilton knew the prisoner's reputation and treated him "with great humanity." Calling Boone to his quarters the very night of the Shawnee's arrival, he interrogated him at length, but with deference and respect. When Boone pressed for an assurance that his men would be well treated, it was given. Then he could not resist the temptation to do some secret gloating. Asked if he had any recent news of General Burgoyne, Boone replied solemnly that the British commander had been defeated at Saratoga and forced to surrender his entire army to the Americans. Aghast, Hamilton begged him not to mention this to the Indians. Boone, ruefully: "You are too late, Governor. Not thinking, I have already told them of it."

He answered Hamilton's questions with consideration. Kentucky, he said, had no great enthusiasm for the revolution and had suffered severe deprivation under the Americans. Within days, Hamilton would be zestfully reporting this account by Boone to the British commander-in-chief in Canada: "The people at Kentucke have not been able to sow grain and will not have a morsel of bread by the middle of June. Clothing is not to be had, nor do they expect relief from their Congress. Their dilemma will probably induce them to . . . come to this place. . . ."

At one point in the conference, Boone casually produced his four-year-old commission in the British colonial forces, which he had lately taken to carrying in case he should have to document his loyalty to the Great White Father across the sea. He had already made it clear that the settlers could yet be turned back to the Crown without use of force; now, without words, he was saying that he might take a hand in persuading them to do so.

His ploy almost worked. Hamilton offered on the spot to pay Black Fish a hundred pounds sterling for Boone, intending to send him back to Kentucky as a British agent. But Black Fish refused. He said that he "loved Boone too strongly" to let him go. A weightier consideration was his need for Boone's services in the coming expedition against Boonesborough.

Regretfully the British turned him back. They wanted to give him "a friendly supply for my wants," as he put it, but he declined, "never expecting it would be in my power to recompense such unmerited generosity." But he did accept Hamilton's offer of a horse and saddle. The other Kentuckians, seeing this, hearing of the great warmth with which Boone had been treated, wondered again whether he had eased their lot or created it. Left behind and shut up in the British prison, there was time enough for their suspicions to fester.

April was nearly gone by the time Boone and the Indians reached Little Chillicothe, for Black Fish had ordered stops at all the villages en route. There he told warriors of the Mingo, Delaware and Shawnee tribes of the planned attack on Boonesborough; they were to be ready to march when the warm weather came.

The chief returned to bad news: Andrew Johnson, the little simpleton they all cherished, had stolen his adopted father's rifle and run away. They had called him Pequolly, meaning Little-Shut-His-Eyes, for his stunning ineptitude at target shooting; they would ask him the direction to Kentucky and laugh with delight when he pointed north. He was such a harmless little fool that they'd left him unguarded—and now he was gone. For three days they searched without even finding his trail and were sure he had lost his way trying to get back to Boonesborough and would perish in the wild country. Wasn't that so? they asked Boone. Boone nodded agreement while calculating that Johnson—an expert woodsman, a crack shot and better than a fair hand at deception—would be more than halfway to Boonesborough by now, carrying word that the salt makers were still alive. More, he would bring back the first detailed intelligence the Kentuckians had ever had about the location of the Shawnee villages north of the Ohio.

Only a few weeks after Johnson's escape, a series of mysterious raids struck the Shawnee hunting camps; scalps were taken, and many horses, and Black Fish thought one of the Indian bands had turned outlaw. Not until weeks after, when a Shawnee scout saw some whites returning to the settlements with stolen horses, was the truth known. And then it was made even harder to bear by the identity of the Long Knife leader. It was little Pequolly.

William Hancock was vexed that Boone could be "so contented among a parcel of dirty Indians"; the other whites at Chillicothe were at least perplexed. They had all heard of captives adopted into a tribe who, learning to love the free, wild ways of the red man, refused, even when the opportunity was presented, to return to their own people. But surely not Boone. He was their leader. He had a wife and family at Boonesborough. And yet, though they were all forced to live the Shawnee life, only Boone had taken a squaw, only Boone hunted with the braves and repaired their broken rifles. And only Boone, seemingly unguarded, showed no interest in escape.

Boone kept his own counsel. He had, as he later wrote, "a great share in the affection of my new parents, brothers, sisters, and friends [and] was exceedingly familiar and friendly with them." Nor was this warmth feigned. There was an almost mystic affinity between Boone and the Indians, and both recognized it. All the secret things he had learned about surviving in the wilderness he learned from them. White men said that he had come to "think Indian" and they did not entirely admire him for it. He wanted land, but he also sensed a certain justice in the Indians' claim that the land remain theirs. They didn't foul it with their swelling numbers and overspreading towns; he had never known Indians to exhaust a country's game because heedless hunters wounded more than they killed and killed more than they needed for food. Oh, the Indian could be a cruel and savage foe, but the whites had given him cause.

And the Shawnee saw in Boone what the white man did not, that he was somehow outside the white man's world. It was true that he stalked the Indians' game and had driven them back on their own land, but he killed neither Indians nor animals for sport, only to defend and feed himself and those dependent on him. He was a true hunter. Like the Indians, he was touched with reverence for the land and the game he pursued.

The Shawnee war chief was happy to take him as an adopted son. He would fill the place of his real son, killed, as Black Fish well knew, in the foolish kidnapping of Boone's daughter. The ceremony of adoption took place soon after the return from Detroit. The chief himself plucked out all the hair on Boone's head except for the scalp lock, a fist-sized tuft left on the crown in defiance of enemies. Then, at the river, he was stripped naked by the village crones and scrubbed raw from head to foot—they had to satisfy themselves that every taint of white blood had been washed away. Finally he was painted with the tribal symbols and, wearing only a breechclout, taken to the council house where all the braves waited. There he was given a tomahawk and proper Indian clothing, and Black Fish declared that he was now a Shawnee and his Indian name would be Sheltowee, Big Turtle. That night there was a great feast of venison, bear fat, corn and maple sugar, and Sheltowee smoked the pipe with his new brothers.

At a certain point, Black Fish spoke to him privately. He said that he and his wife would always welcome their son in their own home. But he understood that Boone was a man, not a boy, and a man who suffered for the need of a woman was a poor warrior and only half a hunter. If his son wished to take a squaw, the old chief said, it would be arranged. Boone did not decline. Soon after, he went to live in his own wigwam with a handsome Shawnee girl who cooked for him and sewed beads on his clothes, and he brought her game and treated her well.

Still, no one, not even Black Fish, was certain of Boone's intentions. In the beginning, he was watched whenever he left camp. Once, when the fresh spring grass was lush, he asked to take his horse out to pasture. "After a little," Black Fish replied. But before giving his approval, he went off to dispatch several braves to hide in the tall grass and keep an eye on his adopted son. Boone, who "could sing a good song," only strolled the pasture while his hobbled horse fed, singing away. Of course he was perfectly aware that he was being watched.

Even after he had demonstrated his trustworthiness, Black Fish took certain precautions. Boone was allowed to hunt alone, as he preferred, but his ration of powder and lead was strictly limited; if he returned empty-handed, he had to surrender it. This he cheerfully did, and confined himself to hunting in the nearby woods where there was only small game, not wanting to cause his brothers alarm. But there was a certain advantage to small game. It did not require a heavy powder charge or much lead, and so he cut his bullets in two and saved considerable powder. These he carefully hid away, along with some jerk that no one knew he had.

Meanwhile, day by day, the affection of Black Fish and his wife for their new son grew and they treated him exactly as they did their other children. The chief boasted openly of Sheltowee's woodland wizardry; the squaw often brought him specially cooked morsels of food. By now it would have been hard to distinguish Boone from the other Shawnee. He was bronzed, painted and, as the weather turned warm, most often clad only in a breechclout. In the greening spring, the Shawnee country turned fair and appealing to him, the land more fertile even than Kentucky's, though not so rich in game. He would have liked to wander through the thickening forests and out into the flat, open clover plains he had only glimpsed.

But he did not. He stayed close to the village, often whistling in obvious contentment as he went about. He joined his new brothers in sports and target shooting, taking care not to make any enemies by winning all the matches. This was not easy, for the Shawnee—and most other Indians—were notoriously poor shots. But he managed it, and any brave who outshot Sheltowee had reason to celebrate. And Sheltowee celebrated with them, passing the whiskey jug, laughing at the jokes and finally staggering home as drunk as any of them.

They were impressed by his talents as a gunsmith and gratefully brought him their broken rifle stocks and jammed hammer locks. He repaired them all with genial good humor, and pocketed the bullets that were sometimes carelessly left in the barrel. Once, at the end of a deer hunt, with the braves all gathered around the campfire, he silently drew the balls from their stacked rifles and dropped them into a pouch at his waist. But this tactic almost turned out badly.

They had broken camp and started home when a deer suddenly broke from the forest ten yards in front of them. The lead man threw his rifle to his shoulder and fired at point-blank range—and the deer sprinted away unhurt. Boone calculated that he now had about sixty seconds before every man in the party discovered that his rifle was somehow loaded with a full charge of powder but no ball. Ten seconds after that, they would turn on him.

"I'm going back to Kentucky!" he shouted, and started racing back down the path. At twenty paces, he spun around, just as half a dozen Shawnee rifles blazed away at him. "Hey, good shooting!" he called, shaking the buckskin apron of his breechclout in front of him as he started back. Standing before the dumfounded braves, he lowered the apron with a flourish and let the stolen bullets fall to the ground. "Here," he said with a broad grin, "take your bullets—Sheltowee big medicine man. He ain't going anywhere."

For a moment more the Shawnee continued to stare at him, mesmerized. Then understanding at last that it was all a joke, they fell to laughing so hard that some of them had to sit down. Soon the whole village was chortling about Sheltowee the medicine man. He was truly one of them.

Yet through all that bewitching, unburdened time, when he could come and go as he pleased without need to answer to anybody, Boone had never forgotten that his little idyll among the Shawnee was stolen from the life of his other self—Daniel Boone, husband and father, frontiersman, settler, commander of a wilderness outpost in Kentucky. He had been waiting and watching for the right moment to escape. Now, as the days lengthened and warmed toward summer, as he saw warriors from outlying villages, Mingos and Wyandots, begin gathering for the attack on Boonesborough, he knew that he must find a way to go back, whether the moment was right or not. He said nothing of this to the other whites, just as he had had little to say to them in the four months of their captivity; until this point, he had been playing a role, and now that he had to shed it, he would take no chances on being given away, innocently or otherwise. The Kentuckians might not be happy as prisoners of the Shawnee, but Boone knew they would not be harmed.

Early in June he went with a party of braves and squaws to make salt on the Scioto. There they were overtaken by a Shawnee war party that had just been badly beaten in a series of battles in western Virginia. Angered by the news, Black Fish decreed that the attack force would set out for Boonesborough without further delay, and they started for home at once.

They had come to an old sugar maple camp about three miles south of Chillicothe by the evening of June 16 when the dogs flushed a flock of wild turkeys. In a flurry of motion, the men grabbed up their rifles and dashed off in pursuit—all but Boone, who was left alone in camp with the women and who sensed at once that his moment had come. He went directly to his horse and cut the salt kettles loose. His adopted mother, hearing them clang to the ground, rushed over:

"My son, what are you doing?"

"Well, mother, I am going home. I have to go and see my squaw and my children, but in a moon and a half I will bring them here and we will all live with you."

"You must not go! Your father will be angry and will catch you and bring you back."

"He will not catch me. His best warriors cannot catch me."

"But you have only an empty gun and no food. You will die on the trail. Do not go, my son!"

Then Boone showed the sorrowing old woman the ammunition and jerked venison concealed in his clothing. He swung up into the saddle and leaned down to touch her arm. And he dug in his heels and galloped away.

The old woman stood silent, but by this time the others had noticed and began shrieking the alarm. Still it was a while before the men heard them over the gunfire and came running. As they freed their horses for pursuit, some said that they would have the ingrate back within the hour, others that he might elude them but would get lost and perish for he knew nothing of their country; no one, not even Boone, could survive such a journey alone and as poorly outfitted as he was. But Black Fish, sadly watching them ride off, said that Boone would go straight as a leather thong to Boonesborough. Then he prepared to send a runner to Detroit with word that the attack on the settlements would have to be postponed.

Until dark, Boone rode the stream beds to cover his trail. He kept going all night and well into the next morning without stopping. Then his horse's legs stiffened and he dismounted and turned the exhausted animal free—Governor Hamilton's gift had served him well. He continued swiftly on foot, walking the length of fallen trees and swinging sometimes fifty yards on wild grape vines to break his track. By the end of the second day he had reached the Ohio.

It was running high and fast. Boone found some logs and bound them together with vine at the water's edge. Then he stripped, threw his clothes and rifle on top and pushed off into the swift, cold flow. Kicking his feet, hanging on with one hand and paddling hard with the other, he reached the far shore just before dark and well downstream from where he'd set out. Weary, feeling himself safe enough for the moment, he stretched out on the bare ground and slept until morning.

He pushed on. His feet burned in his moccasins and, having long since finished the jerk, he grew ravenously hungry. But not until he had passed Blue Licks, where he saw the remains of the salt makers' gear rusting on the ground, did he dare risk a shot. Then he brought down a buffalo and "roasted some meat." He saved the tongue as a homecoming present; it was a particular favorite of his children, now less than forty miles away. His throat caught, realizing this nearness.

He reached the Kentucky River on the afternoon of Saturday, June 20, and sat for a while on a familiar bank below the fort, soaking his sore feet in the water. At forty-three years of age, he had completed one of the most remarkable journeys of the frontier era, covering 160 miles of Indian country and wilderness, mostly on foot, in a little less than four days.

After a time, he crossed at the ford and walked up to the stockade, unnoticed until he was nearly at the gate. Those who saw him first, limping and drawn, stared as at one risen from the dead—and in a Shawnee reincarnation at that, for he still wore Indian clothes and the only hair on his head was a scalp lock. "Daniel Boone," muttered one old companion, tears in his eyes. "By God." And unable to say more, said again, "By God!"

Boone asked for Rebecca. "Bless your soul, she's gone, put into the settlements long ago. She thought you was dead, and so did we all, so she packed up and was off to the old man's in North Carolina." Jemima had stayed, and so had Squire, but the rest of the family, along with many relatives of the other captured men, had returned to the East.

He went alone to the bare cabin and stood a while nursing his bitter disappointment. Then he felt the old family cat rubbing against his leg—well, anyway, she had left him that. But soon Jemima and the neighbors came rushing in with food and thanksgiving that he was back, and he was heartened. This was where he belonged, after all. When someone asked if he would soon start after his family, he said that he could not until they had dealt with the Shawnee. There would be an attack before summer was over—not a raid, an attack.

But not even this grim prospect could dim the settlers' joy to have Boone among them again. Some, it is true, regarded him with a baleful eye—those whose loved ones remained prisoners of the British or the Shawnee; those who had listened too well to the tales of Andrew Johnson, little Pequolly. But most recognized Boone as their natural leader, and his return cheered them. Long into the night they sat talking. Boone said little of himself; he wanted every detail of what had gone on during his captivity.

The taking of the salt makers, twenty-seven good men and the most highly regarded commander in the territory, had been the worst blow yet to strike the settlements. Consternation and confusion followed the return of scouts Brooks and Flanders Callaway with the bleak news. Simon Kenton was among the few men left able to act decisively; with as many others as he could quickly muster, he started off in hot pursuit. But the Shawnee trail, easy enough to find in the "half leg deep" snow, also revealed their overpowering numbers and he was forced to return empty-handed.

Word of the disaster spread swiftly. Many a Kentucky-bound settler, and at least one troop of militia, turned back. George Rogers Clark heard about it, with evident astonishment, in the midst of his campaign against the British on the Illinois frontier: "Came an express from Kentucky here and informed me of Capt. Boone with twenty-eight men (*sic*) being taken prisoners from the salt licks on the Licking Creek without shedding one drop of blood."

Clark's foray into the northwest territory had been brilliantly conceived and was to be daringly executed. He saw clearly that the British forts beyond the Ohio provided the strength and stimulus for the Indian attacks on Kentucky and by early 1779, he would capture them all—and Lieutenant Governor Hamilton in the bargain. But none of these heroics did the settlers any good in 1778 and, in fact, put additional burdens on them. For now the Kentucky forts were made responsible for protecting Clark's rear; bracing to meet the Indian assault that summer, they suffered a further loss of effective defenders when some of the best Kentucky riflemen went off to fight with Clark in Illinois.

At Boonesborough, there was a tangled question of leadership, further complicated by the return of Boone. After the salt makers' capture, Richard Callaway, on no one's order, had assumed command. At some point, he had been replaced presumably because the remaining handful of militia complained of his churlish manner. One, Josiah Collins, draws an indelible image of Callaway in those hard months:

> The pressing necessity of our wants compelled us to trespass on some hogs (we had nothing to pay with) which we boiled and ate without bread or salt. . . . When that was exhausted, Lieut. Hutchings shot down a large steer of Col. Callaway's one morning, for the use of the soldiers. Col. C. was exasperated and swore if another man killed another head of his stock that he w'd shoot him dead.

In any event, the Virginia militiaman, Major William Bailey Smith, was in nominal command when Boone came back, but Callaway had not relinquished his claim and dissension was apparent. Soon, though, Boone's natural leadership, the air of easy confidence that was his gift, asserted itself. In their deepest trouble, the people turned to him, even those who resented his freedom while their own men remained captive. Whatever needed to be done, Boone would do; if anyone could save them, it was Boone. With Smith's tacit consent, Boone took command and Callaway had yet another grievance to mark down for future settlement.

There was much to be done. The fort had fallen into disrepair. Rotted stockade had not been replaced, leaving gaps between cabins that could be stormed by day and infiltrated by night; the gates sagged and either blockhouse would be a death trap in battle, so riddled were they both with openings from fallen and forgotten logs. Outside, a tangle of brush roots and stumps that ought to have been cleared away now provided concealment to within a few yards of the fort. And inside, the well still had not been completed.

Boone said he was willing to stay and die with the rest of them, but if they went to work they could at least make a fight out of it. They did. The stockade and gate were rebuilt. When the two blockhouses were repaired, he ordered two more built so there would be one at each corner of the fort, high and projecting forward enough to cover all walls. Provisions were laid in, lookouts posted and scouts sent to patrol the woods.

Boone appealed to the other settlements for help and Logan sent fifteen men, Harrod five, dangerously reducing their own strength. With the arrival of these reinforcements, the Boonesborough defenders could now muster fifty riflemen, including some boys who had come in as packhorse drivers and bravely stayed. It was not a formidable force, but Boone said that with the fort strengthened it would give a good account of itself, and the people took heart.

On the afternoon of July 17, tensed in expectation of the Indians, they were hailed, instead, from across the river by William Hancock, ragged and half dead. He had escaped from Black Fish's camp nine days before, without a weapon and only some parched corn to live on. Lost more often than not, he once gave himself up for dead, but managed somehow to stagger on to the Kentucky River. Boone himself nursed the wasted man with broth and root poultices.

Hancock brought news that the Indian attack had been delayed by Boone's escape. At first, Black Fish had seemed to lose heart for it altogether, but British officers had come to Chillicothe with many presents and promised more. And so a time had been set, the end of July, and they would come with at least four hundred men and four cannons, and if Boonesborough didn't surrender they would blow it to pieces and kill everyone inside.

"Well, they can try," said Boone dryly.

But some of the others were undone. Suddenly it all looked hopeless. And when Hancock, out of Boone's hearing, began telling of the favors shown to him at Chillicothe and Detroit, and of the agreement Boone had made to return with the Indians and British and surrender Boonesborough, Richard Callaway stomped his foot and demanded an immediate court-martial. Cooler heads prevailed: Boone was here and not with the Indians, and if they were to be attacked, that was just as well. They could always think about court-martialing him afterward—if they survived.

Boone found the waiting more trying than the accusations that inevitably reached his ears. The end of July came and went and some said that perhaps the renewed bustle around the fort had been reported by Shawnee spies and discouraged Black Fish. Boone doubted it. Black Fish would come, he said, no matter what the spies told him.

He had written to the Holston settlements and to Colonel Arthur Campbell in Virginia for help—"we are in fine spirits and intend to fight hard"—and by mid-August, a good supply of corn had been stored in the cabin lofts. Two weeks later there were still no Indians, but he was ready for action. He proposed to do some scouting of his own in the Ohio country. If enough men went with him, they could strike at some Shawnee towns he knew and perhaps weaken the attack force. At the very least, they would spy out the Indian strength and steal enough horses and furs to pay them for their trouble.

This last promptly produced twenty volunteers—despite Callaway's objections. He was stridently opposed to the expedition, ostensibly because it would take rifles from the fort, but actually because he had lately taken to setting himself against any plan Boone offered. Boone paid him little attention—he knew that no substantial Indian force would get past him—and on August 30 the raiders set forth.

By the time they had passed the Licking River it became clear that Boone was more interested in taking prisoners than furs, and the fainthearted turned back. The rest pushed on, crossing the Ohio on rafts and advancing along the Scioto toward Paint Creek town, one of the larger Shawnee settlements. This was the country where Boone had made salt with Black Fish and he remembered it well. He led his men to several small villages that they raided by night, spreading panic among the Indians and making off with several horses. At one point, Kenton, scouting ahead, surprised two braves, seemingly alone, riding a single horse through the woods. He stepped out in their path and, firing head-on, shot both off the horse, one dead, the other dying.

But the two braves had not been alone. The report of Kenton's rifle roused a fair-sized Shawnee war party, the first the Kentuckians had encountered, and soon there were warriors everywhere in the woods. Boone ran up in time to drop one, who had drawn a bead on the beleaguered Kenton.

"Thanks!" Kenton shouted.

"Returning the favor," Boone yelled back.

They fought on, joined now by the other men, and eventually drove the Shawnee off. They moved on toward Paint Creek, where Kenton and another scout, Alexander Montgomery, went ahead to spy, returning to report that there was not a warrior in the place. Some of the men thought this a golden opportunity for a raid and some looting, but Boone now knew that there was no more time to lose. A war party on the move, a town without any warriors at all—it added up to a mustering of Black Fish's expedition.

Leaving Kenton and Montgomery behind to continue scouting, he started back with the rest of the men at forced speed and found the Indian army encamped at the Lower Blue Licks. He took time to gauge its strength from the cover of the circling brush. It was huge, perhaps four hundred braves and forty or more white men; there was a train of packhorses for the provisions and ammunition, but he saw no cannon. Then his little party started off again, reaching Boonesborough toward evening, Sunday, September 6.

Now the attack was coming, he reported. Every hand fell to filling jugs and kettles with water, bringing in horses and vegetables, cleaning rifles and cutting bullets. Only the children slept that night.

The Indians crossed the Kentucky at the ford early the next morning and moved down toward Boonesborough behind the cover of a ridgeline that paralleled the river. But they were not concerned about concealing themselves; when they came opposite the fort, they rode up over the hill in two long dusty files, flags flying, and made straight for the gate.

Squire Boone's young sons, Moses and Isaiah, had just come out to water some horses under the eye of their Uncle Daniel. Supposing the riders to be the devoutly anticipated Holston relief party, they started riding toward them, but Boone called them back. He said the Indians had arrived and the three went back into the fort.

Sentinels had already given the alarm. Men and boys sprang for the blockhouses and took up posts at their assigned portholes. The women set up loading stations beneath them. And all who were not otherwise engaged—slaves, girls, old people—clapped coonskins or beaver hats on their heads and, carrying rifles or reasonable imitations, went marching casually across the fort common. Spies looking over the wall from the high ground across the river would soon report an armed population of at least a hundred. To foster the illusion, Boone ordered the gate kept partially open.

Watching from the southwest blockhouse, he saw the main Indian force stop in the sycamores at the edge of the clearing, while detachments flanked out east and west and rode around to the fort's river side. The braves were generously smeared with red-streaked vermillion, Hamilton later reporting that he had provided the Shawnee with more than six hundred pounds of paint, as well as "150 dozen scalping knives." There were Shawnee, Mingos, Wyandots and Cherokees and, under both the British and French flags, redcoats and French-Canadians. It was by far the largest force ever sent against the Kentucky settlements.

For the moment, at least, the knives were kept sheathed. Across the clearing under a truce flag came Pompey, the black interpreter, calling for Captain Boone. No one answered. To all appearances the people were going about their daily chores; smoke rose from kitchen chimneys and there was no sign of anxiety or unusual ado. Only when Pompey called out a second time did Boone acknowledge his presence and ask what he wanted. He replied that Black Fish had brought letters from Lieutenant Governor Hamilton and wanted to deliver them.

"Tell him to bring them to the gate."

But at this point, Black Fish himself appeared in the clearing and asked Boone to come out. He called him by his Shawnee name, Sheltowee. As Boone prepared to go, several of the men tried to dissuade him, but he had made up his mind. He said that if they saw him taken, they were to slam the gate and commence firing.

They almost did so at the very outset. They saw a swarm of braves close around Boone so that he disappeared from their sight. But the Indians had only drawn near to hear the parley between Boone and Black Fish, who now shook hands and sat down on a blanket spread for them.

"Well, Boone, howdy." Black Fish regarded the hair of his adopted son, now nearly all grown back, with obvious distaste.

"Howdy, Black Fish."

"Well, Boone, what made you run away from me?"

"It was because I wanted to see my wife and children so bad."

"But you didn't need to run away. If you had let me know I would have let you come here." Then the old chief looked around him as if to emphasize the strength of his forces. "Well, Boone," he said, "I have come to take your fort. If you will surrender, I will take you all up to Chillicothe and you will be treated well. If not, I will put all the other people to death and reserve the young squaws for myself." Thereupon he handed over the letters from Hamilton which, in more decorous language, said the same thing, adding only that Boone had promised to surrender his people peacefully.

Boone folded the letters and handed them back. He sighed deeply. He said that since he had lived so long with the Shawnee, "the great Virginia father has sent us a bigger captain here and he does not want to surrender." But he would return now and try to persuade him to do so.

Black Fish rose and handed over a present of seven roasted buffalo tongues. Then he looked straight at Boone and said that his warriors were hungry and had nothing to eat. Boone was well aware that they would take what they wanted as soon as he went into the fort; all he could do was make a point of the settlement's abundance and generosity. "Well, Black Fish, there you see plenty of cattle and corn. Take what you need, but don't let any be wasted."

Before he reached the gate, Indians were already in the cornfield and cows were being shot down. An anxious knot of men clustered around as he came in and he gave a full account of what had happened. He said that if they gave up, the Indians would most likely conduct them to Detroit without harm—they were mainly interested in Hamilton's bounty. But if they fought and lost, few would survive and the deaths would not be pleasant. Then he asked for their decision.

Callaway burst into speech. He said that it was Boone's promises to surrender the people that had brought the Indians here in the first place. First he had handed over the salt makers, and now he would see Boonesborough go down, and if that didn't smack of Toryism then he didn't know what did.

Boone did not reply to Callaway directly. The fact is that during the short time Callaway had yet to live, Boone never addressed him again. Speaking to the others, softly, he said that he had never done anything against the people of Boonesborough, but that everything he had done or said among the Indians and the British was to protect Boonesborough, or so that he could escape to help defend it. His family was in North Carolina, he reminded them, and he could well be there instead of here risking his life. Now he was for resistance, but if the people thought it best to give up, "he would be compelled to yield to the wishes of the majority."

The response was vehement. Squire Boone, only recently returned to Boonesborough, said he would fight there until he died. Smith, Callaway,

Gass and Holder concurred. Of all the men gathered just inside the gate, there was not one who spoke for surrender. "Well," said Boone with a small smile, "then I'll die with the rest."

But defense, not death, was everyone's preoccupation, and at the moment the best defense was delay. Perhaps the men from the Holston would appear, or the troops sent by Colonel Campbell. They could always fight as they stood, thirty men and twenty boys, but so long as the Indians were willing to talk, they would talk.

Sporadic negotiations followed, not one side or the other wholly sincere, but both willing to prolong the charade to avoid the battle neither really wanted to fight. On the afternoon of September 7, Boone went out again, this time with Major William Bailey Smith, the "bigger captain," looking every inch the part in his full dress uniform; Richard Callaway, at his own insistence, accompanied them. Black Fish held court in a sort of arbor, made by chopping the tops off the smaller trees and covering them with blankets and skins. He presented Lieutenant Dagneaux De Quindre, commander of the French-Canadians, and his other white aides, as well as several of the more illustrious chiefs, among them Moluntha, who had taken Cornstalk's place as leader of the Shawnee. Black Fish again said that he had come "to take the people away easily," that he had brought along forty horses "just for the old folks and women and children to ride back."

As arranged, Major Smith served as spokesman and said the people wanted to consider Black Fish's offer. He proposed a two-day truce during which neither side would carry arms into a thirty-yard neutral zone around the stockade. This was agreed to and the envoys returned to the fort heartened by the war chief's inadvertent confession. For if the Indians had brought forty horses for Boonesborough's dependents alone, they must be assuming a force of riflemen far greater than the actual number. That would explain their reluctance to attack and might yet discourage them altogether. Boone's tall tales during his captivity had had an effect.

Seemingly, life at Boonesborough went on as it always had. The women continued to walk out to the spring for water, and though their hearts may have been in their throats when a group of admiring braves gathered round to comment loudly on the white men's "pretty squaws," they pretended absolute unconcern. When the cattle, nervous at the presence of the Indians, refused to come up to the gate for milking, some Shawnee thoughtfully shooed them all the way into the fort; the settlers took the opportunity to keep them there. Meanwhile, behind the palisades, rifles were cleaned and recleaned, bullets were molded and powder measured out. And a rifleman stood at every porthole.

On the afternoon of Wednesday, September 9, a party of Shawnee came up to ask Boone if they could see his daughter, about whom Hanging Maw had told them so much. As this was to be the day of decision, some of the men feared that the Indians had been sent to take her hostage in hopes of forcing a surrender. But Boone ordered the gate opened and brought Jemima to stand, white-faced but calm, just inside. The Indians seemed delighted. Some wanted to shake her hand, but Flanders Callaway, standing by his wife's side with a cocked rifle, told Boone he would shoot the first man who touched her, and finally Boone sent them away.

In the cool of evening, Black Fish and De Quindre approached the fort under a white flag and demanded their answer. Boone himself came out to give it. "The people are determined to defend the fort while a man is living," he said.

The war chief's face hardened with disappointment. It was evident that he had counted on Sheltowee to go back with him and to persuade the others to do the same. Now he felt diminished in the eyes of the other chiefs. De Quindre called him to one side. After they had consulted, the Canadian spoke: Lieutenant Governor Hamilton had sent them on a mission of peace; their orders were to avoid bloodshed and he believed this still could be done. He proposed that nine Boonesborough men meet with the chiefs the following day to draft a treaty. Once it was signed, the Indians would go back to their villages and there would be lasting peace between white men and red.

"This sounded grateful to my ears," Boone later reported, "and I agreed." He had little confidence that the fighting had really been averted—he understood the stony look on Black Fish's face. But it had been put off again, and that was to the defenders' advantage.

The talks continued, and so did a strange round of revelry. The Indians spread delicacies from the British commissary before the negotiators in the sycamore arbor, and the whites, again flaunting their fictitious plenty, set up tables outside the fort and produced a great feast for the leaders of both sides. The pipes were passed and considerable whiskey dashed down. And finally, with the terms still undefined, the treaty-signing was fixed for the same afternoon.

Boone thought it likelier that the fighting would begin then; he could not believe that Black Fish would willingly return empty-handed. At his insistence, the treaty was to be made at the Lick Spring, a clear rifle shot from the fort. He ordered his best marksmen to the northwest blockhouse; they were to stand ready to fire "into the lump" at the first sign of trouble. To give themselves better freedom of movement, the negotiators shed as much clothing as they could without rousing suspicion. Then they went out, unarmed. They were only eight; the ninth could not be spared from his post.

The Indians waited at the table that had been set up on the riverbank, also unarmed. But Boone wondered aloud why so many chiefs who had participated in the earlier parleys had been replaced by warriors.

Black Fish, blandly: These young men were eager to witness the treaty-making.

Boone: Well, then, did there need to be eighteen of them?

Black Fish, imperturbable: Yes, as eighteen was the number of Indian villages that had sent braves to join his army.

But after a ritual request that the settlers evacuate the fort and leave Kentucky within six weeks, which was politely declined, Black Fish made a startling concession: "Friends and brothers! As you have purchased this land and paid for it, you must keep it and live on it in peace."

Then he proposed that the Indians return home and that their white brothers remain here unmolested, retaining all their property; that the Ohio should be the boundary between their two people, but that both be allowed to hunt and trade peaceably on either side; and that there be an end to the theft of horses. To secure these terms, the settlers had only to take an oath of allegiance to the Great White Father across the sea and submit to the authority of his deputy in Detroit, Lieutenant Governor Hamilton.

The whites immediately agreed. Someone wrote it down and they all signed.

"Then we shall live as brothers," Black Fish declared in a ringing voice, "and this treaty shall bind us both as long as the trees grow and water runs in the Kentucky River."

Did Black Fish make this astonishing proposal in good faith? There are historians who believe he did. Certainly Boone and his men were ready to hope so, otherwise how explain their willingness to risk what came next? Then was the bitter struggle for Boonesborough all an accident? There is no unequivocal answer, only the clues of history.

When the pipe smoking was finished, Black Fish said that the agreement must be sealed by "shaking long hands" and drawing hearts close to symbolize long friendship. And as there were two Indians for every white, so would they shake hands. He strode over to Boone and locked arms, a sturdy warrior similarly grasping Boone from the other side. Nervously, the other Kentuckians submitted.

It was at this decisive instant on Friday, September 11, 1778, that the battle for Boonesborough began, accidentally or otherwise. It has been recorded that Callaway, his nerve finally broken, tried to pull free and started the fighting. The other version is that Black Fish, having failed to win the fort by persuasion and now resigned to storming it, first sought to capture its leaders. In either case, there was no turning back.

As the warriors tightened their grips and the frenzied scuffling began, shots were fired from both sides. Black Fish, no less wary than Boone, had hidden a strong force of riflemen beneath the riverbank, and they came up shooting on signal. The fort echoed with the crackle of twenty-five rifles and every visible porthole puffed smoke. But the most desperate fighting was between those who had just talked of peace.

The Indians' intention was to drag the white men down behind the cover of the riverbank, but the Kentuckians dug in their heels and Boone, shaking off his younger warrior, knocked Black Fish flat on the ground with his free hand. The other braves, thinking their chief dead, stood stunned for one fatal moment, and the whites, with the strength of desperation, broke free. Squire Boone, as was later reported by a watcher at the fort, threw off Indians as though they were little children. Then Squire was shot down, but immediately rose and scrambled for the fort.

Major Smith was locked in the arms of a massive brave who was wrestling him steadily backward. Suddenly the Indian stiffened, then fell dead with a bullet in his head. Daniel Boone, charged by a warrior with a contraband tomahawk, ducked his head and took the worst of the blow between his shoulders. Then he straightened and knocked his foe senseless. He began to run toward the gate, shepherding his men ahead, each one trying to disappear inside his skin and seeking the cover of every stray stump. Incredibly, under the whistling hail of two hundred bullets, they all made it back without further injury. In the grandiloquent manner of his time, the historian Draper wrote: "It was an evidence of God's providential care for the feeble band in the wilderness."

Behind the locked gates, all the pent fears of the past days could be heard in defiant cries from the battlements and, below, in the forlorn wailing of terrified children and the screams of women huddled together waiting for the savages to come smashing through the paltry defenses. Dogs bayed, the cattle thundered around the common in wild stampede, dust and smoke from the booming rifles rose into the sky like a pall. In one blockhouse, a marskman fell back wounded by a single ball that had passed between two pickets; in another, a lookout watching from the top log came sprawling down on the backs of the riflemen, his clothes shredded by a volley of bullets but unhurt.

Boone was everywhere, blood clotting on his head and darkening the back of his shirt. He went from post to post shouting assurances and exhorting the defenders to hold fast against the coming assault. At the northwest bastion, above the drumfire of bullets plunking into the logs, someone asked whether they had a chance. Smiling encouragement, Boone said, "If the wind from all that flying lead doesn't blow the stockade down."

Then the Indians charged, a headlong, war-whooping thrust for the north wall by a hundred braves, rifles blazing from behind to cover them. But the Kentuckians had recovered their self-possession. The riflemen picked their targets and fired carefully, as they'd been drilled to do, and the women stood behind handing up reloaded guns. In less than ten minutes the Indians had fallen back, leaving the dead and wounded scattered on the open ground. An eerie quiet settled over the battlefield, broken only by a sporadic rattle of shots.

Boone went off to see to the wounded. Squire, a bullet in his shoulder, thought he had only been grazed. But trying to ram a ball into his rifle, he cried out with pain. When Boone found him, he was still firing, but nine-year-old Moses Boone was doing his loading. Boone cut the shoulder open with his knife and drew out the bullet, then sent Squire back to his cabin to have his wife dress the wound. Persuaded to get into bed, the fighting preacher took a broadax with him for "the last action."

Finally Jemima washed the blood from Boone's head and back and wound a bandage around the gashes. Night came on and with it a lively wind. All firing had ceased when a lookout saw a flash of flame just outside the west wall. The settlers had begun an enclosure there to store flax. Now they knew precisely what had happened: the Indians had found the flax and ignited it against the fence with the expectation that the wind would carry the fire to the stockade.

Someone volunteered to go out and extinguish the blaze, but Boone said the Indians would be watching for just that. Instead he ordered a trench dug under the stockade and out to the burning fence. Then two men crawled out and from the shelter of the trench doused the blaze. A little later, a black man named London, guarding the open trench, fired at a warrior who had crawled up to a stump within a few yards of him. But his rifle failed to discharge and the Indian, aiming at the sound of the falling hammer, shot London dead and fled. They buried him in the night, a good man, the people agreed. He was the first fatality of the siege.

Saturday the sun rose into a clear sky. The Indian casualties were gone from the clearing and the morning stillness was broken not by rifle fire or war whoops, but by the sounds of retreat. Braves shouted for the horses, orders to load up were bellowed loud enough to be heard in the fort's farthest reaches. Then there was a great splashing and clatter as the Indians crossed the river and, finally, the trill of their white ally's bugle growing steadily fainter until it died away on the far side of the wooded hills to the north.

Not even the women were fooled. The Shawnee, who could come and go with the stealth of their ancestors' departed spirits, were advertising their departure for a particular purpose. Let the settlers succumb to the temptation to let the irascible livestock out to water, or to pacify their own nerves by seeking a moment's respite away from the cramped and smelly fort, and the trap would be sprung.

They stayed where they were, waiting. Boone didn't even send out a scout. He knew Black Fish had not gone far.

Sometime during those first days, Simon Kenton and Alexander Montgomery, having completed their scouting mission, returned to find Boonesborough sealed off. They settled down behind the Indian lines to wait for a chance to steal back in, or to pick off an imprudent brave. Another Boonesborough man, William Patton, who had been off hunting when the Indians came, was already hiding in these same hills, anxiously watching the attack. On the night when the Shawnee stormed the fort with torches and blazing arrows, he was so undone that he fled to Logan's Station where he gasped out the news that "Boonesborough was taken; he actually did hear the Indians killing the people in the fort [and] the women and children & men also screaming."

It had not yet come to that. The Indians returned before noon on Saturday and proclaimed the failure of their ruse by blasting away at every sliver of light that showed through the stockade. The gorge of the Kentucky rang and the bluffs behind echoed with their salvos, but to little effect. Watching, the defenders mused aloud that the enemy was certainly not sparing of his ammunition.

Then it became apparent why. A broad streak of silt was seen to swirl out into the river opposite the fort; it spread and thickened, coursing off downstream to muddy the Kentucky from shore to shore. Between rifle shots, the people could hear the sound of axes chopping steadily away. Soon a rumor flew through the fort that the Indians were digging a tunnel to the stockade!

It proved to be more than nervous gossip. A watchtower of stout logs was raised onto a cabin roof and a lookout, clambering up to a height well above the two-story blockhouses, reported the worst. Under the protection of the riverbank, a work party was driving long poles into an unseen excavation, from which Indians emerged carrying buckets full of earth. These were dumped in the water. De Quindre had taught Black Fish something about siege warfare: once the Indians had mined under the fort, they could blow their way into it with one huge powder charge.

Boone ordered a countermine. If they dug under the cabins parallel to the river wall, the Indian tunnel would have to cross theirs. Perhaps they could collapse it. At the least they would have a chance to fire on the attackers as they came through, one or two at a time. Day after day, in the fierce summer heat, men who had just finished a shift on the battlements would go below to do the brutally hard work of digging the four-foot deep tunnel, and day by day it reached out farther beneath the stockade. By throwing the excavated earth out over the wall, Boone let De Quindre know that the Kentuckians were aware of his scheme, and were countering it.

Meanwhile, relays of riflemen manned the watchtower, studying the clearing for any sign of Indian progress or surprise. They also tried to pick off a brave or two at the river, thereby frightening the others away from their work. But as they could report little satisfaction on this score, they took to carrying rocks from the diggings up to the tower and lobbing them out over the embankment. The Indians were furious. They swore so volubly that every female in the fort blushed, and they cried out to the sharpshooters in the watchtower to "fight like men, who do not try to kill warriors with stones."

Mrs. South, a fluttery, lisping, simplehearted little woman, begged the lookouts to quit. "It might hurt some of the Indians and they will be mad and have their wevenge on us." Not surprisingly, this became a jeering theme of the now-seasoned defenders. "Don't get the Indians mad," they would simper out of Mrs. South's hearing, "or they will have their we-venge on us."

The fact is that most of the women behaved admirably, loading guns, making ball patches and running bullets, in addition to feeding the men and caring for the children. Some were a problem. Mrs. Richard Callaway, the most ostentatiously pious lady at Boonesborough, found the elderly potter, Matthias Prock, hiding in fear on the first night of the siege and chased him around the fort with a broom. Poor Prock—no one had ever counted on him for anything more than the earthenware he turned out. "Der potters vass not made to fight," he cried over his shoulder at Mrs. Callaway in Pennsylvania Dutch. But she was relentless: if he would not fight, he would dig the well until he reached water, and she thumped him with the broom for emphasis. Prock dove into the well and came up digging furiously. But as soon as Mrs. Callaway sallied off, he fell into a quivering ball and lay where he was until the next morning, when a more compassionate soul led him away.

A few nights later an Indian torch was thrown against the Callaways' outside cabin door. Unaware, Mrs. Callaway was astonished when her son-in-law, John Holder, who had seen the spreading flames from the blockhouse, tore past her and ran outside. Outlined in the firelight, bullets whizzing by his head, Holder flung a stream of profanity at the Indians, all he had besides a bucket of water. But he put out the fire and ducked back in. His troubles were not behind him. The good Mrs. Callaway backed him to the wall and said that such language was more than she could bear. She said that their danger called for prayers, not blasphemy. By this time, young Holder had caught his breath—obviously he was not short of courage—and replied, "Let me go to my duty now, woman, for if you will not forgive me, God damn it, He will!"

Life went on, full of anxiety, quarrels, sleepless nights and alternating hope and fear: Surely today help would come; but what if it did not—would this day be their last? Dealing with recurrent Indian attempts to set the fort afire and providing for the imprisoned livestock had put a severe strain on the meager water supply. Now, though, there was no one to spare for well-digging and every cloudless day the sun glared hot in the blue sky. Soon they had exhausted the small store of corn and vegetables and there was nothing to eat but the meat of the starving cattle. All the animals were exposed in the enclosure, and every day some were killed by rifle fire from the heights across the river. The people were relatively safe; they had cut openings in every cabin sidewall so they could move around the fort under cover. But it was the final blow to privacy.

And still there were casualties. Jemima was hit in the backside by a nearly spent bullet, a wound more embarrassing than serious; the ball came out with a tug on her underclothing. But one night David Boudrun was standing guard when a chance bullet struck the stone used to close off his porthole. The stone shattered and a fragment drove through his forehead. Taken to his cabin, he sat speechless, rocking back and forth with his head in his hands, blood and brain matter oozing from the wound while his wife kept repeating that it was a good thing he hadn't been hit in the eye. He died before morning and a burial party went to work in the dark.

The Indians were suffering their share of killed and wounded too. One of those to fall was Pompey, the black interpreter. Perched high in a tree, he was sniping at anyone venturing into the enclosure, feeling himself safe enough, as he was barely visible amid the greenery. But a rifle cracked and Pompey was seen to throw up his arms and come crashing to the ground. Later, when his body was found, there was a bullet hole where one eye had been.

The men on the battlements began calling derisively, "Where's Pompey?" When the Indians replied that he had gone to fetch more warriors, one settler gleefully shouted, "He's raising them from the dead, boys—they're coming hot from hell!"

There was a good deal of this mocking raillery between the two sides, including many a bawdy Indian reference to Boone's "good-looking daughter." One day they saw Boone himself hit as he crossed the common. At once they took up the taunt, "We killed your Boone! Old Boone dead now!"

Boone had been shot in the back of the neck, not deeply, though the wound spurted blood. He was forbidden to speak or move until it had been cleaned and covered. Then, about the time the Indians began believing that they might have killed the mighty Boone after all, he rose and called out, "Hey, here's old Boone, back from the grave."

Across the river, on a hillside in clear view of the settlement, one brave dropped his breechclout and, stooping to thrust his rear end at them, gaily invited the whites to "Kick my ass!" As he was out of rifle range, the Kentuckians fumed with frustrated indignation that only burned hotter as other Indians joined in the chant. Finally a marksman loaded his rifle with a particularly heavy powder charge and, praying aloud that it wouldn't blow up in his face, fired. The naked warrior flopped to the ground and with his breechclout still circling his ankles, rolled all the way down the hill while the settlers cheered.

The digging continued. "What are you doing down there?" a white man called.

"Digging hole," came the reply. "Blow you all to hell, maybe tonight. What you do?"

"Digging hole, too—big enough to bury five hundred of you sons of bitches!"

Squire Boone had been building a cannon. Though in pain and still hampered by his shoulder wound, he bored the centers from two tree trunks and bound them around with wagon-wheel iron. Hoisted to the roof of his cabin, the first one blew up with a deafening roar, and the Indians howled their ridicule. In fact a group of them gathered in the peach orchard to do so, and this was a mistake. The second wooden cannon, loaded with rifle balls and packed with powder, worked as well as any machined artillery piece, booming death for several Indians, scattering the rest and "creating considerable havoc among the peach trees." Unfortunately, it was a one-shot marvel; the barrel exploded on the next round.

And still no help came. On the sixth day of the siege, Wednesday, September 16, the heat broke, and toward afternoon a gray mist rolled in from the northwest. The Indian gibes had ended. When night came, their rifle fire, instead of tapering off, intensified. And suddenly an all-out fire attack was under way. Braves with torches concealed behind blankets ran up to throw them against the stockade. Some were shot down but many got through and several fires took hold. Other Indians, shooting from the safety of the river bluffs, dropped blazing arrows on the cabin roofs. And the main body swept the fort with a fusillade of bullets to keep the fire fighters under cover.

A few brave souls scampered across the cabin roofs tearing out burning shingles and throwing them to the ground. Below, others ran out to dash what little water was left on the burning fence. But it was a battle that could not be won. For every fire that was put out, two more started, and even had there been enough men to go after every one, the only water left now came from the women's kitchen jugs. Watching from the dark hills, Kenton and Montgomery thought this the end of Boonesborough.

The people began to come together near the northwest blockhouse. Hypnotized, horrified, they watched the fires spread across the wall that, until now, had stood between them and death. It was their final defense. Without it, they had only one last rifle volley against the onslaught of four hundred Indians.

A few men talked of trying to make a run for it, but Boone silenced them; every man would stay and defend the women and children to the last. In an agony of despair, the people waited for the screaming war whoops that would signal the rush of Indians breaking through to overwhelm them.

Then it began to rain. It was not a strong rain, only the mist thickening in the cool night air and beginning to fall. But the fires sputtered and went out. There was no cheering. Except for a few muttered thanks to the Lord, the people hardly spoke. Without orders, the men went back to their posts and the women to their cabins. They were not saved, only reprieved. The siege went on.

It rained all night and the next day. The catch barrels began to fill, but the mist obscured the defenders' field of vision. They grew tense staring into the murk and imagined nonexistent charges across the clearing and fired at Indians who weren't there. At midday, Boone was called below by the tunnel guards. "Listen," they whispered. He put his ear to the damp ground and heard the faint but unmistakable scrape and thud of men digging through the earth. Someone asked how close he thought they were. He said he was not an engineer and could not tell. He did not say the obvious—that they were a good deal nearer than farther.

But the day passed without incident, except for Richard Callaway's continual harassment of his neighbors. Again asserting his right to command—sometimes by reason of Boone's "betrayal," sometimes because of his rank as a long ago colonel in the Bedford County militia—Callaway browbeat Major Smith and dogged the men's footsteps countermanding orders. Boone ignored him and, in the main, so did the others. And had Callaway produced a commission from General Washington, it would have been the same. The people's lives were at stake. They cared little about what Callaway claimed to be Boone's conspiracy with the enemy. What mattered was that Boone knew the Indians; he could lead.

Still, the discord did nothing to lessen the tensions, nor did the cramped quarters and the endless chill rain that only yesterday had been a blessing. Now it hung over the fort like a shroud, rubbing irritations raw and deepening the gloom. People hungered for something besides a piece of leathery beef, but there was nothing else. They longed for release from this one-acre cage of seventy humans, a milling of cows and horses and the incessant expectation of an abominable death.

Another day passed. Having dug the countermine and stationed men underground, Boone had done all he could, but it was not enough. He knew that an underground thrust, or even a massive powder charge, would be only the beginning of the final attack. The Indians would come across the clearing at the same time, swarming over the stockade on their scaling ladders, and he did not have enough men to stand them off from above and below.

By early afternoon it had grown so dark that the Indians could have crept within ten yards of the gate without being detected. But no one came. The rain began to fall harder. The people, wet and miserable, went to bed with no expectation that they would sleep. Lonely sentinels watched from above but saw little and heard nothing except the crashing rain.

Then, about an hour before daybreak, it stopped. Everyone noticed, for in minutes a sudden, stark quiet had dispelled the insistent drumming overhead. The few who slept were dashed into wakefulness by the hush. The day broke bright and clear.

And strangely still. There were no shots, no Indian cries, not even the sounds of underground digging—only the singing of the birds again. And the lookouts, afraid they were seeing more visions, called to each other to confirm the glorious sight they beheld in the clearing before they sent for Boone. The Indian tunnel had collapsed! From the river to within twenty yards of the stockade, they could trace its path by the sections that had caved in and now lay swimming in mud and rain-soaked earth.

And the Indians were gone.

VII

The Court-Martial of Daniel Boone

The Shawnee were creatures of the wild and did not take to physical labor. Yet they had toiled underground seven days digging a tunnel because the Red Coat chief said that that was the way to force an entry to the fort. But when the rains came and first put out the fires they had thrown against the stockade, and then destroyed their tunnel, they were obliged to conclude that the spirits did not favor these efforts, and they had mounted up and ridden away. Nothing De Quindre said could have stopped them. While some stragglers shot up the cattle at Logan's Station and wounded Benjamin Logan, Black Fish and his badly battered army rode glumly back to Chillicothe to nurse their wounds and gather the will for another attack.

At midmorning, Boone sent scouts out to search the area. Soon the people let the ravenous animals out to feed and water. They themselves walked around the scorched stockade staring with amazement at the heaps of spent bullets, talking compulsively, or suddenly laughing with no reason. None quite believed that they were really delivered. Some who were there said weeks would pass before they could wake in the morning certain the siege was over.

But it was. The Indians had ruined their crops and killed most of the hogs they'd left to root in the woods, but they could not destroy the water or the pasture. These were left, and some cattle, and they themselves were alive. That was enough—everything else they could start again.

They had suffered two dead and four wounded. Boone calculated that the enemy had thirty-seven killed, although Pompey's body was the only one they found; the Indian dead had been borne away lest they be scalped and doomed to eternal dishonor. It was the longest siege ever mounted in Kentucky, the Indian loss the heaviest. Some 125 pounds of shattered lead was carefully collected from the walls to be melted into bullets for the fort's ammunition supply.

By the time Kenton and Montgomery came down out of the hills and crossed the river, the American flag, shot down during the battle, was again flying over Boonesborough. It meant that the Kentucky settlements were still secure, that Clark's army on the northwest frontier was safe to continue its thrust toward Detroit. It meant that this handful, with neither powder nor reinforcements from the state of Virginia or the United States Congress—and certainly without help from Richard Henderson, still in the East busily arguing the claims of his Transylvania Company—these few had saved the West. Thomas D. Clark, the distinguished historian of frontier America, wrote:

> the fact that Boonesboro survived the siege was one of the momentous incidents in the western struggle. Had this fort fallen to the British and Indians the other two Kentucky strongholds would doubtless have capitulated, and Clark would have been left surrounded in the Illinois country with no possible hope of supplies and only the Mississippi and lower Ohio rivers left open for escape.

Several days after the siege ended a relief party of the Holston Valley militia did arrive, and scouring the country, drove out those last Shawnee who had stayed behind to do some private looting. By that time Callaway had had his way. Daniel Boone was arraigned on charges of treason and ordered to stand trial before a court-martial.

As long as the Indians were just beyond the stockade threatening to lift their scalps, no one but Callaway thought anything of the whispers about Boone's friendship with the Indians and British. Afterward, though, they had time to listen. Callaway now insisted that, but for his own watchfulness, Boone would have given them all over to his "father," Black Fish. Weren't Rebecca Boone's people Tories, some of them fighting with the King's army in the East? Wasn't she? Well, so was Boone—and in the pay of Hamilton the Hair Buyer, to boot! He should be "broke of his commission," at the least. And now William Hancock was on hand too, to tell and retell how Boone had betrayed the salt makers and been fawned over by their captors while the others were imprisoned or made to do the savages' dirty work.

Doubt took hold like a summer chill. The people remembered that Boone had never denied these things, and still did not. And for all his parleying with the Indians before the siege, and all the handshaking and whiskey-drinking—to gain time, he kept saying—they'd had to fight after all, and it had been a near thing. Every man, even their wives and children, would have been murdered but for the luck of the rain. Keziah French, Callaway's sister, helped to focus their resentment. "Boone," she said, "never deserved anything of the country."

And yet not a single officer at Boonesborough would join Callaway in preferring formal charges. Sometime in that first week of peace, he rode alone to Logan's Station and persuaded Logan to do it. Ben Logan had nothing against Boone, but he knew that the matter had gone too far; now it would take a court-martial to establish the truth. And so the papers were drawn, a military court impaneled and Boone, accused of attempting to betray the fort and its people to the enemy, was placed under arrest. The sensational news swept the settlements.

Meanwhile Boone, confined to his cabin, wrote a letter to Rebecca in which he gave vent to the bitterness locked in and roiling his innards. Unfortunately, it was so full of uncharacteristic profanity that his scandalized wife cut it to shreds in an attempt to excise the offending parts. Only a single sentence remains intact—"God damn them they had set the Indians on us"—which may be a reference to the panic of some of the treaty makers at the time of the "long handshake." If Rebecca saw fit to pass this blasphemy, one can imagine the censored expressions of contempt for his accusers and the anguished scorn at the ingratitude of those who countenanced their charges.

Because of Logan's wounds, the trial was to be held at his fort, and early in October Boone was taken there under guard. Crowded into a blockhouse, the court and people heard the indictment read out: that the accused, Captain Daniel Boone, favored the rule of the British Government and did therefore, by treasonable acts, seek to surrender Fort Boonesborough and its inhabitants to them and their Indian allies. Then came the specific charges:

> 1. That Boone had taken out twenty-six men [sic] to make salt at the Blue Licks, and the Indians had caught him ten miles below on the Licking, and he voluntarily surrendered his men at the Licks to the enemy.

> 2. That when a prisoner, he engaged with Gov. Hamilton to surrender the people at Boonesborough to be removed to Detroit, and live under British protection and jurisdiction.

3. That returning from captivity, he encouraged a party of men to accompany him to the Paint Lick Town, weakening the garrison at a time when the arrival of an Indian army was daily expected to attack the fort.

4. That preceding the attack on Boonesborough, he was willing to take the officers of the fort, on pretense of making peace, to the Indian camp, beyond the protection of the guns of the garrison.

Asked to stand and plead to these charges, Boone said he was not guilty. But when the trial began and he was challenged to say how they were in error, he could not. The prosecutor was not then interested to hear his explanations.

Then the witnesses were called, and they made a strong case against him. Callaway said that the Shawnee war party was not headed in the direction of the salt makers' camp when Boone was captured, but that he led them there nonetheless and persuaded the men to surrender. Hancock and some more recently escaped prisoners testified that "Boone bargained with the British commander and said he would give up all the people at Boonesborough" in return for which he was indulged with presents and treated with warm consideration; that when he returned to Chillicothe he lived as one with the Shawnee, taking a squaw, making salt with the warriors, hunting with them and repairing their rifles, and though he had many opportunities to escape, was content to stay four months and more in the Indian camp.

Several Boonesborough officers, called to recount events at the fort before the arrival of Black Fish and his army, said that Boone had encouraged a large party to make the expedition to Paint Lick town, promising them furs and other booty. Question: Had not the escaped prisoner, Hancock, warned that the Shawnee meant to strike at that time? Answer: Yes.

Callaway returned to say that Boone later showed the highest regard for the chief Black Fish; and that he tried to lead the garrison's best men out of sight of the fort where, on a pretext of making peace, they were to be taken captive or killed on the spot. "Col. Callaway said that Boone was in favor with the British Government, that all his conduct proved it, for everything he did played into their hands."

There must have been few among the onlookers who doubted Boone's guilt when the prosecutors finished. Some, resenting his prominence, were glad that he was to get his comeuppance; others, even among those who had followed him into Kentucky, had come to blame Boone for his wife's

Tory kin and were now only too glad to lump him with them. There were even a few who harked all the way back to the time of the Regulator troubles in North Carolina and remembered that Boone had sided with Richard Henderson and the other King's magistrates against the people. To those who believed in the gaunt and graying frontiersman sitting in the dock, the outcome looked bleak indeed.

Boone was called to speak in his own behalf. His usual discourse was limited to a terse sentence or two, but now he had a good many things to say and he said them well. He did not deny that he took the Indians to the salt makers and surrendered them; he did not deny the particulars of any of the things he was charged with having done. It was all in the *why*. The salt makers, he said, could have been prisoners or they could have been dead; there was no other choice. Black Fish's scouts had already found their camp and would have secretly surrounded them in the snowstorm, as they actually did the following day, and massacred every last man.

And then? The war party was bound for Boonesborough. Boone well knew that "the Fort was in bad order and that the Indians would take it easily. He thought to use some strategem [and] told the Indians the Fort was very strong, and had too many men for them." At Detroit, too, he had been friendly with the British and "told tales only to fool them."

But, he was asked, hadn't he told Governor Hamilton that he was in sympathy with the British cause and could persuade the people of Boonesborough to come over to the King's side?

Yes, he replied, in order to make Hamilton think he could have Kentucky without a fight. He hoped Hamilton would let him go free to arrange this, and the time gained before the Governor learned otherwise would have given the settlements a chance to better prepare for an attack.

The prosecutor, smiling: Did Captain Boone really believe, or hope to make the court do so, that a man of Hamilton's rank and stature—the Lieutenant Governor of Detroit!—could be fooled by a militiaman's trick?

Boone, expressionless: Yes, reasoning that the best men of Hamilton's rank were commanding armies against General Washington, not sitting in some backwoods headquarters trying to keep George Rogers Clark and his hundred irregulars from breaking in through the back door.

In any event, he went on, the proof of the pudding was in the eating: though imprisoned, the salt makers were still alive; Black Fish had not attacked Boonesborough in February, when it could not have hoped to fight him off. And though Hamilton had failed to buy Boone's freedom from the Indians, he obviously had been agreeable to delaying another march on the settlements until summer because Boone promised him the people would then go north willingly.

Did he live too well with the Indians? Could he have escaped sooner? Perhaps, but remaining had certain advantages. Gaining the confidence of Black Fish might have led to a peaceful settlement; meanwhile he learned a good deal about his plans, as well as the locations of the Shawnee villages north of the Ohio. And so long as he stayed, he knew there would be no attack before summer, a period of time, he said with some small emphasis, "he reckoned would be used to put the Fort in proper order for the Indians' reception." He regretted that this was not done. Still, he escaped in time "to give Boonesborough notice of the attack, to help make what preparations could be made and to fight alongside the people."

As for negotiating with Black Fish and De Quindre, well, he had never heard anyone suggest that the settlers should start the shooting. Talking had won them four days at a time when each hour might have brought the relief party from the Holston. Nor had he taken the officers "beyond the protection of the garrison"; they were covered by twenty-five rifles well within range. There was a risk, yes, but not a man of them was obliged to go. They went because there was a chance they could avoid a battle.

And there came a moment when it seemed that perhaps they had, when Black Fish offered to withdraw and leave them in peace. Whether it was a true offer or not, *at that moment* all eight of the fort's treaty makers, himself included, had been glad to accept it, and meet Black Fish's terms. And so one after another these eight Americans had stepped up to the treaty table—without exception, without a word of protest, not even from Colonel Richard Callaway, who was one of them—and signed an oath of allegiance to the King of England.

Boone looked around the courtroom and asked how this differed from the deception he'd practiced when he was the Indians' captive.

He displayed no anger. His voice remained low so that even in the hushed courtroom people had to strain to hear. He had no responsibility for the politics of his wife's people, Boone said, nor they for his. He did not condemn them for their beliefs, but he did not share them. He said that he was neither a Tory nor a traitor; he was an American soldier who had done his best and now stood falsely accused.

"In the enemy's power, he had used duplicity in an effort to help his own people, and for no other reason." Had it been otherwise, he need never have fled the Shawnee; or, having fled, he ought reasonably to have gone back to Detroit, or returned to his family on the Yadkin. But he had made straight for the people at Boonesborough, and stayed to be "tomahawked and shot, to share their perils and sleepless nights, and risk his very life to save them. He thought that sufficient evidence of his devotion to the American cause." But in deceiving the enemy, he said, it seemed that he had also deceived his friends; he had certainly exposed himself to the malice of those who had other grievances against him.

The verdict was not long in coming. The members of the court found Boone innocent of all the charges against him. To stress how little they thought of them, and in consequence of Boone's "brave actions in saving the settlements from destruction," they then and there promoted him to the rank of major.

A recorder of the proceedings notes that "Col. Callaway was not pleased about it."

In mid-October, Boone started east to get his family in North Carolina. No doubt he took some satisfaction that he had been so sweepingly vindicated, but the court-martial—which, according to historian Clark, was entirely rooted in the "stupid jealousy" of Richard Callaway—and the disaffection of old friends were to sour his remaining years in Kentucky.

Meanwhile, it happened that troubles of another kind would keep Boone in the East for a full year. Rebecca finally had heard that her Daniel was alive, having survived both Indian imprisonment and the long siege. But almost at the same time, mean-spirited neighbors in Boonesborough and the Yadkin made sure that she also heard how Daniel had taken a squaw during his captivity. In other circumstances, after nearly a year's separation her tears and recriminations soon would have been calmed by their joy in being together. Now, though, living amid her Tory relatives, Rebecca was counseled daily "not to return to the dangers and exposures of Kentucky"—the Yadkin was well out of the revolutionary ferment, they reminded her. Finally Rebecca said she meant to stay where she was.

In the Filson autobiography, Boone is made to say that "Nothing worthy of a place in this account passed in my affairs at this time." But only a few paragraphs further there is an intimation of the truth: "To avoid an enquiry into my conduct, I am under the necessity of informing [the reader] that . . . the history of my going home and returning with my family forms a series of difficulties, an account of which I shall purposely omit."

At some point, he went to Virginia to give an account of the siege and report on the Kentucky battlefronts to the governor. He not only mapped the location of the Shawnee villages for the military commanders, but brought them the most detailed intelligence about the British defenses at Detroit that they had yet had.

But mostly Boone spent those rankling months trying to counter the Bryans' pernicious influence and arguing with Rebecca to return with him to Kentucky. By the end of the following summer, when he had organized a new company of settlers and it was clear that he meant to go back whether she did or not, Rebecca reluctantly, but inevitably, began to pack.

They were a substantial party, among them Boone's brothers Edward and Samuel, and his boyhood friend from Pennsylvania days, Abraham Lincoln. Riding west, too, were a good many Rowan County people, for not everyone along the Yadkin shared the Bryans' devotion to George III, and some Virginians to whom Boone had glowingly described the rich lands beyond the mountains.

Kentucky was already changing by the time Boone and his company reached Boonesborough in October, 1779. Clark's widely heralded successes on the Northwest frontier had inspired a rush of immigration. Once more there were settlers' cabins on the north side of the Kentucky, and the buffalo traces and waterways now led to a whole string of new stations—Lexington, Bryan's, Grant's, Ruddle's—all of whose founders entered Kentucky by way of Boonesborough, and Boonesborough had become the busiest post of all. It was full of traders, land speculators and pioneers who had made the long trek over the Wilderness Road and stopped for refitting and a few days' respite. The people prospered. They had raised the largest corn crop yet, incorporated as a town and made plans to establish a ferry across the Kentucky River. They even sent to Virginia for a teacher; he set up his school in one of the cabins and soon had seventeen pupils.

Some things remained the same. The Indian wars went on. The Shawnee had taken to attacking settlers' flatboats coming down the Ohio and that summer, in retaliation, a troop of more than two hundred militiamen struck at Chillicothe and took it by surprise. But the attack was badly mismanaged and the Kentuckians forced to retreat with heavy losses. Black Fish was wounded during this battle and tried to surrender, thinking that Sheltowee, his adopted son, was among the whites and could save his life. But in the turmoil he was left behind and died soon after.

Hearing this last bit of news, Boone walked off alone and for a long time after was more than usually quiet.

He had been chosen a trustee of Boonesborough, but so had Callaway, and Boone declined to serve. In little more than a year, the settlement he had founded had changed beyond toleration. His real friends—Floyd, Kenton, Stoner—had moved on or were dead; there was no game worth shooting within twenty miles, and the fort itself sometimes seemed more crowded than Salisbury on Saturday night. Before long, he loaded some packhorses and took his family five miles northwest to the bank of a small stream where he had a land claim. There he built a log house and stockade that became known as Boone's Station. It was the year of the Hard Winter, a time when the rivers froze and deep snow covered the ground from November until the end of January.

The new year, inauspiciously begun, turned worse for Boone as the old hunger for land sent him back to the East. With the voidance by the Virginia legislature of all the land titles granted by the Transylvania Company, state agents came to Kentucky to hear the settlers' claims. Boone seemed to have established clear title to over three thousand acres, which he promptly sold to raise money for warrants, the right to survey new and larger claims. As Boone set off for Richmond in the early spring to buy the warrants, Thomas and Nathaniel Hart and some of his other friends entrusted him with their own money and commissioned him to act on their behalf. Riding east with a traveling companion, William Grymes, Boone carried nearly fifty thousand dollars in his saddlebags, all in cash.

They were already close to their destination when they stopped for the night at a Virginia inn, ate a meal and fell into a heavy sleep. When they awoke, their locked door had been opened and the money was stolen. They found the rifled saddlebags under the stairs, and even a few hundred dollars of the money hidden in the cellar. Where was the rest of it, Boone demanded of the innkeeper, holding him nearly off the ground by his shirtfront. The man swore that he didn't know. Boone was convinced that he did, and that he had put a potion into his food to deaden him to the intruder's footsteps. And who else could have unlocked his door? But suspicion wasn't proof. The money was gone, never to be recovered, and once again Boone had been done in by the sharp practices of "civilization." On the verge of the riches in land that he craved, he found himself, as he later wrote, "left destitute."

He was especially stricken because most of the stolen money belonged to others. Some, typically, blamed Boone and held him to strict account;

over the years he paid them back, one by one. But the Harts, who lost more than anyone, did not lose faith in their old friend. That summer, when he learned of the misadventure, Thomas Hart wrote to his brother:

> I feel for the poor people who, perhaps, are even to lose their pre-emptions; but I must say I feel more for Boone, whose character, I am told, suffers by it. Much degenerated must the people of this age be, when amongst them are to be found men to blast the reputation of a person so just and upright, too pure to admit of a thought so base and dishonorable. . . . I will freely grant him a discharge for whatever sums of mine he might have been possessed of at that time.

Boone returned to the understandable hazards of the wilderness. The end of the bitter winter had brought a new time of blood to the frontier. The Indians infested the country, usually in strength now, lusting to smash the isolated stations south of the Licking. Not even their British patrons, who would have preferred to go after Clark at the Falls of the Ohio, could temper the red man's lust for settlers' scalps. Morgan Bryan noted in his journal nine Indian raids during a five-day period in March; three settlers were killed and two taken prisoner. One of the dead was Richard Callaway.

Callaway had applied for and been granted the ferry franchise—"3 shillings for each man or horse"—and as soon as the snow was gone went with four men to cut timber for the boat at Canoe Ridge, about a mile from the settlement. There a party of Shawnee surrounded and trapped them, only one escaping and racing back to the fort for help. But when help reached the scene the Indians were gone and Callaway was dead, his scalp taken and his body abused. Another man, shot and tomahawked, lived only a short time, and the other two, Negroes, were taken away and never heard from again.

Boone, returning not long after, set out alone to scout the woods. Close to the Licking he stopped to drink at a spring and someone thumped a bullet into a tree just above his head. He dove into the brush, then scrambled downhill to a little creek and crossed to hide in a canebrake on the far side, waiting: if the Indians decided to track him, they would take the easy route first. Sure enough, two braves soon came walking cautiously down the creek, rifles at the ready. Now Boone was confronted with the eternal problem of the frontiersman: two enemies and a one-shot muzzle loader. This time forest cunning was blessed with a little luck. As Boone held the lead Indian in his sights, the other momentarily stepped into line.

Boone squeezed the trigger. The first brave, shot through the head, was dead before he hit the water; the second threw up his rifle, and with blood gushing from the hole in his shoulder, turned and fled. Boone came out and examined both rifles. He took the better one and went back up the hill to finish his drink.

He was often alone those days. Even when he was out with a large patrol, he sat quietly at the campfire, cleaning his rifle or sewing up a tear in his hunting shirt while the other men talked. Many times something that no one else heard or sensed would make him get up and slip into the woods without a word. Then the rest would wait uneasily, not bedding down until he returned to say that all was well.

Sometimes it wasn't. Once, hunting meat for the settlement with a large party, he came back to the camp and reported that he had found signs of Indians not far away. He told them to stuff their blankets with whatever they had and leave them by the fire—just a group of hunters in innocent sleep. But at his orders, the hunters dispersed themselves in the circling woods, rifles trained on the firelit camp. Hours passed. Some men began muttering sleepily that old Boone was beginning to see Indians in his dreams and they should return and bed down. But no one moved, and just at dawn there was a roar of rifle fire and the empty bedrolls danced. When the Indians came storming into the camp, the Kentuckians let them have a full salvo, killing three and stampeding the others back to the woods in frantic retreat.

Elsewhere the white men were not so lucky. In June, an expedition of nearly seven hundred Shawnee and Great Lakes Indians commanded by a British regular, Captain Henry Bird, moved into Kentucky. This time they brought artillery, attacking first at Ruddle's Station on the South Fork of the Licking. The people fought back but had no chance against the solid shot of the British cannon and soon gave up. It was the first fort ever surrendered in Kentucky. The second yielded a few days later when Bird moved on to Martin's Station, a little further along the South Fork. At two other stations the people were warned in time to flee, but the Indians burned every building to the ground. All were about a day's march from Boonesborough.

Boonesborough was safe for the moment. The Indians had taken three hundred prisoners and a long train of plunder and were willing to return to Detroit. The march, "too barbarous to relate," was one of the grisliest episodes in the annals of frontier history. The weaker prisoners were killed before it even began, their bodies thrown together in a pile. The rest were "seized and scattered and, bewildered and agonized, loaded down with spoils from their own cabins." In spite of Bird's efforts to protect them, those who fell under the weight of their burdens were tomahawked and scalped and left unburied by the side of the trail. The survivors disappeared into a captivity that, for some, lasted nearly fifteen years.

The horrifying news was sped from post to post. Clark ordered an immediate attack on the Indian towns in reprisal. But the settlers, though more than eager for revenge, sensed with deepest fear that the massive Indian assaults below the Licking were only a beginning, and that their militia's expedition across the Ohio would not be the end. Boone, Logan and the other Kentucky commanders knew it. Having burned Chillicothe and other Shawnee villages, they hurried back to brace for the Indians' counter raids. They came and were beaten off, though more lives were lost. Events were building inexorably toward the culminating disaster of the settlement of Kentucky.

In the fall of the year, Boone went with his younger brother Edward to make salt. Ned, as everyone called him, was then one month short of his fortieth birthday. He had married Martha Bryan, Rebecca's sister, and had six children. Since he'd brought his family to Kentucky the year before, he and Daniel had become particularly close; they never spoke of Ned's liaison with Rebecca nearly twenty years before.

They spent several days at Blue Licks, then started back by way of Hinkston Creek, stopping to let their horses rest and feed in a pleasant glade not far from home, the trees around vivid in autumn reds. When a bear suddenly appeared across the creek, Boone took a hasty shot and only wounded it. It bounded off downstream, Boone following. Ned sat on the bank, cracking hickory nuts between two stones and keeping an eye on the horses.

Boone's shot had not been off by much. The bear had gone only a hundred yards before it fell dead and Boone already had his knife out to begin the butchering when shots rang out through the woods upstream. Before their echo died, he heard the Shawnee shouting: "It's Boone! We killed old Boone!"

He stood rooted to the spot. In a bizarre flash of time, the years fell away and he was remembering his return to Virginia after all the long months of the Cherokee wars—the new baby in the cradle, Rebecca saying how lonely it had been, that Ned had come to comfort her, *that he had looked so much like her Daniel. . . .*

And so Ned was dead.

An Indian dog, having picked up his scent, came yowling downstream. Turning to run, he dropped his ramrod and dared not go back. He darted into a canebrake. The Indians were now close behind, but that was not his dilemma; alone he could lose them in the cane. But the dog would not be shaken off. It came baying after him, then running back to make certain its masters were closing the gap. And without a ramrod his empty rifle was useless.

But Boone's moment came. Gaining enough of a lead to pause, he slashed down a stalk of cane with his knife and made it serve as a ramrod. With his rifle loaded again, he crouched in wait for the dog and shot it dead. He could hear the Indians cry out in rage when they came on the body, but by then he had slipped into the depths of the canebrake and was beyond pursuit.

Next day he came back to bury his brother. Ned's body still lay near the bank, but the Indians had cut off his whole head and taken it away, along with the horses and salt. Boone tracked them all the way to the Ohio, to no avail. He hunted a winter's supply of meat for the widow and her children. He grieved. But life went on.

Kentucky, its population swelled to nearly twenty-five thousand, had been divided into three counties. In November Boone was promoted to the rank of lieutenant colonel in the militia, appointed sheriff and deputy surveyor of the newly created Fayette County. In April 1781, he was sent to Richmond to represent the people in the Virginia General Assembly.

He was in distinguished company. Former Governor Patrick Henry was in attendance, and Thomas Jefferson, serving the final days of his term, presided. However, when the Americans under the Marquis de Lafayette fell back before a British army commanded by the turncoat Benedict Arnold, the legislature abandoned Richmond and reconvened in Charlottesville, eight miles to the northwest. Early in June, hoping to capture Jefferson and the members of the assembly, Colonel Banastre Tarleton and a troop of cavalrymen swept down on the improvised capital. Most of the legislators escaped, Jefferson barely, galloping out the north end of town as Tarleton rode in the south. Among the handful caught was Daniel Boone.

Certain of his ability to outride or outfox the British, he had lingered behind to help "load up in waggons some of the public records." Hearing the approaching redcoats, he casually mounted his horse and, with a companion, began riding slowly down the street. Halted, he turned his frank blue eyes and most guileless manner on the British and easily convinced them that he was but an innocent farmer glad to be bound home from town; he was wearing buckskin and moccasins and looked anything but a member of the General Assembly. But as he started off again, his companion called out, "Wait a minute, Colonel, and I'll go with you."

"Colonel, is it?" exclaimed an alert British officer, and Boone was promptly taken into custody. That night he was locked up in a coal house where he passed the time singing songs. In the morning, thoroughly begrimed, he was presented to Tarleton for questioning.

What sort of colonel was he, the redcoat commander, a Tory, asked him. No sort, Boone replied with an innocent smile. He had once held a commission from Lord Dunmore, but the whole thing was more a joke than anything. People just called him colonel. There were a few more questions, but Tarleton was so obviously taken in by the plainspoken "farmer" that though he listed all his other prisoners by name, he never even mentioned Boone and soon released him. By June 18, Boone had made his way to Staunton, another forty miles west, where the lawmakers had resumed their sessions. In August, he came home and found that Rebecca had given birth to a son, Nathan; he was to be their last child. A few months later, he returned to Virginia to take up his legislative duties. But by the spring of 1782, the Year of Blood, he was back in Kentucky fighting Indians.

In the East, the fighting was over. After five years of hit-and-run warfare, Washington finally had the advantage of numbers and position. In October 1781, with the support of his French ally Lafayette, he had pressed Lord Cornwallis to the sea at Yorktown and forced the surrender of the largest British army in America. Except for the treaty-signing, the Revolution was won.

But that was in the East. In the back country, the war raged on more fiercely than ever. The British may have lost their colonies, but they could still prevent the loss of the territory taken by Clark, and toward that end they whipped up the Indians to ever more fearsome attacks. In March, a band of Wyandots killed a young girl and captured a black man just beyond the gates of Estill's Station, fifteen miles from Boonesborough. Captain James Estill and his garrison of twenty-five men, returning from a scouting mission, tore off in pursuit. But when they caught up with the Wyandots, the Indians turned and fought savagely, at one point stunning the whites with a daring thrust from the flank. The result was a devastating defeat, Estill and all but five of his men killed. It was the most somber sort of news for the settlers. Apart from suffering a terrible loss, they knew now that the Indians no longer would flee at the approach of white militia.

Far from it. In June, the Delawares routed a column of five hundred militiamen and captured the commander, Colonel William Crawford. While the white renegade, Simon Girty, watched without any effort to intervene, they scalped him and slowly burned him alive. In July, Nathaniel Hart was killed within a mile of Boonesborough, and soon after two boys were kidnapped from nearby Hoy's Station. Captain John Holder rode after the raiders with some sixty men and fell into an ambush at the Lower Blue Licks. He managed to extricate his men with only a few casualties, but it was another sharp defeat for the whites, and this one was the prelude to disaster.

The Kentuckians were not unaware that worse was coming. But they did not have a standing army; the men had crops to care for and families to feed, and there were not enough of them to patrol the enormous wilderness. It was also a bleak fact that the strength they did have was undermined by rivalry among the county commanders and by the persistent demands of Clark in the West. Boone, who had won Clark's agreement to take a hundred men to build a fort at the mouth of the Licking, soon had counter-instructions: he was to send the men to the newly laid-out town of Louisville, where they were to "build a strong garrison and a row galley." As Boone later reported to the governor,

> Our militia are called on to do duty in a manner that has a tendency to protect Louisville, a town without inhabitants, a fort situated in such a manner that the enemy, coming with the design to lay waste our country, will scarcely come within one hundred miles of it, and our own frontiers open and unguarded.

Clark's "row galley," a long, heavily armed craft propelled by oars, was meant to patrol the Ohio and prevent the Indians from crossing into Kentucky, its riflemen able to pepper either bank behind the protection of its high gunwales. The trouble was that the Indians, understandably, did not elect to cross within sight of this awesome floating fortress. Certainly the galley saw no sign of the three hundred Wyandots and fifty white rangers who slipped over in early August. They were led by Captain William Caldwell and Simon Girty and were bound for Bryan's Station.

Girty was one of the more intriguing characters of frontier history. In an earlier time he had fought with the Americans, known Boone well and once saved Simon Kenton's life. But he and his brothers had been taken captive as boys and grown up among the Indians, and this, along with real or fancied slights in later life, persuaded them to defect to the enemy in 1778. Since that time, Girty had dressed like an Indian, led them in raids and so outdone them in ferocity that, in the settlements, the specter of Simon Girty was enough to command the instant obedience of every child. Before leaving Chillicothe for Bryan's Station, he had warmed the Indians for the task ahead with an emotional speech:

> Brothers! The fertile region of Kentucky is the land of cane and clover. There the bear and the beaver are always fat. The Indians from all tribes have had a right to hunt these wild animals and bring off their skins to purchase for themselves clothing, to buy blankets for their backs and rum to send down their throats after the fatigues of hunting and the toil of war.
>
> Brothers! The Long Knives have overrun your country and usurped your hunting grounds. They have destroyed the cane, trodden down the clover, killed the deer and the buffalo. The beaver has been chased from his dam and forced to leave the country.
>
> Brothers! Was there a voice in the trees of the forest, every part of this country would call on you to chase away these ruthless invaders who are laying it waste. Unless you rise in the majesty of your might and exterminate their whole race, you may bid adieu to the hunting grounds of your fathers.

Bryan's Station had been built by Rebecca's relatives and others from North Carolina in 1779. It was a few miles northeast of Lexington, a typical frontier parallelogram, but longer than most, with forty cabins and palisades twelve feet high, and soon became the strongest outpost between the Kentucky and the Licking. When feebler stations were abandoned, the people often forted up at Bryan's.

Early on August 15, it was secretly surrounded by Caldwell and his force of Wyandots and rangers. They came within hours of finding it altogether defenseless, for the garrison, like others from Boonesborough to Harrodsburg, was preparing to march off to the relief of Hoys' Station— exactly what Caldwell was counting on. But someone, a scout or a lone hunter, had come galloping in with news of the Indian force descending on them and the people at Bryan's began preparing for a long battle.

It began with one of the most remarkable acts of community bravery ever recorded. The day's supply of water had not yet been carried up from the spring. If they were about to be besieged, they had to have water—but how? The fact that the Indians were concealing their presence could only mean that they were waiting to ambush the men when they came out. To go for the water, then, would play into their hands, leaving the station defenseless.

They would have to send the women, Captain John Craig, the fort commander, said stoically. There was no choice. But he believed no harm would come to them, for in the very act of going to the spring, they would persuade the Indians that the fort remained unaware of any danger and that Caldwell's ruse was working. Captain Craig thought the Indians would not expose their presence to take the women.

It all sounded plausible, but to the thirty-five wives and daughters who picked up their bottles and jugs and went out under the hidden guns to test the theory with their lives, the next moments were endless, every stirring of the morning breeze a preface to disaster. But having first knelt in prayer, they walked resolutely to the spring, sixty long yards beyond the stockade, chatting and feigning unconcern. They filled their containers and started back as slowly and casually as they had gone, fighting down the temptation to break and run. But once the gates were closed behind them, they fell into the arms of their waiting menfolk, some women weeping with relief.

As the day wore on and the men did not emerge from the fort, Caldwell realized his mistake. Somehow the Indians had been detected; no one was coming out. Had he taken the women hostage, he would at least have had something to bargain. Now he would have to fight. Rifles and firebrands were brought to bear, and by midday the settlers' fate hung in the balance. But two messengers had slipped through the enemy line and ridden to Lexington for help, and in the early afternoon a troop of militia fought its way into the station.

The tide of battle swung the other way. Having failed to take Bryan's Station by surprise, the Indians now faced sixty well-protected sharpshooters, and had no doubt that more were coming. Caldwell tried one final trick: he sent Girty to bellow out a demand for surrender, promising leniency now but death by evening when the British artillery would arrive. The answer was given by an impetuous youth named Aaron Reynolds, whose blistering invective had gained him a certain reputation along the frontier:

> We all know you! As for me, I have a good-for-nothing dog named Simon Girty because he looks so much like you. Bring on your artillery if you've got any, and be damned to you! We, too, are expecting reinforcements; the whole country is marching to us, and if you and your gang of murderers stay here another day we will have your scalps drying in the sun.

It was a large statement for so small a force, outnumbered three to one even with the reinforcements, but it must have had an effect. In the morning the Indians were gone, having first taken time to reduce the crops to ruin and slaughter all the livestock, six hundred head of cattle, hogs and sheep. The relief from Boonesborough, led by Boone, and troops from Lexington and Harrodsburg arrived in time to see the devastation while the people of Bryan's were still gaping at it, too stunned yet to do anything else.

The military commanders gathered inside the fort to plan the pursuit. There was no question but that the savages must be hunted down and punished. It was only a matter of whether to set off at once or wait for the arrival of Benjamin Logan with nearly five hundred men from the farther settlements. But in the highly charged hours just after the siege, those who counseled caution were shouted down and there was even some muttering about "damned cowards." Hugh McGary, a hotheaded major of the Lincoln County militia who had favored delay, smoldered under this affront to his courage.

But Captain Craig and the men from Bryan's were passionate to have their revenge, and Lieutenant Colonel John Todd, the ranking officer, felt they had more than enough men to deal with the raiders. So at noon they galloped north on the Wyandots' trail, 182 strong. Boone commanded the men of Fayette County; with him was Israel, his eldest son, barely recovered from an illness but insisting he was well enough to ride. The third commander was Lieutenant Colonel Stephen Trigg.

There was no difficulty following the Indians' track. In fact, it was so readily apparent that the whites pressed confidently forward without once having to stop and search it out. They covered more than thirty miles before making camp for the night a few miles below the Licking, certain they would overtake the enemy early the next day.

Boone did not doubt that, but wondered why the Indians were making it so easy for them. Instead of scattering, they were withdrawing in a body, pounding down a trail a child could follow, making no effort to conceal their campfires, even blazing the trees in their passage. These were not the signs of a band of raiders trying to escape pursuit. Boone, troubled, read them as an invitation to an ambush.

Soon after daybreak the Kentuckians moved on to the river. From the heights overlooking the Blue Licks they saw what appeared to be a few stragglers vanishing over the ridge on the far shore. All was quiet. But Boone, who knew this country from bitter experience and never forgot any piece of ground he ever crossed, urged Todd not to be deceived; the enemy meant to fight and the terrain was all in his favor. They would be better advised to wait for Logan.

Todd refused. He was afraid the men would think him weak. The glimpse of the retreating braves encouraged him to believe that he could strike at the Indians' rear and overrun them. When they came down to the riverbank he called the commanders together and said they would advance in three columns. He would take the center, Boone the left and Trigg the right. They would march straight ahead.

Boone repeated his misgivings. He said that he was familiar with the ground opposite, and though all they could see seemed safe enough, there were hidden ravines on the far side of the ridge providing perfect cover for an ambush. Furthermore, he had counted the Indian campfires the day before and believed the Kentuckians to be badly outnumbered. He pleaded with Todd to wait.

Todd did not want to flaunt the advice of Daniel Boone, for no one knew better what Indians were apt to do. But he sensed the fighting heat of the men milling behind him. What would his own people say if he let himself be overruled by another county commander? Temporizing, he decided to send two scouts across the Licking to reconnoiter the ridge. Boone predicted that they would see nothing; the trap was already too well prepared. They soon returned to report not an Indian in sight.

Those who heard this pressed forward. McGary, still seething at what he took to be his humiliation at Bryan's Station, blustered that they were letting the murdering savages get away. Then, looking directly at Boone: "We do not have time to wait for old ladies."

Boone replied that anyone fool enough to fight on the enemy's terms ought not to be offering advice to others. He continued to plead with Todd not to march into the trap. If he was determined to move without Logan, let it at least be with caution. He proposed that he himself would take some men across the river further upstream and advance on the ravine from the flank. If the Indians were gone, the main force could cross in safety; if there was a fight, Todd would be forewarned and free to strike the other flank.

Perhaps Todd would have yielded; he was properly nervous by now. But McGary cried out that they had come to fight Indians and he, by God, meant to do it. With that, he spurred his horse down to the river, calling over his shoulder, "All who are not damned cowards follow me and I'll soon show you where the Indians are!" It was this moment that decided the tragic outcome of the Battle of Blue Licks.

In a better regulated army, McGary would have been shot dead on the spot for usurping command. But in Kentucky, command was largely by consent, leaders and followers social equals. Todd made no move and within a few seconds the river was churned white by the horses of those who prided themselves that they would go where any man led, and those who didn't want to be thought afraid to do so. The commanders had no choice but to follow.

When they came ashore on the far bank, most of the men dismounted and moved forward on foot, an advance guard some fifty yards in front. They followed a buffalo trace to the hilltop and started down. The ravines Boone feared, timbered, full of thickets, angled away from each other on either side of the advancing men. But they were still; there was nothing to be seen but trees and scattered brush, no sound but the hum of the summer woods. And so the Kentuckians blundered on to disaster.

The Wyandots, well hidden in the ravines, waited until the last of the whites cleared the top of the ridge. Then, at a range of forty yards, two hundred rifles blazed, a volley so ravaging that all but three of the twenty-five man advance fell dead or wounded.

That part of the debacle that could be called a battle lasted less than five minutes. Boone's troops actually drove the Indians back, fighting valiantly as they advanced from tree to tree clearing the ravine on the left. But in the center Todd had been shot dead and his men, caught in the open, were cut down by a withering fire, the survivors breaking ranks to run for their lives. On the right, the Indians turned Trigg's flank and, charging in behind the shattered line, swept the remnants of his troops across Boone's route back to the river. Trigg himself had been shot off his horse and lay dying.

As the stunned Kentuckians wheeled and fled in panic, the shrieking Wyandots discarded their rifles and leaped forward with tomahawks and scalping knives. The rout became a slaughter. The wounded, even brothers and lifelong friends, were abandoned in the frantic race for life. The terrified survivors had only one thought, to reach their horses, but they were so closely pursued that most who tried to mount were cut down with only one foot in the stirrup. Then the Indians swung into the saddle and began riding down those still running for the river, splashing in after them, tomahawks flashing, cleaving their heads open even as their arms flailed desperately toward the far shore.

There were moments of selfless gallantry. Benjamin Netherland had already gotten back across the river with his horse and was about to gallop off to safety when his eyes—and his heart—were caught by the devastation on the other side. Leaping to the ground he rallied a handful of riflemen to stand and fire on the Indians, permitting some hounded and beset whites who had reached the bank to get safely across.

Aaron Reynolds, already known for his ability to outswear men twice his age, added a new dimension to his reputation by saving the life of his commanding officer, Captain John Patterson. Finding Patterson exhausted on the riverbank, Reynolds got off the horse he was escaping on, lifted the helpless officer up into the saddle and sent him across the river. Reynolds then swam for it but when Patterson looked back, he saw a band of Indians surround and capture his comrade.

Boone, meanwhile, seeing the line collapse and his escape route cut, called his men together and started them westward through the woods; he knew a ford near Indian Creek and they would cross there. Israel remained crouching behind a tree covering the retreat. When Boone caught a stray horse and pressed it on the boy, he replied, "Give it to someone else, Father, and we will go together."

Boone had just surrendered it when, out of the welter of shots, one cracked close and he turned to see Israel driven to the ground by the impact of a ball striking his chest. He started at once to rise, but blood filled his mouth and he fell again, and by the time Boone reached him only his frightened eyes moved.

Boone took him up in his arms and carried him into the woods, making his way down the hill toward the ford at Indian Creek. At one point he sensed movement behind him and spun to see a charging Wyandot. He dropped to one knee and holding the boy in his left arm, fired with the right and shot the brave dead at a range of four feet. Then he went on.

At the ford, he saw the last of his men into the river, then started across himself, struggling to hold his son's head up out of the water. He carried him to a cave he knew, putting him down tenderly, murmuring encouragement. But Israel's eyes no longer moved and the blood had dried in his mouth. For a time Boone sat beside this second of his eldest sons to die at the hands of the Indians. He would never be able to speak of that moment without tears. Finally, alone, he started back to Boone's Station to tell Rebecca.

Early on Monday, August 19, Benjamin Logan reached Bryan's Station to learn that Todd had already marched off without him.

"Dreading the consequences," he soon formed up his Lincoln County militiamen and started north. But at 1:00 P.M., when he had gone only a few miles from the fort, the first of the Blue Licks survivors came pounding down the trail, spent and haunted men, riding their horses too hard, flying from nightmares that had come true. And so the awful news came home.

Thinking the Indians might be in hot pursuit, Logan set up a defensive line. But only more tattered, battle-weary Kentuckians appeared, a few riding, most on foot. They were escorted back to Bryan's. There the women beseeched every new arrival for news of loved ones, but if there was any news at all, it was bad. The one moment of cheer came when the irrepressible Aaron Reynolds appeared. He had broken away from his captors and escaped after all. Captain Patterson, who thought Reynolds had died saving him, was so glad to see his rescuer that he promised him two hundred acres of land.

They kept coming all through the night until nearly a hundred were accounted for. Then, toward morning, the trickle stopped and it became clear that those who had not returned would never return. Messengers were sent to the other stations. Back came a clamor for word from the battlefield, a demand that the dead be decently buried. On August 24, Logan and his men again started north for Blue Licks. Boone, alone among the commanders to survive, went with them.

They were still far from the river when they saw the scavenger birds sailing overhead. But the battlefield was more appalling than the worst they were prepared for. The mutilated bodies had swelled beyond recognition. Those with hands tied behind their backs offered mute testimony to the Wyandot treatment of their prisoners. Boone later reported to the governor that they buried forty-three men, but that "many more we expect lay about that we did not see." In fact, seventy-seven of the men who had so boldly dashed into the Licking five days before were now dead, a loss felt in virtually every frontier home.

Israel Boone was not buried in the common grave at Blue Licks. After that work was done, Boone went across the river and found the body of his son in the cave where he had left it and brought it back to Boone's Station. There he and Rebecca laid the twenty-three-year-old boy to rest, a final victim of the last battle of the American Revolution.

VIII

Glory and Grief

When the dead were buried, the recriminations began. The county commanders accused Clark of "weakening one end of the country to strengthen another," and Clark blamed "these unfortunate gents" for allowing the enemy to slip past their guard and then go stumbling into his ambush. McGary came in for bitter criticism as a "vain and seditious fool," and Logan for his late arrival at Bryan's Station. Decrying the "shameful" loss of so many valuable men, Colonel Arthur Campbell wrote,

> Logan is a dull, narrow body, from whom nothing clever need be expected. What a figure he exhibited at the head of near 500 men, to reach the field of action six days afterwards.

Everyone now lamented the fact that Boone's advice had been ignored. But Boone, in his report to Governor Benjamin Harrison, did not even mention it and had not a word of censure for his fallen comrades. Nor did he blame Logan, to whom he had barely spoken since the court-martial; he was, in fact, willing to have the governor accept Logan's own account of the disaster. He only renewed his plea for aid:

> I know, Sir, that your situation is something critical. But are we to be totally forgotten? I hope not. I trust about 500 men sent to our assistance immediately. . . . may be the saving of our part of the Country. But if you put them under the direction of Genl. Clark, they will be little or no service to our Settlement, as he lies 100 miles West of us. . . . I have encouraged the people here in this County all that I could, but I can no longer encourage my

neighbors, nor myself, to risque our lives here at such extraordinary hazards. [Another] Indian campaign into our Country will break these settlements.

Governor Harrison responded to the various reports with an expression of sympathy to the bereaved and a gentle chiding of both sides in the quarrel. By early November, they had put aside their differences and Clark led over a thousand men under Boone, Logan and Floyd into the Shawnee country. For four days they systematically burned villages, grain and crops, and for a time the Indian threat diminished. But not until 1794, when General Anthony Wayne won a decisive victory over the northern tribes at Fallen Timbers, was there real peace in the West. In the meantime, another fifteen hundred settlers were killed or carried off and, as Boone put it, "Kentucky was full of the freshly widowed and orphaned."

He remained at Boone's Station until 1783, hunting, surveying and, much against his nature, raising tobacco, for it brought ready cash, of which he was steadily in need. For a time all went well. He was building up his land holdings and providing valuable parcels for his children. But there were auguries of his financial undoing. He gave land away or sold it cheaply to buy warrants for new lands. Sometimes his surveys were faulty or supplanted by other claims; often he had to pay damages. And then a charming rogue from New Jersey came west and defrauded him of some prime land.

His name was Gilbert Imlay, an adventurer and land speculator, and he persuaded the ever trustful Boone that he could interest men of great wealth in the western lands. So saying, he contracted to buy a choice ten-thousand-acre tract and gave Boone his note for a thousand pounds. Three years later, having sold off the land, he wrote to tell Boone sadly, that "I have been unable to receive a pound" and could not redeem the note.

And yet he did not forget the old pioneer, and in a certain historic sense, finally did discharge his obligation. Some say it was Imlay who first directed John Filson's attention to Boone, leading to the enormously successful "autobiography." It was certainly Imlay, fleeing a Virginia court, who spread the frontiersman's fame abroad. As the lover of Mary Wollstonecraft, the leading feminist of the period, he was welcomed into the radical literary circles of France and England; soon, the European journals were extolling Boone, the "natural" man, and offering firsthand accounts, usually vastly exaggerated, of his life and woodland prowess. Eventually Mary Wollstonecraft's daughter married the poet Shelley, whose friend, Lord Byron, was to celebrate Boone in his unfinished epic, *Don Juan*.

None of this would have made much impression on Boone if he had known about it and, meanwhile, his fortunes continued to decline. It turned out that even his title to the land at Boone's Station was flawed and the sheriff came and said he would have to leave. He had not yet absorbed this news when he had another encounter with his Shawnee brothers.

He was working in the shed where he cured his tobacco, raising the dried leaves to an upper tier to make room below. And as he stood well off the ground, four braves walked in and leveled their rifles at him. He bid them a pleasant howdy and, unable to think what else to do for the moment, went on hanging tobacco.

"Well, Boone," said one of the Shawnee, "we got you good this time. You no get away any more. We carry you off to Chillicothe. Damn!"

Boone looked down more carefully. Now he recognized the Shawnee as among those he had cavorted and hunted with during his captivity five years before. "Well, old friends! I'm glad to see you," he responded. He asked about other warriors he had known and said that old Sheltowee would enjoy a trip back to the Shawnee town. Perhaps he would bring his squaw. Would that be all right?

"Come down, Boone! Now!"

Well, if he could just finish hanging the tobacco. You see, tobacco was peculiar stuff and if it didn't dry just right you might as well throw it away. There was some almost ready he could let them have. And so he chattered on and the Indians, half-angry, half-hypnotized by his glib prattle, continued to stare up at the disembodied voice. Boone, meanwhile, was busily accumulating a mountain of dried tobacco, and suddenly swept it all down on their upturned faces.

Caught in the storm of leaves and dust, the blinded Indians groped helplessly around the shed, choking and cursing, while Boone leaped down and ran for his cabin. Once locked safely inside, laughing uproariously, he made Rebecca come and watch as his "brothers" staggered off, still coughing and swearing up a streak because "Godammit Boone" had tricked them again.

He would not have cause to laugh so heartily again for a long time. In April, John Floyd was killed by Indians. It turned out to be a double blow to Boone because Floyd, a bold, strapping figure of a man, was his good friend and because he had entrusted the legal management of his land contracts and claims to him. Floyd was one of the most colorful characters of Kentucky's formative years. He had survived the early Indian wars and later led a regiment in Clark's campaigns into the Shawnee territory. In between, he commanded a privateer in the waters off Cuba, was captured by the British and imprisoned in England. Escaping, he fled to France and was befriended by Ambassador Franklin, nearly lost his life to smallpox and finally, in 1778, returned to America to marry and prosper. Governor Harrison thought so highly of Floyd that he appointed him the first judge of the Kentucky judicial district. He was then thirty-two years old. Five weeks later, he was shot down from ambush and died soon after. Afterward Boone's papers were lost and, with them, many of his unsecured titles. It is likely that whatever evidence he had to support his claim to Boone's Station was among those missing documents.

Once more Rebecca packed up and the Boones moved on, but this time not happily. A brother, Edward, and their son Israel were buried at Boone's Station; they had cleared the land and built the cabin and stockade with their own hands. Ahead was not adventure but the dreary work of farming, for some land Boone owned at Marble Creek, five miles west, seemed the only place to go. He stayed two years, raising crops and hunting whenever he could get away.

By 1786 he had had enough and, handing the farm over to his daughter Susannah and her husband William Hays, he went north to Limestone on the Ohio River, which was becoming Kentucky's leading port of entry. Most of the new settlers now came down the river and struck out for the interior to find their fortunes, more than three thousand in the year after Boone's arrival. Barges full of livestock and provisions for the settlements landed at Limestone, too, and it seemed a good place to Boone. He turned to surveying land for newcomers and buying and selling some on his own account. He also opened a tavern where Rebecca set a table whose food, one traveler noted, "was the best I had eaten in many a day," and where a month's board came to around eight dollars. He also built a warehouse to store goods waiting transshipment. With it all, he eked out a bare livelihood.

But Limestone had other attractions. It became the point of departure for raids into the Indian country and old friends were frequently on hand. All that first summer preparations were made for an expedition intended to take enemy prisoners who could then be offered in exchange for the whites held captive by the Shawnee. Clark, Logan and McGary arrived, and late in September Boone gave up being a tavern-keeper and businessman to join them on the march north. Some twenty warriors were killed during this campaign, among them Big Jim, who had tortured young James Boone to death in Powell's Valley nearly fifteen years before. Seventy-five were captured, and one of these was Moluntha, the old chief Boone had known in Chillicothe.

Moluntha was not reluctant to go with the Kentuckians—he even brought his squaw—for he had been trying to effect an exchange of prisoners for some time. He was especially glad to see Boone, and they chatted all the way back to camp. There, Hugh McGary, still smarting over the censure that had been heaped on him for the defeat at Blue Licks, broke into the circle of men around the old Indian. "Were you at the Blue Licks?" he demanded.

Moluntha, who had not been but did not understand the abrupt question, nodded amiably, thinking to please the white man.

"Well, damn you, I'll send you to hell for it!" Before anyone could stop him, McGary swung his ax and split the chief's head open. As his horrified squaw ran to catch the falling man, already dead, McGary turned on her, but she covered her head with her hands and lost only three fingers. Finally the other whites tore the raging McGary away.

It was a brutal, irrational act—Moluntha had actually been working with the Americans. But this time McGary paid a price for his savagery. Boone and some of the others were revolted by the murder; they pressed for a court-martial and McGary was stripped of his commission.

Boone at fifty was little changed from the agile frontiersman who had brought his family to Kentucky a decade before. His hair was grayer and the lines around his mouth a little deeper, but his step was quick and his sharp blue eyes still keen. Dressed in the buckskin and homespun he had always worn, he looked as ready as ever to set off on a long winter hunt. But he hunted only once or twice a year now that he was involved with surveying and tavern-keeping. His "Indian Book," an account of the provisions he supplied during the exchange of prisoners, might indicate that his business was flourishing. Vouchers presented to the government for payment October 22, 1787, totaled more than a hundred pounds—a very substantial part of which covered whiskey for both the prisoners and their guards. But that was a full year's accounting and, in the meantime, he had to spend a good deal of time trying to collect money owed for his other work.

To one surveying client he wrote that "times were a little difficult [and] I must be plain with you. I am entirely out of cash and the Chain men and Markers must be paid on the shot and I want 2 or 3 guineas for my own use." That his legal troubles were not over is evidenced by another letter in which he reveals that "I will have to pay a huge sum of money at Court on Tuesday" and urges the recipient to "settle on Monday." Somehow, though, he always had a few dollars to lend to old comrades passing through.

Of his children, young Rebecca and the three boys, Daniel Morgan, Jesse and Nathan, were still at home. Nathan was only a toddler, but Rebecca did her full share of work at the tavern, and Daniel Morgan and Jesse were usually at their father's side when he was out surveying, or trading land, horses, furs, rifles—whatever anyone wanted that enterprise or ingenuity could provide.

He had a way with young people. A friend of his sons', a lad named Hanks, went hunting with the Boones one day, so awed by the presence of the legendary woodsman that he said scarcely a word. Then, as he later remembered the episode, "Daniel Boone lent me his rifle in place of my own, saying, as I carried it on my shoulder, that if I saw any buffaloes, it would twist around until it pointed straight at them. We had a very good hunt."

Another friend of Daniel Morgan's was Blue Jacket, the young Shawnee chief; he came to owe Boone his life. When a peace with the Indians was signed in the summer of 1787, Blue Jacket invited eighteen-year-old Daniel Morgan to go hunting with him to commemorate the event. But the peace was uncertain at best, and one spring day Blue Jacket was brought into Limestone under guard, charged with stealing horses from Strode's Station. He was turned over to Boone, who locked him in an empty cabin to await the people from Strode's. There could be little doubt that they would mete out extreme punishment. But somehow a knife was left in the improvised prison and next morning, in place of Blue Jacket, there was only the cut rope that had bound him. Boone was properly contrite when the men from Strode's arrived, but later he told Nathan and Daniel Morgan that perhaps the spirit of old Moluntha was resting a bit more easily.

A little boy who had never heard of Daniel Boone would have reason to be grateful for this compassion. Not much older than Boone's Nathan, he had been kidnapped by the Shawnee, who decided to raise him as an Indian and concealed the fact that he was their prisoner; his parents thought him dead. But Boone saw him in the Shawnee camp one day and, with the special favor he now enjoyed among them for having saved their chief, managed to secure the boy's freedom. The arrangement was that an Indian prisoner would be released in his place.

This didn't sit well with some officious militiamen directing the prisoner exchange; it had not been done according to the rules and they ordered the boy returned. Boone, who seldom displayed his anger, this time gave it free rein. He told the officers that he had a half-dead jackass with more spirit than they had and, in a stinging letter to their commanding officer, wrote, "I am here with my hands full of business and no authority. But if I am not indulged in what I do for the best then it is not worth my while to put myself to this trouble." Then he took the boy back to his parents. Soon after, an Indian prisoner was sent home.

By this time, the legend of Daniel Boone was known around the world, given wings by the Pennsylvania schoolmaster, John Filson. He had come west to write a book about Kentucky, and spent the summer of 1783 with Boone, coaxing tales of his life on the frontier. When his book appeared the following year, it had an appendix entitled, *The Adventures of Col. Daniel Boon.*

It was a sensation. Though only 33 of its 118 pages are devoted to the Boone narrative, written in what Filson pretended were the frontiersman's own words, the account of his exploits was so immensely popular that the entire work soon came to be known as "Filson's Boone." And despite the stilted language, despite the inaccuracies and the passages that came straight from an eastern pedagogue's imagination, the essential appeal of one man against the wilderness thrilled readers throughout America and Europe. Here was the natural man as hero, living the life others only dreamed about. Filson's Boone strode the frontier with unconquerable spirit, the very model of the daring trailblazer, little read but with a native wisdom that fitted him for everything he needed to do, brave, upright, God-fearing—and an absolute dead shot.

Some writers would plagiarize Filson and others would embellish even his inventions. The real Daniel Boone receded farther and farther behind the haze of myth. In later years this irritated the old woodsman, but of Filson's book, which started it all, he would only say that it was true, every word, and with the merest trace of a smile, "Not a lie in it."

In the four years to 1786, Boone executed about 150 separate surveys, some for newcomers to Kentucky, more for wealthy Virginians who were willing to invest in good land if someone else would undertake the hazardous business of finding and marking it, and then provide them with a clear title. Boone was far from the most qualified or experienced surveyor in Fayette County, but he had two virtues that made him one of the busiest: he knew where to find the best land, and he was not afraid to strike off into the still dangerous forests to lay it off, cross-staff and compass in one hand, rifle in the other.

Most frequently his chainmen were Jesse and Daniel Morgan, but another of his assistants was Isaac Shelby who, in 1792, would become the first governor of the new state of Kentucky. Boone's usual fee came to something less than three dollars, which would never enrich him, but he often worked on shares and was paid in property, sometimes as much as half the acreage surveyed. He was slowly building up a fortune in land, and by 1786, he had filed claims on nearly one hundred thousand acres.

For a time it appeared that at last his hopes were being realized, the long years of defeat and disappointment far behind. But as before his hopes were built on sand, his faith in what he conceived to be simple justice misplaced. Like most other frontier surveyors, he was often careless about proper filing procedures, and sometimes otherwise violated the letter of the law. This provided an opening for shrewder land-seekers to preempt lands he had already claimed, and sometimes he had to repay clients from his own holdings.

But the core of his difficulties was that the loose regulation of the public lands made it possible for officials, some venal, some merely inept, to issue more warrants than there was land available. By the time the land rush was all over, enough of it had been promised to cover Kentucky four times over. Those who eventually won out in the resulting tangle of conflicting claims and overlapping boundaries were those who stood closest to the bureaucracy and best understood both the law and the little acts of patronage that could make it more amenable.

Boone was not one of them. As he generously put it, "Unacquainted with the niceties of the law, the lands I was enabled to locate, through my own ignorance, were swallowed up by better claims."

Nor was he alone in adversity. Many another pioneer who knew nothing of the statutes but who had cleared the land and planted it and fought for it was one day confronted with a stranger who had never before set foot in Kentucky, but who carried a piece of paper that said the land was his. Simon Kenton was so stripped of all his property and wound up in debtor's prison. The legal brief had replaced the long rifle as the weapon that won Kentucky. The brave people who defended Bryan's Station with their lives found themselves trespassers there; the true title had been granted to Colonel William Preston, who was chief surveyor when Kentucky was Fincastle County, and Preston traded the land to another Virginian who, like himself, had never been there.

Boone did not lose everything overnight, but he fought only a spiritless rear guard action against the lawyers and sheriffs and writs and subpoenas that steadily chipped away his holdings. He hadn't the heart for that kind of fighting—disputing another man's word, challenging rulings he couldn't understand. Nor did he ever argue with the parade of men who now came to say that land he'd surveyed or sold them had been lost to a prior claim; he simply sold off still more of his property to pay them.

Bad luck dogged him. In an effort to raise cash, he took to digging the medicinal root, ginseng, and with his sons started up the Ohio to sell it in Philadelphia. His keel boat ran up on some driftwood and overturned, and the soggy ginseng brought scarcely half what he had counted on. He tried riding Kentucky horses east for sale, but they arrived in such poor condition that he didn't realize enough to pay the expenses of the trip.

Discouraged, disillusioned, he left Limestone and ferried his family along the Ohio to Point Pleasant on the Kanawha River where, thirty-five years before, Cornstalk and the Cherokees had gone down to defeat in Lord Dunmore's War. Boone, of whom it was said that he could smell a salt lick thirty miles away, found one at the mouth of Campbell's Creek. There he built a comfortable home, a double log cabin of two stories with a porch in front, and tried to forget his troubles.

He doesn't seem to have spent much time there. In the fall he was off deer hunting with Nathan, now old enough to begin learning the secrets of the wild. One frosty autumn night, camped along the Ohio, they were awakened by the sounds of axes at work across the river. Indians building a raft, Boone told the boy; no doubt they had seen their fire. Boone packed all the gear into the bottom of their canoe, then slipped back into his bedroll. Shouldn't they push off, Nathan asked uneasily; weren't the Indians coming? Yes, they were coming, Boone replied softly, but not before they had finished their raft. Meanwhile, he and Nathan could take their rest. Not until near daylight, when the chopping sounds stopped, did he shake the boy awake. Then, having heaped some more wood on the fire, they went down to the canoe and slipped silently downstream.

As the claims against him mounted and he lost one suit after another, he came more and more to depend on the solace of the woods. But now he was overtaken by rheumatism, sometimes so severe that he needed Rebecca to go along and carry his rifle. Once he took the entire family and, sheltered only by a bark lean-to, they passed all fall and winter hunting and trapping. The catch was good that year and they sold the skins and salted bear meat at Point Pleasant.

When the rheumatism let him, he was the Boone of old. One day, alone, he presented himself at the home of Daniel Huddleston near Kanawha Falls and asked to spend the night. When the family awoke the next morning, the stranger was gone, but he was back at breakfast to tell them that he had spotted beaver in the river. Afterward he said to the Huddlestons' young son, Jared, "Well, come with me and I will show you how to trap beaver." They caught more than a dozen in the next few days and Boone gave one of his traps to the boy in thanks for the Huddlestons' hospitality. Another time, nearby, a family named Flinn had been killed by Indians, all except the mother and her ten-year-old daughter Chloe, who were carried off. Boone tracked the raiders to their village and one night stole Chloe back from them. Since her mother had died on the trek north, Boone took the child home with him. A year later he found some of her relatives along the Ohio River and brought her to them.

Though others plagued him with lawsuits and even impugned his honesty, Boone still had the confidence of his neighbors. By popular petition he was appointed commander of the Kanawha County militia, and he set off on a scouting trip along its hundred-mile northern frontier. Returning, he recommended to the governor that, among other defense needs, "Spyes will be necessary at the point (Point Pleasant) to search the river crossings; these spyes must be composed of Inhabitants, who will know the woods and waters." In 1791, he was again elected to the Virginia assembly and is said to have walked all the way to Richmond. "After tiring with legislation," recalled a friend, "he picked up his gun and came home."

But the fact is that Boone was no longer a real leader in the affairs of Kentucky. He was almost the only one left of those towering figures who had wrested the country from the Indians and the wilderness—Floyd and Harrod were dead, Clark discredited, Kenton gone to Ohio where he fought only poverty and was as much an anachronism as the old forts rotting among the weeds. The people didn't live in forts anymore, but in towns, and they kept coming in ever increasing numbers. By 1795, there were seventy-five thousand of them in Kentucky, now the fifteenth state of the Union. And with them came new problems, new interests and new leaders.

The names one now heard—Breckenridge, Shelby, Todd, Wilkinson

—were not those of the men who had manned the stockades, but of a new aristocracy. Manor houses were rising; there were regular streets in the towns, and they were full of merchants, lawyers and land speculators. There were already three hundred people in Louisville. Lexington was building a university. And in places like that a man wearing buckskin and leggings caused heads to turn.

Boone sought a contract to provision the militia, but was not successful at it. He moved around, hunting again in Tennessee and going as far as North Carolina. Once he took Rebecca and young Nathan east for a last visit with loved ones in Pennsylvania. A friend years afterward remembered how "[Daniel Boone] and his wife came from Kentucky on horse back and their little son rode behind his father the whole journey, and they visited their relations and friends through this section of the country."

Meanwhile the Kanawha settlements were growing, spreading. It was the old story: people crowding in to displace the game, shattering the serenity of the countryside with their nervous energy. Civilization cost too much in wear and tear on the human spirit, Boone decided, and in 1795, he and Rebecca went west again, settling on ten acres of uncleared land owned by their son Daniel Morgan at Brushy Fork. It was not far from Blue Licks, where so much of the Kentucky saga had been written. But to Boone, now past sixty and seeing newcomers move in to farm land bloodied by the best fighting men of two races, it was a lifetime away.

The following year he read a notice in the Kentucky *Gazette* that the Wilderness Road he had cut twenty years before was to be widened for wagons all the way to Lexington, and he wrote to ask his old surveying aide, Governor Isaac Shelby, for the job:

> Sir: After my best respects to your Excellency and family, I wish to inform you that I have some intention of undertaking this new Road that is to be cut through the Wilderness, and I think myself entitled to the offer of the business as I first marked out that Road in March, 1775, and never received anything for my trouble and suppose I am no Statesman. [But] I am a Woodsman and think myself as capable of marking and cutting that Road as any other man. Sir, if you think with me, I would thank you to write me a line by the post the first opportunity at Mr. John Miller's on Hinkston Fork. . . . I am, dear Sir, your very humble servant, DANIEL BOONE.

But the name of Boone had been reduced to a romantic memory in the new Kentucky, calling up images of a quaint old pioneer ambling through a barely remembered past. Shelby didn't even reply to his letter, and the road contract went to someone else.

The endless litigation over land continued to harry and enmesh him. He lost every suit brought against him. In the same year that Kentucky decided to name a new county in his honor, two other counties seized ten thousand acres of his property and sold them for taxes. Even other people's troubles became his. As one who knew the country from end to end, he was called regularly to testify in the suits and countersuits between rival claimants to the same land, and inevitably he made an enemy of the loser. Some went about saying that Boone had lied and been bribed to do it. Others even threatened his life. He began to feel that he could no longer travel in safety, that "in time of peace my own Kentucky has become more dangerous to me than it had been in Indian times."

He was by now good and weary of recrimination, of living among those who had looked to him to fight their battles, and had come to hate him over the ownership of a piece of land. He told a nephew that "he did not want to die among them." He had left one large tract on the north bank of the Licking that had not been "shingled over" with other claims. In 1798, he conveyed this to John Grant, his sister Elizabeth's son, and directed him to deed it piecemeal to any man who presented a claim against him, and never after inquired about its disposal. He told his children that he was finished contesting lawsuits, and instructed them not to do so, now or after his death, that even if they won the cost in "vexation" was more than any land was worth. Then he prepared to leave Kentucky altogether.

In 1795, Daniel Morgan Boone, then twenty-five years old, had journeyed west to look at the Spanish lands beyond the Mississippi, no doubt with his father's blessing. Like his grandfather, who had come to scout America for *his* father, Daniel Morgan liked what he saw. The country was open and full of game, the trapping excellent. Captivated, he paid a visit to the lieutenant governor himself, Don Zenon Trudeau, who armed him with still more good news. Should so distinguished an American as Daniel Boone decide to emigrate to Missouri, the Spanish government would reward him with a substantial grant of land, and provide lesser grants to each family he brought with him.

Lieutenant Governor Trudeau was an unusual man, considerably more enlightened than most colonial officials. While his compatriots shuddered at the thought of American immigrants crossing the Mississippi into Spanish territory, he encouraged it; only when there were people on the land would it be secure from Indians and the relentless ambitions of the British. When Spain's King Charles IV decreed that all his subjects must be of the Catholic faith, Trudeau stretched the decree until it all but vanished in subterfuge, permitting any religion at all in Missouri so long as it was practiced privately. And Trudeau, who knew all about Daniel Boone, also knew that where he went others would follow. Soon he was writing to the old pioneer to repeat the offer he had made to Daniel Morgan, adding that Boone might well merit a public office under the Spaniards.

For four years more, Boone clung to the hope that Kentucky, the land he had idealized and fought for over nearly half a century, would yet fulfill his dreams. Then, one spring day in the year 1799, when all his lands were gone, and the dreams with them, he chopped down a giant yellow poplar and began hewing out a canoe that was to measure sixty feet from stem to stern.

He had been through a dark time, one that might have finished a lesser man. But there had always been a special resiliency in the Boones—it was the darkest hours that seemed to touch off their brightest dreams—and every new dream led them west. So it was that through that summer of 1799, Boone worked away on the long canoe that was to take him, his family and everything they owned to the country marked on the maps as Upper Louisiana, six or seven hundred miles away. That was the year George Washington died, but Daniel Boone, age sixty-five, was going west to start a new life.

He did not go alone. Squire Boone, his body scarred from old wounds that would torment him until his death, once again answered the westering call sounded by his brother. Others—Bryans, Callaways, friends and neighbors—who also had lost out in the Kentucky land scramble but still stood willing to go where Boone led, assembled with their boats and possessions. Kentucky was already behind them—the years, the effort, the loved ones buried in its earth. Ahead was another new land, another chance.

They left on a clear morning in mid-September. People came from considerable distances to see the departure and kept appearing until the little fleet was well up the Ohio, some to bid old comrades goodbye, but many out of human curiosity, having heard that Daniel Boone was leaving Kentucky forever. Squire, Daniel Morgan and Nathan manned the Boones' canoe, the women—Rebecca, Jemima, Susannah—and the small children riding among the household goods. Boone, with his sons in law, Flanders Callaway and William Hays, and a few others drove the cattle and pack-horses overland. "The old man," wrote William S. Bryan, "walked every foot of the way."

At Cincinnati, the two groups were briefly reunited before traveling on. Again crowds flocked to the riverside for a glimpse of the legendary Daniel Boone. They asked him why he had left Kentucky. Boone kept his troubles to himself; he merely said that he wanted more elbow room. But they pressed him: what had decided him, what had happened? And Boone, whose stories now improved with the size of his audience, finally replied that he had had a visitor at Brushy Fork, and when the man said he lived only seventy miles away, *that* decided him. "I went to my wife and said to her, 'Old woman, we must move, for now they are crowding us.' "

MISSOURI

IX

Moving On

In the courthouse square of St. Charles, Missouri, there is a red granite boulder with a plaque commemorating the Boone's Lick Road,

> the trail followed by Daniel Boone when he discovered the Salt Springs, afterward called Boone's Lick, which gave to the road its name; the main highway out of which grew the Santa Fé Trail, the Salt Lake Trail and the Great Oregon Trail.

All his life, wherever he went, Boone was linked with the paths that led people through the wilderness. Sometimes, as in those last years in Missouri, he did not follow them all the way to the new lands of the South and Northwest. But even then, pathfinders and pioneers—Lewis and Clark, Lieutenant Zebulon Pike, Manuel Lisa—came to seek his counsel about the unknown territory beyond the young settlements for he had traveled as far west as the Yellowstone country and hunted the length of the Missouri and the Platte rivers. Among the first Americans to settle in what is now the state of Missouri, in the end, Boone became as important to its development as he had been to the development of Kentucky, and he was to live there almost exactly as long.

The Kentucky immigrants followed the Ohio to its turbulent juncture with the Mississippi, then turned north, the boatmen paddling against the current. By the end of October they had come together at St. Louis, a trading post on the river with a population of less than five hundred, mostly French, and were greeted with flourishes and fanfare. Spanish and American flags snapped in the autumn wind, drums rolled, the garrison paraded and rifles cracked out a welcoming salute. Boone, who never before had been publicly honored, enjoyed the show but couldn't quite believe it was for him.

Lieutenant Governor Trudeau, who had been summoned back to Spain, waited to greet the distinguished arrival with his replacement, Carlos D. Delassus. Trudeau had made certain that Delassus understood the importance of the new settlers, and that the promises made to them would be kept. They were. Boone was to be appointed syndic, or chief administrator for all the Femme Osage district, an immense area north and west of the Missouri River; he was given a thousand arpents, about 850 acres, and empowered to distribute four hundred arpents to each of his followers.

When the ceremonies and business were finished, the travelers, greatly pleased, moved off to begin their new life. While the boats wound slowly around the sweeping bends of the Mississippi and the Missouri, Boone mounted up and rode the sixty miles due west to where Daniel Morgan had already picked out some land for himself and built a home. It was on a bluff overlooking the Missouri, and here Boone began cutting logs for a small cabin, a colonist for the fourth and last time. Eventually he selected a tract for himself adjoining Daniel Morgan's, rich bottomland on the north bank of the river, but he didn't bother to move.

Before long, the Boones, Bryans and Callaways were again established within a few miles of each other around the Femme Osage Creek, their cluster of homes the farthest white settlement on the Missouri. Someone suggested calling it Little Kentucky, but there was no enthusiasm for that. Squire, who had a particular feeling for stone houses, had begun building a new one; but when two of his sons came to visit him and found the country not to their liking, the old preacher went back to Kentucky with them. He always regretted it. He saw his brother Daniel only once more after that, and lived out his last years in poverty, victimized by land sharks, imprisoned for debt and finally forced to leave Kentucky still again, this last time for Indiana.

Meanwhile, life in Missouri seemed to promise the expatriate Americans everything they had come seeking. They found game in good supply; they got on well with the largely French population, traditionally more interested in fur than in land; and the Spanish rule intruded only lightly on their lives. The fact is that the American experience was working out so well that the lieutenant governor asked Boone if he could bring in another hundred Kentucky families; if he did, his reward would be an additional ten thousand arpents. It took only a few letters and it was all arranged. Boone was becoming a substantial landholder again.

It remained true that the necessity to pretend adherence to the Catholic church sometimes went against the grain, but no one ever really interfered with the newcomers' true faith. The commandant, for example, was enjoined "to watch that no Protestant preachers introduced themselves," but the commandant, Daniel Boone, never seemed to notice— although he was sometimes in attendance when a traveling Baptist held services in one of the cabins. And when young Daniel Morgan won the hand of Sarah Lewis and the marriage had to take place in the St. Charles parish church, even though both bride and groom were Protestants, no one afterward ever asked them what creed they followed or taught their children.

To Boone, born a Quaker but resistant ever after to any doctrinal expression of religion, it was all a small matter. His faith was his own, and it was unshakable. Some Missourians used to say that God would never cross the Mississippi; Boone never doubted that He was already there when the white men arrived. Yet when a visiting missionary entreated, "Don't you love God?" in an effort to get him to join the church, he replied, "I have always loved God, ever since I can recollect," and feeling that to be sufficient, departed.

For the first year he and his sons hunted only meat for the pot, carrying it home on their shoulders. Soon, though, they were after deer and beaver in a serious way. They got a good enough price for the deer hides in St. Louis, but Nathan took the fur all the way to Lexington, where it brought three dollars a pelt. His father's share went toward paying off some of that still considerable Kentucky debt. One February, Boone and Rebecca went alone to live for some weeks on the open land and made maple sugar—about four hundred pounds of it!

Early in the summer of 1800, Boone received his commission as syndic. Besides being the leading citizen of the Femme Osage district, he was now its most powerful official—sheriff, judge, jury and commandant. He held court under a great overspreading elm, which came to be known as the Judgment Tree, and there he dispensed a rough frontier justice, settled disputes, allocated lands and managed the public affairs. As his knowledge of the law was limited to his own experiences in court, which had been largely calamitous, he cheerfully ignored all formal procedures and spurned conventional rules of evidence, telling all who came before him that he wished to know only the truth.

Sometimes his decisions were stunning. A poor widow and a landholder were in dispute over a cow. It was clear that the man had the better case, and Boone ruled in his favor—then ordered the next defendant, a chronic disturber of the peace, to turn over one of *his* cows to the widow as punishment. More than once both parties to a suit were compelled to divide the costs and be gone.

But the most common penalty in Boone's court, as it was everywhere along the frontier, was the whipping post. He saw no sense in sending a man to prison when he was needed to till the land and provide meat for his family; the lash, "well laid on," was quick and effective and discharged an offender's debt to the community. Once whipped, he could again hold his head as high as anyone. A horse thief, sentenced to thirty-nine lashes, the maximum penalty, was asked how he felt when it was done. "First rate," he declared. "Whipped and cleared." Brawls, a common enough occurrence, were fierce, no-quarter affairs. Confronted with one man who had bitten off another's ear, Boone ordered twenty lashes laid across his backside so that when he sat down he would be compelled to think it over.

But not every case was straightforward, and one, a murder, was especially trying for Boone, for the accused was his friend, and the victim was the husband of Susannah, his first daughter. The indictment was unsparing:

> That one James Davis, being moved and seduced by the instigation of the Devil, on the 13th day of December, in the year of our Lord 1804, did make an assault with a certain rifle gun, four feet long, and of the value of five dollars, loaded and charged with gun powder and one leaden bullet, and then and there fired and killed William Hays.

But Boone knew his son-in-law. He was a good and brave man; he had been there at the cutting of the Wilderness Road and fought the Indians at Boonesborough, Bryan's Station and with Clark's expeditions. But he was also a man of high hot temper, grown worse as he aged. The facts were that he had had an argument over money with Davis, a shoemaker and Boone's frequent hunting companion: Davis had gone to the Hays' house to collect; Hays ordered him away; Davis persisted. But not until Hays threatened his life and went for his own gun had Davis fired the fatal shot.

Saddened, grieving for his daughter and grandchildren, Boone bound the defendant over to the grand jury in St. Charles, fixing his bond at three thousand dollars. Then he himself signed it and Davis was released. When the trial was called, Davis satisfied the jury that he had acted in self-defense and he was acquitted.

Long after Boone's commission had been superseded, Missourians kept coming to the Judgment Tree and Boone, dignified, terse, continued to dispense justice. The people were satisfied with Boone's court. They understood it. And there is no record of even a single appeal from the decisions of Daniel Boone.

For a few dazzling years, Napoleon had visions of restoring the French colonial empire in the New World. But no sooner had he coerced Spain into ceding back the Louisiana territory, lost in 1762, than a depleted treasury and the prospect of still another war with England turned Louisiana into a luxury he could not afford. It was at this turning point in history that President Thomas Jefferson, fearing the French would close the port of New Orleans to the growing American trade along the Mississippi, instructed his envoys to negotiate for the purchase of New Orleans and a guarantee of free navigation on the river. When, instead, Napoleon offered the whole of Louisiana, the ministers were prompt to accept, although they had no constitutional authority to do so and Jefferson was the first to admit that.

It was the signal achievement of his administration. The year was 1803, and without war or even the loss of a single life, he had doubled the size of the young United States and made it into a continental nation. The Louisiana Purchase, a vast new territory of more than eight hundred thousand square miles, extended the American frontier from the Mississippi to the Rocky Mountains. A whole new country was opened to settlement, and the restless men who pushed westward, ever westward, would one day shape from it all or most of thirteen new states. The cost had been $15 million, or about four cents an acre.

Most of the nation rejoiced with patriotic fervor, but the people in Missouri were uneasy. The French foresaw in the coming of the Americans an end to their Arcadian way of life. Wherever the Yankees went, they cut down forests, built towns and factories, and spread the noise and bustle of their commerce across the countryside. And the transplanted Kentuckians, hopeful the broad Mississippi would remain an effective barrier to such an invasion, feared the loss of their lands and an imposition of the taxes and regulations they had fled at least once.

For a time nothing changed. Not even the arrival of the new

American governor, Captain Amos Stoddard, in March 1804, disturbed the even tenor of life in the Femme Osage. Stoddard's instructions were to leave the people in peace to the extent that he could, and Delassus, his predecessor, encouraged him to keep most of the current officials. Of the syndic, Delassus wrote:

> Mr. Boone—a respectable old man, just and impartial. He has already, since I appointed him, offered his resignation owing to his infirmities. Believing I know his probity, I have induced him to remain, in view of my confidence in him, for the public good.

Boone's "infirmities" were diplomatic. He had no desire to impose himself on anyone. Assured that he was wanted by the new administration, he was glad to stay on. His real problem with the Americans—once more!—was the title to his lands.

The newly arrived land commissioners were not anxious to appropriate anyone's property; mostly they confirmed the Spanish grants. And when Boone appeared before them bearing Trudeau's letter of invitation to Missouri and his certificates of survey—bitter experience had taught him how important papers could be—he had no concern. Ten minutes later, he had been stripped of every acre.

Had his grants been approved by the Spanish governor in New Orleans? the commissioners asked. Well, no, Boone replied, he had been busy and never seen to it. But he had been told that the lieutenant-governor's signature was sufficient, and he had that.

Commissioners: Well, had he cultivated any part of his holdings, as required by Spanish law, or cleared some?

Boone: No, he was a hunter, not a farmer.

Commissioners: Had he built a house on the land? Did he even live on it?

Boone: No, he had built his house on the land of his son, Daniel Morgan, adjoining, and lived there. Now he lived on the land of another son, Nathan.

Commissioners, regretfully: The law was clear. To guard against speculators, it said that a man had to cultivate, improve or live on land ceded to him by the government. As Boone had done none of these things, nor even obtained a definitive title from the Spanish authorities, they had no choice but to take his lands into the custody and keeping of the United States.

Boone, stunned: Thank you.

And so, incredibly, Daniel Boone, who had led the people to Missouri, as he had led them to Kentucky, was now left as landless in the one place as he had been in the other. But somehow he was not nearly so aggrieved. His sons still had land and the country remained open and full of game. And in Washington, D.C., there were some good men who found the old pioneer's plight intolerable in light of his services to the United States, and they went to work on his behalf.

But the years passed and nothing happened and sometimes Boone thought he would move on again, to still another frontier. It was not so much the lost land as the old tugging toward the unknown, the lands yet unseen. Missouri was filling up, and now was the time to move on, before he was finally tethered by his aching old bones.

But suppose he did? Would the outcome be different? He remembered the golden days of the long hunts in Kentucky before the others came, when the land was a legend crossed only by buffalo traces and cold clear streams, the woods teeming with game, the clover meadows rolling all the way to the sky, and not a white man to be seen and rarely a red one. But it didn't stay that way. Soon enough the settlers came, and now Boone puzzled over the paradox that he, more than any other man, had shown them the way.

All his life seemed a paradox. Happy in the wilderness, fulfilled, he returned again and again to live the hemmed-in life of a farmer. Needing nothing but his rifle and his wits, he hankered for the eminence that came with land and wealth. And loving the empty land, he had led the multitudes to fill it.

So he did not go, and then the seasons seemed to rush through his life. Boone in his seventies spent the summers holding court under the Judgment Tree, a leathery, white-haired old man who still listened more than he spoke, and visiting one or another of his children, intriguing a growing flock of grandchildren with his tales, chopping trees for the winter's wood and even, reluctantly, lending a hand in the field. But with the first crisp crackle of autumn, he had to be off hunting, trapping or just wandering.

He rarely went alone anymore—Rebecca opposed that—but he always had a faithful companion in Derry, a young black servant who kept his camp and skinned out the game. Sometimes one or more of his sons went along, or Flanders Callaway, and later a grandson or two. William Hays, Jr., was with him in the fall of 1808 when they had to flee a band of Osage Indians. Afterward the boy was flushed with excitement at the adventure, but Boone groused because they had lost their traps. He must be getting old. Soon, though, his confidence was restored. Some other Osages invaded his camp and demanded his winter's catch of beaver pelts. Boone offered them the business end of his rifle instead and this time it was the Indians who fled.

He always said that the Osage were no match for the Shawnee or the Wyandots. But the smaller tribes to the northwest were another matter, more interested in the white man's scalp than his furs. Trapping in their country one winter, alone this time, Boone found himself cut off and dependent on a wilderness cunning he had not had to fall back on in twenty years. He had followed the Missouri to the Grand River, then turned north under the headlands of western Iowa. Having brought down enough game to see him through the trapping season, he tied the canoe in a protected creek and made camp in a cave. But soon after his traps were set, he began finding unmistakable signs that he was roaming in the very midst of an Indian hunting ground. By this time the creek was frozen over, his canoe iced in. And though a heavy snow had fallen, concealing his traps, it would also proclaim his trail if he tried walking out.

Boone stayed where he was, camouflaging his camp, making only a small, shielded fire to cook each night, and did not venture out for twenty days. Sometimes he heard Indians passing within a few yards of where he lay hidden, rifle ready, but they never suspected his presence. Well fed, essentially secure, he just waited. Finally there was a thaw. As the snow melted and the ice broke up, Boone collected his traps and gladly paddled out to find a safer country. But he was perversely cheered by the little episode.

Settlers along the length of the Missouri and its branches were no longer surprised to see Boone's long canoe glide by, the old gentleman paddling steadily away no matter how many others might be aboard. One autumn he came walking into Fort Osage in westernmost Missouri, and the commanding officer, with some astonishment, noted that, "We have been honored by a visit from Col. Boone . . . the colonel cannot live without being in the woods."

On one of these expeditions, Boone discovered the salt springs in present day Howard County that became known as Boone's Lick. With Nathan and Daniel Morgan, he established a bustling little industry there that soon employed six men and produced thirty bushels of salt a day. This was shipped up to St. Louis by keelboat and for years supplied all the settlements north of the Missouri River. Even more important in the eye of history, the salt works led to the opening of the Boone's Lick Road, which for the next half century remained the pioneers' highway west.

Boone had not been permitted to fight in the War of 1812, although he was among the first to volunteer when word of the new hostilities with Britain reached the Femme Osage that summer. The government said that seventy-eight was too old for soldiering. But his sons and grandsons of age joined up.

It was a Westerner's war. While the avowed cause, freedom of the seas, was little understood on the frontier—and less appreciated in the maritime states, which feared the war would ruin their commerce—no one in the West failed to see that another good trouncing of the redcoats and their Indian allies would open still more land to settlement. The men marched off enthusiastically, Daniel Morgan and Nathan to command ranger units on the Missouri River frontier.

But the war could not be contained on the frontier. Again spurred and supplied by the British, the Indians raided the Missouri settlements, sending the people flying to fort up. For Boone, who stood ready with his rifle but did not get to use it, it was a sad and trying time. He could not fight or travel, and soon he was overtaken by a particular grief. At maple sugaring time in 1813, he took Rebecca to Jemima's, where the sturdy old woman went into the woods to boil sap. Suddenly she sickened and came back to the house. Within a few days, on March 18, she was dead.

When the body had been prepared, Boone asked to be alone with it for a time. Rebecca Bryan Boone had spent fifty-six of her seventy-four years as his wife, most of the time in log cabins with dirt floors. She had borne their first child when she was only seventeen, and their tenth when she was well past forty; together they had buried three. They had had their difficulties, nearly all of them the result of Boone's eternal wandering, but in loneliness and poverty and danger, Rebecca was at his side whenever he let her be, and he could not conceive of the years ahead without her. Finally he rose heavily and helped to carry her coffin to the grave on a high place above the Missouri that he had chosen for the two of them.

Almost exactly two years later, after the peace had been signed but before the news reached Missouri, Jemima's boy, James Callaway, was killed in a battle at Loutre Creek.

The Indians fought on. On a spring morning a few weeks later, they struck at the home of Robert Ramsey, Boone's near neighbor. Ramsey was shot down but managed to sound a distress call on his old trumpet. Fearing it would bring the rangers, the Indians left, tomahawking three of the Ramsey children in the yard as they rode off. Boone, who heard the alarm, came at a gallop. It was too late for the fighting, but he was needed all the same for the doctoring skills he had built up over a long lifetime of ministering to wounds and frontier mishaps. He arrived just as Mrs. Ramsey went into premature labor.

"Quiet and unexcited," as a witness remembered him in those grim hours, the old man went to work. For two of the children, skulls shattered and their life's blood draining away, there was nothing to do but let them slip mercifully into death. The third, though, would live, and Boone cleaned and bandaged his bloodied head. Then he probed for the bullet in the wounded man's groin and brought it out. There was little beyond an occasional word of comfort that anyone could offer Mrs. Ramsey; after a long and torturous labor, she delivered a healthy baby, but died a few hours afterward.

For a time, Boone retreated again into a brooding silence. But by October, as though he had confronted the end of his own life and accepted it, he wrote a revealing and remarkably perceptive letter to Sarah Day Boone, the widow of his older brother Samuel; it was Sarah who, half a century before, had taught him to form his letters:

Dear Sister,

With pleasure I read a letter from your son Samuel Boone, who informs me that you are yet living and in good health, considering your age. I write to you to let you know I have not forgotten you and to inform you of my own situation since the death of your sister Rebecca. I live with Flanders Callaway, but am at present at my son Nathan's and in tolerable health. You can guess at my feelings by your own, as we are so near one age. I need not write you of our situation, as Samuel Bradley or James Grimes [nephews] can inform you of every circumstance relating to our family and how we live in this world; what chance we shall have in the next, we know not. For my part, I am ignorant as a child. All the religion I have [is] to love and fear God, believe in Jesus Christ, do all the good to my neighbors and myself that I can and do as little harm as I can help, and trust in God's mercy for the rest. I believe God never made a man of my principles to be lost, and I flatter myself, dear sister, that you are well on your way in Christianity. Give my love to all your children and all my friends. Farewell, my dear sister.

DANIEL BOONE

But the old man was far from finished. Some years before, a Kentucky legislator and property owner, Major General Green Clay, had written to ask him to return and testify in a court case over some disputed land; Clay promised Boone that he would "provide for the support of yourself and your lady all your lives afterwards; and a handsome legacy for you to leave to your children."

Boone had declined. When he left Kentucky, he vowed never to set foot on its soil again. "If I was compelled to lose my head on the block or revisit Kentucky," he wrote General Clay, "I would not hesitate to choose the former."

But as he grew older, this passionate aversion cooled; he was simply incapable of sustaining such animosity. He did go back twice, and in 1810, the legislature, which had had a hand in depriving him of his land in Kentucky, passed a resolution urging the federal Congress to restore the lands taken from him in Missouri:

> The Legislature of Kentucky, taking into view the many eminent services rendered by Col. Daniel Boone in exploring and settling the Western Country. . . . and that from circumstances over which he had no control, he is now reduced to poverty, not having so far as appears, an acre of land out of the vast territory he has been a great instrument in peopling. . . .
>
> Resolved—By the General Assembly of the Commonwealth of Kentucky —That our Senators and Representatives in Congress be requested to make use of their exertions to procure a grant of land in said Territory (of Missouri) to said Boone.

The resolution disappeared into the legislative maze in Washington, surfacing now and then to spark Boone's hopes, only to disappear once more. Sometimes he sat by the river and wondered if he should be in Washington fighting for what was rightfully his; perhaps he should have fought harder for his land from the first. But he knew in his heart that he was incapable of such fighting, the courtroom bluster and the backroom toadying, and so what happened to him had been inevitable.

It did not make him feel any better. He had set out in life with only a rifle, a horse and a good woman to his name, and he used to say that that was enough. But deep down he was the same as any man: he wanted more, and for a time had had it. Now he was near the end and what he had was less than when he started, for his Rebecca lay moldering in her grave.

Around this time he made his first trip back to Kentucky, visiting his brother Squire in Indiana where the old preacher was building his last stone house. Sometime during this journey, Boone met an engaging young man who seemed to have no business other than to go tramping through the woods drawing pictures of birds. His name was John James Audubon, and the two plainly enjoyed one another's company. Boone showed Audubon how to "bark off" a squirrel, shooting at the tree limb just beneath the creature's feet so that it was killed by concussion from the splintering wood, neither fur nor meat damaged; and Audubon sketched the old woodsman's weathered face. Though the portraits he later made from these sketches did not become as famous as his ornithological paintings, they are among only a handful ever done of Boone.

In Kentucky Boone paid off some more of his debts, mainly with money he'd earned trapping, and appeared as a witness in still another land suit. This time the dispute was over a corner Boone had surveyed long before, that he had said was marked by a certain poplar tree. When the court adjourned to the site and Boone pointed out the tree, an attorney asked how he could be so sure it was the same one. Because, replied Boone, he had jammed an empty rum bottle into the crotch to mark it, and if they now chipped away the new growth, they would find it. This was done and the bottle pulled out; the case was decided on the spot.

Eight years after his move to Missouri, in February 1814, President James Madison signed into law a "special act of Congress" restoring to Boone the title to exactly one-tenth of the land conveyed to him by the Spanish crown. After all the years, all the travail, the Missouri delegate had made an incredible blunder at the last moment; brushing aside the 8,500 acres Delassus had given Boone in 1800 for bringing a hundred pioneer families to Missouri, he assured the Congress that all the old frontiersman really sought was the return of his original 850-acre grant.

Boone didn't even get to keep that. Some enterprising Kentuckians, reading about Congress's well-publicized show of generosity in the newspapers, promptly journeyed out to Missouri to present him with their twenty-year-old claims, and he had to sell off every last parcel of land to pay them.

When it was all gone, when the old man had nothing left, still another Kentuckian came, a man named Ballard. He was the husband of Chloe Finn, the orphaned child Boone had rescued from the Indians years before and taken into his home. He had deeded her some land then, and now Ballard said that the claim had been ruled invalid; he thought Boone ought to make good the loss.

Boone replied that he had given the land as a gift. He was sorry they'd lost it, but it had been handed over in good faith and never cost Ballard or his wife a single penny. Now, having lost his own property, Boone said he was dependent on the bounty of his children and had neither land nor money left to give anyone, even if he'd wanted to. But the Kentuckian persisted: he felt he was entitled to some recompense for his trouble. And finally Boone told him that he had come a long way to suck a bull and would have to go home dry. Then the old man went into his cabin and closed the door.

He returned to Kentucky for the last time in 1817. Three more seasons of trapping had put some money in his pocket again and he sought out every man who claimed a debt from him. He asked only one thing, what was owed, and paid it over without further question. At the end, he had barely enough to get back to Missouri, but he was much relieved.

Wherever he went, aging companions came to see him and brought their children and grandchildren so that in years to come they could say that they had once shaken the hand of Daniel Boone. Returning along the Ohio, he stopped for a last visit with Simon Kenton, who had been made a brigadier general of the Ohio militia, but who also hadn't an acre of land to his name. The two old veterans, both white-haired but still standing straight, lived over their long ago adventures and parted, knowing they would never meet again, with tears in their eyes.

Boone had just fifty cents left when he reached home, but he was content: "I have paid all my debts and no one will say when I am gone, 'Boone was a dishonest man.' I am perfectly willing to die."

But he was some way from death. As long as he could walk, he could wander, and there still was half a continent to see. Those lands of the far West, like a lodestar, drew him on. Having explored the plains of Missouri, Kansas and the Dakotas, he set out on the Platte River one year and followed it all the way to the Rockies. Then he struck out overland and spent the winter season trapping in the Yellowstone country, a fantastic land of steaming geysers and mountains taller than any he had ever seen. It would have been a spectacular journey for anyone in that time, at least six hundred miles across absolutely barren country; even for Boone it was noteworthy—he was well past his eightieth birthday.

But he was no sooner back than he told Daniel Morgan, "I intend by next autumn to visit the salt mountains, lakes and ponds about five or six hundred miles west of here." The farther slopes of the Rockies intrigued him; so did California. But he was not destined to see them. The wandering was coming to an end.

Although he had been in good health except for his rheumatism, he began to feel intimations of his mortality. Once, hunting along the westernmost reaches of the Osage with Derry, he fell sick and decided that death was not far off. In the past, he had often sworn the servant to carry him home, dead or alive. For all his wilderness wandering, Boone had a horror of being buried far from his loved ones. But now he relented; the way back was long, and for Derry, alone and burdened with a corpse, it would be full of peril. Instead, Boone, lying weak and pale on the ground, directed the faithful black in preparations for his burial: Derry was to wash the body and wrap it in a good blanket; the grave was to be on the highest hilltop around—*there*—and properly marked; afterward, it must be covered with rocks and logs so the wolves couldn't paw it open. Once the grave was dug, he said, he would give the youth some messages for his family and show him exactly how to get home. But when the grave was dug, Boone felt somewhat better, and the next day the two resumed their hunting.

Still, he knew that old age had finally overtaken him. His eyes began to fail and he had to mark his rifle sight with a slip of white paper. Trapping with his grandsons, he was satisfied to stay close to camp now, to do the cooking and skin out the game. But he remained spry enough to help Nathan build a substantial stone house, three rooms below and four above, and to carve seven mantels with a sunburst design for the fireplaces.

There was no end of cherished grandchildren to distract him, fifty-two in Missouri alone, and then there were *their* children. Long after, one of their playmates would say that she felt no safer in her own parlor than she had sixty years before when borne over the hills on the shoulders of Daniel Boone, or than when he paddled her across the Missouri on a log.

He was well aware of his fame toward the last, for often travelers, total strangers, sought him out and wanted him to tell the tales of his fighting days in Kentucky, and sometimes he did. The myth makers were already at work. Someone gave him a copy of a book in verse called *The Mountain Muse*; it had been written by Daniel Bryan, a nephew of Rebecca, and purported to be an account of Boone's life on the frontier. Asked to comment on it, he said that though he could not sue the author for slander, he thought such publications should at least be left until the person alluded to had been put under the ground. "This book," he said, "represents me as a wonderful man who killed a host of Indians. I don't believe the one has much to do with the other."

It all troubled him, somehow. He did not want to be remembered as an Indian killer. He knew he was not the first white settler of the West, as

some said, or the discoverer of Kentucky, or its chief military defender—
and he had never claimed to be. He used to shoot straight and run swiftly;
he had been a hunter, a woodsman and had had a hand in opening the
wilderness. He had done his duty, that was all.

On fair afternoons, he would sit near the riverbank and watch the
brown Missouri roll by. Sometimes, in that last summer of his life,
westering parties passed beneath the rise where he sat, his rheumatic old
bones at rest against a tree, rifle close at hand. And sometimes they
climbed the bank to visit with him, agile, sharp-sighted young men, their
faces still unweathered, and a new life and days without end before them.

Had he been west along the river? they would ask.

Yes.

How far? Was the way hard?

How far? Why as far as it goes, and beyond. For a while they would
talk of the things he had seen in that big outreaching land to the west, but
soon their sharp eyes strayed back to the river, where their women waited.
They were anxious to move on, and when they had gone he felt suddenly
outdistanced by time, a stranger in his own skin.

They were off to open a new country, these people, traveling in
proper wagons and keelboats loaded with household goods, and sometimes
a hundred or more head of cattle following along. And all he could do was
sit and watch them go by. Well, it would be no different—they would fill
their west just as his people had filled Kentucky and Missouri, and they
would drive off the game, too. For in the end, settlers were all the same: all
they knew for sure was how to clear a farm and tag after the rear end of an
ox, up one furrow and down another.

How did he find Missouri? one asked him. Crowded, he replied, and
with a glint in his eye told how he had moved from North Carolina to
Kentucky seeking space and repose, retreating before the flood of settlers.
And again the settlers followed him, and again he moved on, to Missouri.
"Here I hoped to find rest," he said, "but still I was pursued, for I had not
been at the licks two years before a damned Yankee came and settled
within a hundred miles of me!"

His wry little jokes were a last defense against a world in which, for all
his fame, he seemed to have overstayed his welcome. An artist, Chester
Harding, came from St. Louis to paint his picture that summer, but
couldn't find anyone who even knew where he lived. "The nearer I
approached the home of the old man," Harding later wrote, "the less

interest was felt by his neighbors." Finally, when a man who lived only two miles away said that he did not know any Colonel Boone, his wife spoke up: "Why, yes, you do. It is that white-headed old man who lives on the bottom, near the river."

Harding's own attitude seems to have been akin to the neighbor's. Recalling the visit in a letter, he wrote that as he had been a backwoodsman himself, "I took very little interest in the old man, or his adventures." Boone sensed this at once. When Harding idly asked if in all his travels he had ever been lost, Boone tartly replied, "No, I can't say as ever I was lost, but I was once bewildered for three days."

When the portrait was finished, his grandchildren oohed and aahed over it, but he himself felt it made him look like a cadaver, cheeks all sucked in and mouth clamped tight over his toothless gums. But it was the only portrait of him ever painted from life.

Sometimes when he sat by the riverbank and thought about the years sped by, he wondered if he could have lived a different life. Suppose he had settled in Philadelphia or Baltimore—that was where the money went, to the towns, and that's where it stayed. But this mood passed quickly, for the old man knew it to be pure foolishness. He hadn't been made to sit, and especially not in the press and smell of a town. Then what? What was it that smoldered inside him now, at the very end? And of course he knew; it was just that—the end. Does any man come happy to his old age? What rankled was that there would be no more long hunts, no more winter treks to the end of a trapline, no more roving alone into the blue and beckoning distance.

Those had been his rewards, the best part of his life. He could not put them into a bank or leave them to his children, but they were real enough. He had seen the land when it was new, and it had gladdened him as riches never could. And so, finally, he came to understand why he had not been able to build a fortune. He had never really cared about it enough; his heart was not in it. It was the seeking that mattered.

Well, he need not be ashamed of that. If he had nothing else to pass on to his children, he had given them his feeling for the land. They would find their own frontiers.

And he supposed they would see some sights, too. The country was different now, but it was still young. It would grow and change in ways that he could not imagine. All those settlers pushing west—they were building it. What would it look like fifty years from now? Where would the frontiers be then? Well, that was something for his children to find out, and their children, and that wasn't such a bad legacy.

And so the old man sat near the riverbank, musing and finally at peace, waiting for the one last adventure still ahead of him.

He died just after the end of summer in 1820, a month shy of his eighty-sixth birthday. He had been taken with a fever at Jemima's house, but had shrugged it off and ridden over to see Nathan, as he had promised he would. There he had a generous helping of sweet potatoes, his favorite food, and feeling sickly again, retired to the sunny corner room that was reserved for him in the fine stone house. And on September 26, his great wealth of children and grandchildren nearby, he slept quietly away.

Next day they moved the cherrywood coffin the old pioneer had made himself up to Flanders Callaway's barn, for not even the big stone house could hold all who came to the funeral. Nathan's son-in-law, the Reverend James Craig, preached the service. He said little about Boone the pathfinder, for everyone knew that, and spoke instead of Boone's attachment to his family and his essential decency. "He was a good man," the Reverend Craig said, and left the rest to history.

In St. Louis, the convention drafting a constitution for the state to be, hearing the news, adjourned; they wore black crepe on their sleeves for twenty days, one for each year that Daniel Boone had lived in Missouri. And across the West, though hardly any of his old comrades were alive to remind them, the people knew that a giant had died.

X

Afterword

The years passed and his legend grew. In 1845, the Commonwealth of Kentucky claimed the bones of the founding father and, to its later regret, Missouri yielded them. Amid military flash and pageantry, Boone and Rebecca were reinterred under a great monument of Italian marble. By then the wildly inflated "biographies" had appeared, one author forthright enough to concede that his "was not made for use, but to sell." In genuine admiration, Lord Byron wrote of him in *Don Juan*: "Of the great names which in our faces stare/ Is Daniel Boone, backwoodsman of Kentucky"; and James Fenimore Cooper made him the model for the heroes of his *Leatherstocking* stories. By the bicentennial of his birth, eight counties, twenty-two towns and any number of roads, rivers and mountains had been named in his honor.

But the real Boone, whose life is the essential American story, had all but disappeared in a cloud of myth. And counterpointing the legends of his greatness, there were even some stern scholars who reevaluated his place in history and judged it insignificant.

But between the two extremes, Boone somehow lives on. For the remarkable thing about the American past is not how far back it goes but how, as the years pass, it tells us more of what we need to know. Anyone who has ever worried about the man-made burdens of life in the late twentieth century—broader roads and a shrinking wilderness, more taxes and less freedom, greater cities and an end to privacy—anyone who even once has felt the urge to flee from it all will know Daniel Boone's true place in the annals of America. He found his way west. We shall have to find ours.

Daniel Boone—A Chronology

1713   George, Sarah and Squire (Daniel Boone's father) leave England for America.

1717   Their father, George Boone the elder, brings the rest of his family to Philadelphia.

1718   The elder Boone moves his family to Oley (later Exeter) Township, Berks County, Pennsylvania.

1720   Squire Boone marries Sarah Morgan.

1730   Squire Boone buys land in Oley adjacent to his father's farm.

1734   Daniel Boone born November 2, the sixth child of Squire and Sarah.

1744   Squire buys grazing land; Daniel spends next six summers as herdsman.

1746   Given first rifle.

1747   His brother Israel "marries out" of Quaker faith; father expelled from Exeter Meeting.

1750   Squire sells his land; Boone family starts for North Carolina.

1751   After a year in the Shenandoah Valley of Virginia, the Boones continue on to North Carolina, settling in the valley of the Yadkin River.

1755   Daniel Boone a wagoner in Braddock's expedition against Fort Duquesne.

1756   Marries Rebecca Bryan.

1758   Cherokee Indian wars begin; Boone member of Forbes expedition against Fort Duquesne.

1759   Boone moves family east to Culpeper County, Virginia.

1760   Crosses Blue Ridge Mountains for first time and explores Tennessee.

1762   Cherokees defeated; Boones return to Yadkin.

1763   Boone meets Richard Henderson, who defends him in suits for debt, later engages him as land scout.

1764 Moves west to Brushy Mountains.

1765 Leads a party to Florida.

1767 Reaches Kentucky without realizing it.

1769 With John Findley and four others, finds Cumberland Gap and crosses into Kentucky bluegrass country; spends next two years hunting and exploring Kentucky.

1772 Returns twice to Kentucky; works to interest Cherokees in selling their claim to it to Henderson's land company.

1773 Leads settlement party toward Kentucky; attacked by Indians at Wallen's Ridge; five killed, including Boone's son James; all turn back.

1774 Visits James' grave.

— With Michael Stoner, covers eight hundred miles in sixty-one days to warn Kentucky surveyors of Indian uprising.

— Commands three Clinch forts in Lord Dunmore's War.

1775 Makes final exploratory trip to Kentucky.

— Present at Sycamore Shoals when Henderson buys Kentucky from Cherokees.

— Leads party of road-cutters blazing the Wilderness Road to Boonesborough.

— Among delegates enacting laws for Transylvania Colony; assumes leadership as Henderson's influence declines.

— Returns east to get his family.

— Continental Congress declines to accept Transylvania as fourteenth colony.

— First Indian attacks.

1776 Jemima Boone, Betsey and Fanny Callaway kidnapped by Indians; Boone leads rescue party.

1777 Indian raids mount; Boone wounded in attack on Boonesborough.

1778 Arranges surrender of salt makers to large force of Shawnee under Black Fish and British officers.

— Taken to British commander in Detroit; persuades him not to attack Boonesborough until summer.

— Lives four months in Shawnee camp as Black Fish's adopted son.

— Escapes, returning to Boonesborough in four days to lead preparations for defense against Shawnee attack.

— After unsuccessful negotiations with Black Fish, Boonesborough settlers, under Boone's command, withstand ten-day siege.

— Boone tried by military court for treason; acquitted and promoted to major.

— Goes to North Carolina for Rebecca; spends a year persuading her to return.

1779 Leaves Boonesborough to build own settlement, Boone's Station.

1780   Robbed of fifty thousand dollars, mostly money entrusted to him by friends to buy land warrants.

     —Richard Callaway, Edward Boone killed by Indians.

     —Boone becomes member of Virginia legislature.

1781   Captured by British raiders in Charlottesville; persuades them he is local farmer and is released.

1782   Siege of Bryan's Station.

     —Boone one of three commanders as fewer than two hundred Kentuckians pursue strong Indian force and are defeated at battle of Blue Licks; Boone's son Israel killed.

1783   Boone moves to Limestone, becomes tavern-keeper and land surveyor.

1786   Has filed claims on more than one hundred thousand acres, but counter-claims and loose regulation chip away at his holdings.

1789   Moves to Kanawha County; nominated militia commander.

1795   Land troubles mount; moves to Brushy Fork, near Blue Licks.

1796   Applies to Governor Shelby for job of widening old Wilderness Road; no response.

1798   A thousand acres of his land put up for sale by Mason and Clark counties; new county named Boone in his honor; conveys last of Kentucky land to nephew with instructions to deed it piecemeal to any who present claim against him.

1799   Leads party of Boones, Bryans and Callaways to Missouri to make new settlement; eventually granted eleven thousand arpents (more than nine thousand acres) by Spanish governor.

1800   Appointed syndic for Femme Osage district; continues to dispense justice under Judgment Tree even after Americans take over.

1804   Following Louisiana Purchase, American commissioners rule Boone's claims invalid; he loses Missouri lands.

1812   Volunteers for second war against British; turned down because of age.

1813   Rebecca dies.

1814   U.S. Congress awards Boone a thousand arpents; Kentucky creditors besiege him and he surrenders all of it.

1815   Boones flee Indian attack; Flanders Callaway's canoe overturns and Boone's hand-written biography lost.

     —Boone continues hunting, wandering; visits Fort Osage, near present Kansas City at eighty-two; journeys to Yellowstone country.

1817   Makes last trip to Kentucky; pays all debts.

1819   Chester Harding comes to paint his portrait.

1820   Dies at Nathan's home, September 26.

1845   The remains of Daniel and Rebecca Boone removed to Kentucky for reinterment at Frankfort cemetery.

Chapter Notes

I. THE BOONES: MOVING WEST

The most comprehensive Boone genealogy is by Spraker. Many new details of Daniel Boone's English antecedents were uncovered by the Van Noppens, who made an exhaustive search of old Devon records. For the young Boone in Pennsylvania, the primary sources are the records of the Oley-Exeter Friends and the Draper manuscript life of Boone (Series B). It ought to be said at the outset that Draper—particularly the Life, the Boone Papers (C), the Notes (S) and the Kentucky Papers (CC)—is consistently rewarding for every phase of the Boone story.

(Abbreviations: FCHQ, *Filson Club Historical Quarterly*; *Register, Register of the Kentucky Historical Society*; MVHR, *Mississippi Valley Historical Review*; MHR, *Missouri Historical Review*.)

4– ". . . never had an aching bone. . . ." Spraker, p. 19.
4– The term quitrent, rarely heard today, was gallingly familiar to colonial settlers. It represented the fixed rent, usually a small amount, but payable in perpetuity by all who bought land from the King's proprietors.
4– "Because one may hold. . . ." Van Noppen, p. 54.
5– "Dear Friends. . . ." *Ibid.*, p. 36.
5– To the Boones the date was the sixth day of the sixth month. Although the Gregorian, or New Style, calendar was adopted by most European nations in 1582—and is the one we use today—Great Britain did not drop the Julian calendar, which began with the month of March and was eleven days shorter, until 1752. Further, the Quakers scorned the use of pagan names to identify months and referred to them in numerical sequence. Long after Parliament adopted the modern calendar many people of the time,

including Daniel Boone, continued to use the Old Style for the rest of their lives. For consistency's sake, all dates in this book are given in the New Style.

6– The American settlers seem to have devised the word trace for trail or path; it was in use on every frontier.

6– "600 miles nearer. . . ." *Daniel Boone in Pennsylvania*, Paul A. W. Wallace, Pennsylvania Historical and Museum Commission, 1967.

6– Oley, an Indian word meaning kettle, was a broad hollow circled by heavily timbered hills on the very edge of the western frontier. The earliest settlers had come only a few years before and even the cleared land was studded with stumps and boulders. The cattle were turned loose to find grazing. Oley was located a few miles southeast of the present city of Reading and was then in Philadelphia County, a part of which was separated in 1752 to form Berks County. This, and the similarity between Berks and Bucks, misled some early biographers about the site of Boone's birthplace.

7– "At a solemn assembly. . . ." Spraker, p. 32.

7– "thanks to God. . . ." *Olden Time*, John F. Watson, p. 60. (Collected at the instance of the Gwynedd Monthly Meeting from Manuscript records.)

7– "free to the people. . . ." *The New World*, Richard B. Morris, 1963, p. 85. (*Life History of the United States.*)

8– "Our condition at present. . . ." Pennsylvania Archives (Samuel Hazard, ed.), 1852, pp. 215–18.

8– The Shawnee in Pennsylvania were led by a remarkable chieftain named Kakowatchiky who had no intention of taking the warpath, asking only that a wounded warrior's rifle, lost in the battle, be returned. But the incident left its mark. Years later, when a Moravian missionary sought his conversion to Christianity, the old chief demurred, remarking that he was an Indian of God's creation and satisfied with his condition. In any event, he said, it seemed to him that white men prayed with words but the Indian prayed in his heart. (Wallace, p. 123)

8– "There were several notices. . . ." Draper 1C, pp. 19–19². (From a letter by John F. Watson, March 4, 1853, containing the "extracts and gleanings made from an inspection of the *Records of Friends Meetings at Exeter, in Berks County*," for Draper.)

9– The children of Squire and Sarah Boone were: Sarah, born 1724; Israel, 1726; Samuel, 1728; Jonathan, 1730; Elizabeth, 1732; Daniel, 1734; Mary, 1736; George, 1739; Edward, 1740; Squire, 1744; Hannah, 1746.

9– A handsome stone house, built some time after Squire Boone and his family left Pennsylvania, stands on the original foundations of Daniel Boone's birthplace. A spring, used by the Boones as a source of fresh water and cool storage for milk and butter, still flows in the cellar. It is now known as the Daniel Boone Homestead and is maintained by the Pennsylvania Historical and Museum Commission.

9– "Thee naughty boy. . . ." Draper 2B, p. 19.

10– "If thee has not. . . ." *Ibid.*, pp. 26–27; 6S, p. 44.

10– Many stories about Boone's childhood and youth were later told by him to his son Nathan, who authenticated them for Draper. Thirty years after the old trailblazer's death, Draper spent a month with Nathan Boone and his wife in Missouri, carefully writing down their reminiscences. See also "The Ancestry and Boyhood of Daniel Boone," William B. Douglass; *Kentucky School Journal*, vol. 13, September, 1934.

11– "when grandfather died. . . ." Spraker, p. 23.

11– Daniel Boone was not yet eight when Count Zinzendorf's Moravian Indian mission organized a well-remembered convocation in John De Turk's barn for a group of visiting Mahicans. It lasted all night and in an emotional climax the chief and two warriors were baptized. Transported with joy, they went rushing through the streets to tell every white man they encountered what a great favor had been bestowed on them.

11– For Boone's early relationships with the Indians, see Draper 2B; and Douglass, *op. cit.*

12– "When he was about fourteen. . . ." Draper 2B, p. 27.

12– "Let the girls. . . ." Douglass, *op cit.*, p. 18.

12– "This was coppyed. . . ." Durrett Collection, University of Chicago.

12– An apparently genuine Boone assertion in bark is on display at the Filson Club in Louisville and has haunted generations of scholars. Though distorted with age, it seems to read, "D. Boone Kill a Bar / 1803 / ZOIS." There have been some intriguing theories, but no certain explanation of what ZOIS means.

12– Several members of the Boone family were men of considerable learning. John's son James was a mathematician of note and eventually went to Philadelphia where he became a teacher and a member of Benjamin Franklin's circle of friends. Another of Daniel's cousins, also named James, became the family historian and wrote a highly regarded Boone genealogy. In 1760, the distantly related Thomas Boone was appointed royal governor of New Jersey and the following year assigned to the government of South Carolina, "where he served some years with much acceptance." (Draper 2B, p. 6.)

14– "Where did thee learn. . . ." Draper 19C, p. 46.

15– "that he was in a great streight. . . ." Draper 1C, pp. 24–24¹.

15– "found the truth. . . ." *Exeter Monthly Meeting of Women Friends*, June 6, 1743.

15– "produced to this Meeting. . . ." *Ibid.*

15– "The Boones were active. . . ." Draper 1C, p. 24¹. This note, and some others, came to Draper from a Quaker lady of Reading, Rachel D. Griscom, who copied pertinent sections of the Exeter Meeting books for the historian in 1888. This time, though, she added a prim caution: "It is not necessary to put these minutes of this sad story in print to annoy the very respectable family of Boones now living in this vicinity."

16– "so many bears. . . ." Draper 1B, p. 39.

16– "countenancing his son's. . . ." Draper 1C, p. 55.

16– "Whereas Squire Boone. . . ." *Ibid.*

16– In 1750, preparing to leave, Squire sold his land to his wife's relative, William Maugridge, for a pittance. Maugridge had no better luck with it and in the end had to mortgage it to a prominent friend in Philadelphia, Dr. Benjamin Franklin. So it seems clear that Squire finally left Pennsylvania not only because his standing in the community was decisively undercut but because he had not fared well financially. The primitive agricultural methods of the time—the same crops in the same fields, year after year—had depleted the land; and though he had five looms, they often sat idle for want of customers. Of all the Boone brothers, Squire appears to have been the least prosperous. His brother George, with whom he had come to America, left, at his death, fifty pounds for each of his ten children, and seventy-five pounds for each grandchild, a substantial sum for the time, as well as land holdings, mill and waterworks.

II. THE PRIDE OF KINGS

Wall's *History of Davie County* has considerable new material about life on the southwestern frontier and the Boone family in North Carolina. See also Doddridge for the best personal account of the effects of the Cherokee Wars on the pioneer family.

21– "Our grandfather told Boone. . . ." Van Noppen, p. 77.

22– "there were not above. . . ." Wall, p. 21.

22– Inhabitants flock. . . ." *Ibid.*

23– Squire probably paid the rent in Spanish dollars, the most important coin of the colonial period and ancestor of the American dollar. English coinage was so rarely seen, nearly all of it quickly flowing back to the mother country toward payment of the unequal balance of trade, that the social historian William B. Weeden aptly termed it more a medium of expression than a medium of exchange. The Spanish dollar of the 1750s was worth about eight shillings in North Carolina.

23– No part of Squire Boone's house is still standing. Its logs were used to build a temporary kitchen for a second house on the same site, but that was torn down around 1925.

24– "Well, if it has come to this. . . ." Draper 2B, p. 41.

24– Rowan County was again divided in 1836 and the section the Boones lived in became present-day Davie County.

25– A company of brave Jesuits, concerned with the salvation of Indian souls, marched with the French fur traders. A familiar sight outside the trading posts along the western rivers was a bound-together wooden cross.

26– "The Indians had killed. . . ." Draper 2B, p. 40.

26– "The frowns of war. . . ." *Ibid.*, p. 42.

26– "They told me. . . ." *Montcalm and Wolfe*, Francis Parkman; vol. 1, p. 38, Boston, 1901.

27– The site of the contested fort is at the confluence of the Allegheny and the Monongahela rivers, the "Forks of the Ohio." When the British took Fort Duquesne in 1758, they renamed it Fort Pitt for the new prime minister, and around it grew up the city of Pittsburgh.

27– "The savages may be. . . ." *History of the United States*, George Bancroft, vol. IV, p. 190.

28– It is said that Findley's careless disposal of the dried grass was the introduction to Kentucky of its famed bluegrass, which spread throughout the central region. Boone repeated this story to Daniel Bryan, who told it to Draper.

28– "Death [was] always snapping. . . ." FCHQ: October, 1932, p. 372.

29– "colors flying. . . ." Draper 2B, p. 45.

29– Ironically, the French commander had been on the point of abandoning Fort Duquesne. He believed his force of fewer than 250 French and Canadians and 650 reluctant Indians to be badly outnumbered. But a brave young officer, Captain Daniel de Beaujeu, shamed the Indians into following him in an assault on the British by exclaiming, "I am determined to go out and meet the enemy! Will you suffer your father to go out alone? I am sure we shall conquer." De Beaujeu was shot dead in the opening volley, one of only 40 French and Indian casualties.

30– "a great number of bloody scalps. . . ." *American History Illustrated*: July, 1970, p. 36.

30– "(They were) stripped naked. . . ." *Ibid.*

31– "We shall know better. . . ." Bancroft, *op. cit.*, p. 192.

32– "You, like my hunting shirt. . . ." Draper 6S, 17½.

33– The Boone anecdotes are quoted by the Van Noppens; see also Draper 2C and 6S.

33– The children of Daniel and Rebecca Boone were: James, born May 3, 1757; Israel, January 25, 1759; Susannah (Mrs. William Hays), November 2, 1760; Jemima (Mrs. Flanders Callaway), October 4, 1762 (see note for p. 40); Lavinia (Mrs. Joseph Scholl), March 23, 1766; Rebecca (Mrs. Philip Goe), May 26, 1768; Daniel Morgan, December 23, 1769; Jesse, May 23, 1773; William, June 20, 1775 (died in infancy); Nathan, March 2, 1781.

35– "declared that he had killed. . . ." This is Boone's own account of the episode. He told the story to a young friend, R. Clayton, who years afterward recounted it in a letter printed in the St. Louis *Christian Advocate*: July 25, 1877. See also Draper 7C, p. 44.

37– "The whole family were instantly. . . ." Doddridge, pp. 39–40.

37– "What are you doing? . . ." Draper 2B, p. 76.

40– "Well if the name's the same. . . ." Draper 2C, p. 53. The story of the new baby is told by Thomas Norman, whose father migrated to Culpeper from North Carolina with the Boones and later fought alongside Daniel with Waddell's rangers. It was obviously not a secret at the time, but the tale grew blurry with the years and Rebecca's illegitimate child was variously said to have been Susannah, Lavinia or Rebecca. But two facts are incontrovertible; first, that Norman is the only witness among the many who afterward claimed to know the truth to testify from direct knowledge—his father had returned to Culpeper with Boone later in 1762, saw the new baby and, of course, knew that it could not be Daniel's; and second, that none of the other Boone children's birthdates, as given by either Spraker or Douglass, accords properly with any of Daniel's subsequent long absences from Rebecca's side. Along with Norman's account, Draper reports all the inaccurate ones, which were probably kept alive by Richard Callaway's animosity toward Daniel, and by the fact that many in Rebecca's family sided with the Tories during the Revolution. But, remarkably, either piety or a misplaced protectiveness toward Boone has kept all his earlier biographers from dealing with the false rumors or reporting the plain truth of Jemima's birth.

III. O MY DEAR HONEYS, HEAVEN IS A KENTUCKY OF A PLACE

Wall has a thorough account of the Regulator movement in North Carolina, as well as the best bibliography of primary sources for that period in Boone's life. Archibald Henderson's articles and *The Conquest of the Old Southwest* are rich in the facts of Boone's relationship with Richard Henderson. One must be wary of his interpretations, however (Richard Henderson was his ancestor), and for a more dispassionate view of the respective roles of Boone and Henderson in the settlement of Boonesborough and its defense, see Thomas D. Clark, *Frontier America* and *Kentucky, Land of Contrasts*. For the Florida trip and Boone's growing closeness to his son James, the Draper life shines. Excellent surveys of the Long Hunters' way of life and their influence on the western settlement are given by Emory L. Hamilton in *Historical Sketches of Southwest Virginia* (see Bibliography), and Brent Altsheler, FCHQ, October, 1931. There are sound accounts of Boone's first long foray into Kentucky by Thwaites and Bakeless.

41– On his return to North Carolina, Squire Boone, now sixty-five years old and still trying to establish himself in some profitable and lasting occupation, "was licensed to operate a Publick House at his own Plantation." The rates, set by the Rowan County Court, were posted as follows: "Rum and whiskey and other spiritous Liquors—6 shillings per gallon; Dinner of Roasted or Boiled Flesh—1 shilling; Lodging per Night in a good bed—2 pence." The venture did not prosper. Rowan Court Minutes, 1753–1795; quoted in Wall, p. 43.

41– "vicious habits. . . ." Draper 2B, p. 115.

43– "had the honor of having. . . ." Van Noppen, p. 99.

44– "I can never look upon. . . ." Henderson (*Conquest*), p. 106.

45– "he wished to be informed. . . ." *Civil and Political History of Tennessee*, John Haywood (1823), p. 35. (Quoted in FCHQ: January, 1947, p. 10.)

45– "Wisdom comes. . . ." Van Noppen, p. 191.

47– Squire Boone's is the oldest known gravestone in present Davie County, but the lettering is still legible: "Squire Boone, died in the 69th year of his age in the year of our Lord, 1765." Daniel's mother, Sarah Morgan Boone, died twelve years later and was buried beside her husband.

49– "Ah, Wide Mouth. . . ." Bakeless, p. 42.

49– Once, camped along the New River, Boone and Benjamin Cutbirth cached their haul of skins and meat and went off looking for ginseng, a medicinal root for which there was always a cash market. Cutbirth remembered that Boone knew exactly where to find the obscure little plant. But it turned out to be a bad day. Returning to camp, they discovered that some animals— wolves or wildcats—had broken into the pen and dragged their meat off. Thereafter, the place was known by the ironical name they gave it: Meat Camp. Still, they returned with their peltry. Another time, hunting on Rowan Creek, they were overtaken by Cherokees and robbed of their deerskins and all their equipment. For Boone, it meant more debt.

50– "2300 Deer Skins Lost. . . ." Caruso, pp. 69–74.

51– Boone took his son Nathan back to the site of the winter encampment in 1796, and Nathan's account to Draper identified it as being only a mile or so from the present-day town of Louisa. The trace followed by Boone and his companions is now covered by U.S. Highway 23.

51– "I never have heard. . . ." Draper 2B, p. 165.

52– The Falls of the Ohio is a rock ledge that divides the river's water levels. In 1773, the city of Louisville was laid out on the site.

52– Dr. Thomas Walker had found the pass at Ousioto twenty years before, naming it Cumberland Gap. Within a decade of Boone's trip, the Indian usage was all but forgotten.

53– "I have known Boone. . . ." *American Historical Review* (Henderson): vol. 20, 1914, p. 98.

54– "It was on the first of May. . . ." Froncek, p. 68.

55– "O my dear honeys. . . ." Moore, p. 24.

57– "thinking to have. . . ." Draper 4C, p. 45.

58– "Now brothers, go back. . . ." Draper 2B, 187–88.

60– Some sources contend that Squire never encountered the camp-keepers, but instead found Boone and Stewart in their camp after the others had departed. This follows Peck and Flint, whose accuracy must be held suspect when unsupported by other documentation. Draper (2B, pp. 194–95) gives the sequence of events as he got it from Nathan Boone and that is the version I believe correct.

60– "and robbed John Findley. . . ." FCHQ: July, 1969, p. 215: *John Findley First Pathfinder of Kentucky*, Lucien Beckner. For an account of Findley's first trip to Kentucky, see Beckner's "Eskippakithiki: The Last Indian Town in Kentucky," FCHQ: October, 1932.

61– "to recruit his shattered circumstances. . . ." *A Memorial to the Kentucky Legislature*, 1812. (Quoted by Henderson in *Conquest*, p. 153.)

62– "Thus situated. . . ." *Kentucke*, Filson, pp. 53–54.

62– "Without bread, salt. . . ." *Op. cit.*

62– The salt lick, a circle of salt-impregnated ground around natural saline springs, was a focus of life on the frontier. Game usually abounded there, for buffalo, bears and deer came to lick at the salty earth. Pioneer farmers traveled dozens of miles, hauling their heavy iron kettles and spending sometimes weeks in boiling off gallons of water for every precious cupful of salt.

IV. A DARK AND BLOODY GROUND

Boone's tragic first attempt to settle Kentucky is competently covered by Kincaid and, more recently, by James William Hagy in FCHQ: July, 1970. The best accounts of the journey by Boone and Stoner to warn the Fincastle surveyors are by Neal O. Hammon in the *Register*: October, 1972, and FCHQ: January, 1973. Hammon, a professional architect and Kentucky's leading authority on pioneer trails and roads, has also shed new light on the opening of the Wilderness Road ("The First Trip to Boonesborough," FCHQ: July, 1971). There are many books about the Wilderness Road, Kincaid's the most satisfactory, but nearly all rely for detail and a sense of immediacy on the contemporary journals—Henderson's and Walker's, reprinted in Ranck; Calk's in Sosin's *The Opening of the West*. Ranck's account of the Boonesborough settlement, from its conception to its demise, remains the most comprehensive ever written.

69– "the spirit of an enterprise. . . ." Morehead's *Address* at Boonesborough, 1840.

71– "when a halt was called. . . ." Van Noppen, p. 116.

72– Many accounts of this episode hold that Russell delayed his start from the Clinch, and that Boone sent James back to get flour and farm implements from him. Returning, James, Henry Russell and the others are then said to have been overtaken by darkness on the night of October 9–10, camping some miles behind the main party. When one wonders what need Boone had for flour and farm implements on the trail, this version of the prelude to the massacre fails to stand up.

74– "James was a good son. . . ." Draper 6S, p. 80.

74– "the worst melancholy. . . ." *Ibid.*, p. 83.

75– "I have engaged. . . ." Draper 3QQ, p. 46.

75– "I am in hopes. . . ." *Register*: vol. 36 . . . 1938, pp. 372–73.

76– "Alarmed by finding. . . ." *Ibid.*, vol. 70, no. 4, October, 1972, p. 289.

76– Most sources have Boone and Stoner reaching Harrodsburg before the Indian attack and say that Boone took time to help lay out the lots, including one for himself. This would have been a gross betrayal of his mission. More to the point, it is inconceivable that Boone and Stoner could have covered the three hundred miles to Harrodsburg with still time to build a cabin in the twelve days between their departure and the date of the Indian attack. See also FHCQ: July, 1974; Hammon: "The Legend of Daniel Boone's Cabin at Harrodsburg."

77– "Since I began this letter. . . ." Kincaid, p. 87.

77– "Mr. Boone is very diligent. . . ." Thwaites, p. 109.

77– The story of Rebecca and the sham attack is from Draper, 11CC, pp. 224–27 (from an interview with Mrs. Samuel Scott, in the Shane papers).

78– "What will you do? . . ." Caruso, p. 136.

78– The peace required the Shawnee to surrender prisoners, horses and all property taken from the whites, and to give up hunting, or even visiting, on the south side of the Ohio. All the chiefs were present for the treaty signing but Logan. "I am a warrior, not a councilor," he said, then cried out to humanity with a primitive eloquence that has rarely been equaled: "I appeal to any white man to say if he ever entered Logan's cabin hungry, and he gave him not meat; if he ever came cold and naked and he clothed him not. . . . Now who is there to mourn for Logan? Not one."

78– "be acquired by treaty. . . ." Caruso, p. 143.

78– "to support each other. . . ." MVHR: vol. 1, no. 3; December, 1914, p. 348.

79– "Proposals for the encouragement. . . ." *Ibid.*, p. 351.

79– "one Richard Henderson. . . ." Henderson (*Conquest*), p. 241.

79– "infamous company. . . ." North Carolina *Gazette*, February 24, 1775. (Saunders, ed. IX, 1122–25).

79– "Pray, is Dick Henderson? . . ." Archibald Neilson to Andrew Miller, quoted in MVHR: *op. cit.*, p. 351.

80– "The whites have passed. . . ." Kincaid, pp. 97–98.

81– "I do not love to walk. . . ." Ranck, pp. 158–59.

81– "Why do you always ask? . . ." *Ibid.*

83– "for work making roads. . . ." *Ibid.* (Henderson Company store ledger), fn., p. 25.

83– "We put off from the Long Island. . . ." *Ibid.* (Walker's journal), p. 163.

83– True to their word, the Cherokees never molested the settlers in Kentucky. But as Dragging Canoe prophesied, other tribes would contest the white man's incursions with blood and terror; chief among these were the Shawnee.

85– "Dear Colonel. . . ." Ranck, pp. 168–69.

86– "Once beyond the great. . . ." *Register:* October, 1974, p. 392.

87– "from Mr. Luttrell's camp. . . ." Ranck (Henderson's journal), p. 171.

87– "With me, it was beyond. . . ." *Ibid.*, pp. 184–85.

87– "good Queen Anne's musket. . . ." *Ibid.*, p. 186.

89– "Camped that night. . . ." *Ibid.*, p. 172.

89– "Captain Boone related. . . ." *Ibid.*, p. 192.

V. THE FOURTEENTH COLONY

For events at Boonesborough and the settlers' response to the challenge of their new lives in the wilderness, Ranck again is the most satisfying source. See also FCHQ: January, 1947 ("The Transylvania Company Study in Personnel: James Hogg," Archibald Henderson; and "The Henderson Company Ledger," John Shane) for both a traditional account and many warm little human asides of Boonesborough's first years. Lester's work on the Transylvania Company is sound and especially useful for an understanding of its ultimate failure. Not surprisingly, Draper has the best account of the kidnapping of Jemima and the Callaway girls (Series B, C and CC), and Floyd's own story of this most sensational event, originally told in a letter to Colonel Preston, is reprinted in FCHQ: vol. II; October, 1928 to July, 1929; pp. 171–73.

90– "the established authority. . . ." Henderson (*Conquest*). Preliminary leaf.

91– "an honest, open countenance. . . ." Ranck's (Henderson's journal), p. 174.

91– House of Delegates. . . ." *Ibid.*, p. 196.

92– "was at some loss. . . ." *Ibid.* (Henderson's journal), p. 172.

92– "the only commodious place. . . ." *Ibid.*

92– Some historians have read Henderson's dissatisfaction with Fort Boone to mean that the first site was poorly chosen for defensive purposes; Boone detractors have condemned it as a malarial hollow commanded by the wooded hills on the far side of the Kentucky. This requires a word. Apart from the fact that Boone was no more anxious to expose himself to Indian rifle fire than any man—and knew better than most how to avoid it—the range from the hills to the first fort was well beyond the carrying capacity of the day's weaponry. It seems clear enough that additional land, not tactical position, was the reason Henderson chose a new location.

92– "We Begin Building us. . . ." Sosin (*Opening*: Calk's journal), p. 44.

92– "We all view our loots. . . ." *Ibid.*, p. 43.

93– "that he would have nothing. . . ." Ranck (Henderson's journal), p. 174.

93– "Should any successful (attack). . . ." *Ibid.*, pp. 188–89.

93– Shane puts the general uneasiness with Henderson's leadership this way: "None of them (the proprietors of the Transylvania Company) had seen the country which they purchased. They took it entirely on Boone's representation. . . . Hence the origin of the Company is to be attributed to Boone's representations."

93– For Henderson's problems with whiskey, see Lester and FCHQ: January, 1947, p. 29.

94– "Hunters not returned. . . ." Ranck (Henderson's journal), p. 177.

94– "You, perhaps, are placing. . . ." Ranck, p. 198. A transcript of the convention of the Transylvania Delegates is provided by Ranck (Appendix N, p. 196); Lester offers a lucid analysis of the delegates' work.

95– "In Kentucky, one man's trigger. . . ." *A History of the South*, Francis Butler Simpkins, 1953, p. 40.

95– "that set of rascals. . . ." Lester, p. 116.

95– "abhorred independence. . . ." and "most permanent harmony. . . ." FCHQ: January, 1947, p. 13.

95– "A greater absurdity. . . ." (a sentence deleted from) *Common Sense*.

96– "Flattered themselves. . . ." and "If the United States colonies. . . ." Ranck, pp. 215–16.

96– "The proprietors have no grant. . . ." FCHQ: January, 1947, p. 13.

98– "If she found a man. . . ." *Ibid.*, p. 46.

99– "Whilst some of your petitioners. . . ." *Petitions of the Early Inhabitants of Kentucky*, James Rood Robinson (ed.), p. 149.

99– Although Virginia and North Carolina maintained rival claims to Kentucky, it was Virginia that exercised more effective control, incorporating it first into its westernmost county (Fincastle), then organizing it into a separate county (Kentucky) whose boundaries conformed to the present state, and in 1780, dividing it into three counties (Fayette, Jefferson and Lincoln). Kentucky achieved statehood in 1792.

100– "I want to return. . . ." FCHQ: January, 1941, p. 9.

103– "You Boone's girl. . . ." Draper 6S, pp. 78–79; 16C, p. 76.

105– "How are you feeling? . . ." Draper 11CC, p. 14.

106– "unless you set a store. . . ." *Ibid.*, p. 16.

107– "For God's sake, man. . . ." Draper 4B, p. 474.

108– "the first home-grown watermelons. . . ." Ranck, p. 145.

VI. BOONESBOROUGH: THE BATTLE JOINED

The standard histories of Kentucky—Cotterill, Marshall and especially Collins, and Mann Butler's *Valley of the Ohio*—remain useful for an overview of gathering events and the menace of the Indian raids. Details of the salt-maker's capture and Boone's subsequent life among the Shawnee are mainly from information given to Draper by Joseph Jackson, one of the prisoners (11CC, pp. 62 ff., and 5B, 533 ff.); Bradford; Daniels Trabue's diary (Draper 57J, pp. 44 ff.) and Draper's biography of Boone (B). For the British and Indian side, and especially for Black Fish's visit to Hamilton in Detroit, see Haldimand. The siege itself is most completely covered in Draper's biography, which unhappily does not continue beyond the year 1788, with considerable personal detail to be found in contemporary accounts, like those of Moses Boone (Draper 19C, p. 9 ff.), Isaiah Boone (Draper 19C, p. 57 ff.), William B. Smith (Durrett) and those in the manuscript collections of Shane and Tipton.

110– "We are surrounded. . . ." Lester, p. 174.

111– The adventures of Richard Burke, known in the settlements as "Fool" Burke for his habit of getting lost, sometimes in sight of a fort, provided some tension-breaking laughter. Burke, captured by a raiding party that spring, managed to get away close to the Kentucky, then wandered days in the forest without any idea where he was. When a search party finally found him, Boone asked how he contrived to get lost so close to the river. He had been following a buffalo, "Fool" Burke replied, hoping it was bound for a salt lick where he would find a path leading home. But after two days the buffalo had taken him back to the very place they'd started from. "That stupid critter was as lost as I was," he wailed. (FCHQ: January, 1947, pp. 27–28).

More typically, the tales carried from one settlement to another were of sudden death. A free Negro called Hynes was known in Boonesborough as being "as good a soldier as any we had." He farmed a fine tract of land about five miles downriver from the settlement but was always there in time of trouble, often volunteering to ride for meat. He was killed on one of these sorties and, said Boone, "sorely missed." (*Ibid.*, p. 40.)

113– "Back to the fort. . . ." Draper 5B, p. 498.

114– "Well, Simon, you behaved. . . ." Kenton, p. 88.

115– "We found a poor. . . ." and "The people in the fort. . . ." Lester, pp. 195–96.

116– "Howdy, Captain Will. . . ." Draper 5B, p. 526.

117– "Tomorrow we will kill. . . ." Van Noppen, p. 139.

117– "When the Red Coats came. . . ." *Ibid.*

117– "Cornstalk will not rest. . . ." Draper 57J, p. 27 (Trabue's diary).

119– "Brothers, you have got. . . ." *Ibid.*

119– "The savages could not. . . ." Hamilton to Sir Guy Carleton, April 25, 1778; Haldimand, Microfilm designation A-687, p. 35, Ottawa.

121– "We will see which. . . ." Draper 11C, p. 64.

121– "No, they won't. . . ." Van Noppen, p. 192.

122– "You are too late. . . ." Draper 5B, p. 548.

122– "The people at Kentucke. . . ." Hamilton to Carleton, April 25, 1778; Haldimand, Microfilm designation A-687, p. 35; Ottawa.

123– "A friendly supply. . . ." Froncek, p. 75.

124– "a great share. . . ." Ibid., p. 76.

126– "I'm going back. . . ." Draper 16C, p. 7.

127– "My son, what. . . ." Draper 11C, p. 62.

129– "Daniel Boone, By God. . . ." Draper 5B, p. 568.

130– "The pressing necessity. . . ." Shane, quoted by Lester, p. 204.

131– Half the men taken prisoner at the salt licks eventually escaped; two were killed, a few chose to remain with the British in Canada, and the rest returned home after the Revolution.

131– Hancock said that he had become so discouraged during his wanderings that he had lain down beneath a tree to die. But just before he closed his eyes for the last time he noticed his brother's name carved in the tree and remembered that they had once camped there, only four miles from Boonesborough. Heartened, he rose and managed to make it back.

134– "Well, Boone, howdy. . . ." Draper 12CC, p. 74. (Josiah Collins); 5B, p. 588.

135– "Well, Black Fish. . . ." Draper 11CC, p. 12.

135– "he would be compelled. . . ." Draper 5B, p. 582.

136– "Well, then I'll die. . . ." Ibid., p. 94.

136– "to take the people. . . ." Draper 19C, p. 79.

137– "The people are determined. . . ." Ranck, p. 84.

137– "This sounded grateful. . . ." Draper 5B, p. 594.

138– Boone, Major Smith and Richard Callaway led the negotiators; their subalterns were Squire Boone, Flanders Callaway, William Hancock, Stephen Hancock and William Buchanan.

138– These young men were eager. . . . Bradford, p. 44.

138– "Friends and brothers. . . ." Draper 22C, p. 5.

138– "Then we shall live. . . ." Draper 6S, p. 141.

139– Cotterill, among other historians, believes the Indians might well have withdrawn peacefully. He writes (p. 145): "It is by no means settled that the Indians were acting in bad faith in taking the hands of the white men. Rather is it to be believed that the lamentable outcome was a result of the panic on the part of Colonel Callaway. . . . If [the Indians] had meditated treachery they had had several, and better, opportunities before. Only the day before they had had nine men in their power and did not offer to molest them. . . . It remains at least an open question whether the trouble at the spring was due to treachery on the part of the Indians or a panic on the part of the white men."

141– "Boonesborough was taken. . . ." Draper 57J, pp. 27–28 (Trabue's diary; Trabue was at Logan's Station during the Boonesborough siege).

142– "fight like men. . . ." Draper 11C, p. 76; 57J, p. 27.
142– "It might hurt. . . ." *Ibid.*
143– "Der potters vass. . . ." Draper 12CC, p. 200.
143– "Let me go to my duty. . . ." Draper 11CC, p. 13.
144– "Where's Pompey? . . ." Draper 5B, p. 613, 622; 11CC, p. 13. Less reliable sources have it that it was Boone who shot Pompey, but this seems unlikely.
144– "We killed your Boone. . . ." Draper 5B, p. 618.
144– "Kiss my ass. . . ." Draper 4C, pp. 24–26.
145– "What are you doing? . . ." Bradford, p. 45; Draper 6C, p. 143; 11CC, p. 14.

VII. THE COURT-MARTIAL OF DANIEL BOONE

All the official documents pertaining to Boone's court-martial have disappeared, probably at the instance of some misguided partisan who believed he was protecting the pioneer's reputation. Fortunately, Daniel Trabue was present throughout the trial and his account of it in his diary (Draper 57J), followed in Draper's biography, preserves the essential facts. Many Boone biographers refer obliquely to his "troubles" in North Carolina; not one makes the obvious connection to Rebecca's family and her reluctance to return to Kentucky. For Boone's capture by Tarleton's raiders in Charlottesville, see John Cook Wyllie's excellent article in the *Magazine of Albemarle History.* There is still no better account of the battles at Bryan's Station and Blue Licks than the solidly documented Filson Club Publication No. 12, "Bryant's Station," the combined work of Durrett, Ranck and Bennett H. Young. Long out of print, it deserves a place among those other fine Filson Club publications that have been republished in recent years.

149– "the fact that Boonesborough. . . ." Clark (*Frontier*), p. 20.
150– "Boone never deserved. . . ." Draper 11CC, p. 94.
150– "God damn them. . . ." Draper 11C, p. 61.
150– In this account of the court-martial, all paraphrased dialogue is from Trabue, all direct quotation from Draper's biography.
154– "stupid jealousy. . . ." Clark (*Kentucky*), p. 26.
157– "I feel for the poor people. . . ." *Journal* of the Presbyterian Historical Society: vol. 14 (1930–31), p. 343.
158– "too barbarous to relate. . . ." The words are attributed to Boone by Filson and quoted in Durrett ("Bryant's Station"), p. 114.
159– "It's Boone. . . ." Draper 22C, p. 7; Bradford, pp. 115–17.
160– "load up in waggons. . . ." *Magazine of Albemarle History*, p. 8.
161– "Wait a minute, Colonel. . . ." *Ibid.*, p. 9.
162– "Our militia are called. . . ." Durrett ("Bryant's Station"), p. 206.

163– "Brothers! The fertile region. . . ." Butterfield, pp. 190–91. There is some question about whether Girty actually used such well-rounded phrases. It may be that in this case, as in others involving Indian speeches translated into English, the interpreter indulged his literary gifts.

163– Both Bryans and Bryants were involved in the building of that station and it was known by both names.

164– "We all know you. . . ." Durrett ("Bryant's Station"), p. 115.

164– Girty, against whom many a Kentuckian had sworn personal revenge, served the British throughout the Revolution, acting as Hamilton's interpreter and participating in many battles, including Fallen Timbers. He died in Canada, in his bed, at the age of seventy-seven.

166– "We do not have time. . . ." Draper 6S, pp. 151–53. McGary seems to have been a born troublemaker. When Harrodsburg had been under fire, he stormed so at James Harrod about neglected defenses that the commander went for his rifle and the two might have killed each other if Mrs. McGary hadn't intervened.

166– "All who are not damned. . . ." *Ibid.*

168– "Give it to someone else. . . ." *Ibid.*, pp. 164–65.

169– "many more we expect. . . ." Boone to Governor Harrison, August 20, 1782; Durrett ("Bryant's Station"), p. 216.

VIII. GLORY AND GRIEF

The best accounts of Boone as a surveyor are by Jillson (*Kentucky School Journal*), September, 1934; and the *Register*: July, 1946. For a broader understanding of Boone's land troubles and the problems of land distribution in Kentucky before statehood, see "Discontent in Frontier Kentucky," Patricia Watlington, in the *Register*: April, 1967. The story of the remarkable John Floyd is well told by Hambleton Tapp in FCHQ: January, 1941. For Boone at Limestone, see David I. Bushnell, Jr.'s account in the *Virginia Magazine of History and Biography*: January, 1917. For Boone in the Kanawha, see the *Register*: vol. 11, no. 32 (1913).

170– "weakening one end of the country. . . ." Durrett ("Bryant's Station"), p. 206.

170– "these unfortunate gents. . . ." Clark to Governor Harrison, October 18, 1782; *Ibid.*, p. 207.

170– "vain and seditious fool. . . ." Campbell to Colonel William Davies, October 3, 1782; *Ibid.*, p. 222.

170– "Logan is a dull. . . ." *Ibid.*

170– "I know, Sir. . . ." *Ibid.*, p. 215.

171– "Kentucky was full. . . ." Draper 6S, p. 165.

171– "I have been unable to. . . ." *Ibid.*, p. 215.

172– "Well, Boone, we got you. . . ." Draper 16C, p. 8.

173– Limestone became Maysville a few years later and remains a busy little river town of eight or nine thousand, about fifty miles southeast of Cincinnati.

173– "was the best I had eaten. . . ." *Register*: July, 1936, p. 219 (Journal of Joel Watkins, from the Durrett Collection).

174– "Were you at the Blue Licks. . . ." Draper 22C, p. 235.

175– "Daniel Boone lent me. . . ." Draper 12CC, p. 144 (Shane).

176– "I am here with my hands. . . ." Draper 26C, p. 17.

176– "not a lie in it. . . ." McClung, p. 79.

177– The dangers of surveying the Kentucky wilderness are vividly described by Jillson: ". . . every surveyor actually took his life in his hands each time he ventured into the vast forested stretches of the new country. Lest anyone think this point overplayed in an attempt to aggrandize Boone, it is perhaps proper that the tragic deaths of Captain Hancock Taylor, Colonel John Floyd and John Filson be recalled. Each of these men were able woodsmen, well known and highly regarded by Boone. But none of them took as many, nor as great, chances in the savage-infested wilderness as did he." (*Kentucky School Journal*: September, 1934, p. 31.)

177– "Unacquainted with the niceties. . . ." Tipton Papers, p. 351.

178– The chaos inherent in the land distribution systems on the western frontier is described by Thwaites: "Each settler or land speculator was practically his own surveyor. With a compass and a chain, a few hours' work would suffice to mark the boundaries of a thousand-acre tract. There were as yet no adequate maps of the country, and claims overlapped each other in the most bewildering manner. A speculator who 'ran out' a hundred thousand acres might, without knowing it, include in his domain a half-dozen claims previously surveyed by modest settlers who wanted but a hundred acres each. A man who paid the land-office fees might 'patent' any land he pleased and have it recorded, the colony, and later the State, only guaranteeing such entries as covering land not already patented." (Pp. 121–22.)

178– "Shouldn't they push off? . . ." Draper 6S, pp. 200–201.

179– Kanawha Falls was on the site of the present-day West Virginia town called Boone.

179– "Well, come with me. . . ." Hale, p. 169.

179– "Spyes will be necessary. . . ." *Register*: vol. 11, no. 32 (1932), p. 10.

179– "After tiring. . . ." Draper, see under the year 1791 in C series.

180– The Boone visit to Pennsylvania was well-remembered. Old Thomas Lincoln talked about it until he died.

180– The Brushy Fork cabin is the only one built by Daniel Boone to have survived the years.

180– "Sir, After my best. . . ." Draper 6S, p. 205.

181– "in time of peace. . . ." *Ibid.*, p. 219.

181– "he did not want to die. . . ." *Ibid.*, p. 309.
183– "I went to my wife. . . ." Draper 15C, p. 26.

IX. MOVING ON

Although Boone lived in Missouri as long as he did in Kentucky, there has been only one special study of this final phase of his life, a series of articles written by Rebecca's descendant, William S. Bryan, appearing in MHR in 1909–1910. Bryan also contributed a Daniel Boone biography to *A History of the Pioneer Families of Missouri*. Unfortunately, neither the articles nor the book are documented and are, in fact, burdened with errors. But Bryan did collect a good deal of family tradition and his account has color and warmth. Contemporary periodicals and later issues of MHR are invaluable, as, of course, is Draper.

187– "the trail followed. . . " MHR: vol. 19, p. 588.
189– "To watch that no Protestant. . . ." MHR: vol. 4, p. 30.
190– Stories of Boone presiding under the Judgment Tree abound in MHR: see vol. 3, pp. 92–98, 199–203; vol. 4, pp. 85–91; vol. 19, p. 386; vol. 31, pp. 185–88; vol. 37, p. 347.
190– "First rate. . . ." MHR: vol. 31, p. 188.
190– "That one James Davis. . . ." MHR: vol. 3, p. 200.
192– "Mr. Boone—a respectable. . . ." Draper 15C, p. 64.
192– Had his grants been approved. . . ." American State Papers, Public Lands, II, p. 473.
193– Boone's children had to surrender much of their land, too. But between them, Daniel Morgan and Flanders Callaway managed to retain some nine hundred acres.
194– "We have been honored. . . ." MHR: vol. 16, p. 27. On the visit to Fort Osage, Boone wore "the dress of the roughest, poorest hunter," noted the commander. "He goes hunting twice a year to the remotest wilderness he can reach (and) left here for the River Platt, some distance above." Boone was then eighty-two.
195– Boone's sons continued to operate the salt licks after the old man's death, shipping salt as far away as New Orleans. Jesse Boone died only three months after his father, but Daniel Morgan and Nathan lived long, full lives. Daniel Morgan became a justice of Gasconade County, Missouri, then, in the Boone fashion, moved west to Kansas, where his son, Napoleon, became the first white child born in that territory. Nathan was a delegate to the Missouri constitutional convention, served as a captain in the Black Hawk War and had a distinguished military career on the western frontier.
196– "Dear Sister, With pleasure. . . ." Spraker, p. 59.
197– "If I was compelled. . . ." Letter to Clay, May 5, 1806; quoted in the *Navigator*: 1814, p. 249; Draper 6S, p. 221.

197– "The Legislature of Kentucky. . . ." Draper 6S, pp. 148–49.

198– "and now Ballard said. . . ." *Ibid.*, pp. 251–52.

199– "I have paid all. . . ." Bryan (*Pioneer Families*), p. 47.

200– Among the other myths, newspapers around the country once printed a vivid account of Boone's "death," all about how he had been found at a salt lick with his rifle cocked and ready to fire at a buffalo. Someone signing himself "Truth," perhaps one of Boone's sons, thereupon wrote to the Missouri *Intelligencer* to say, "Col. B. [is] living in a populous settlement with his son, Major Nathan Boone, and quietly making ready for a crop of corn. . . . Until two years past he was in the habit of hunting a few weeks in each year for amusement—the last attempt he made was in the latter end of the year 1816. He was attacked by a pleurisy at Loutre Lick, on his route to the hunting ground. That was the first time he had even been obliged to have recourse to medical aid."

200– "This book represents me. . . ." Draper 7C, p. 43.

201– "Here I hoped to find rest. . . ." MHR: vol. 34, p. 431.

201– "The nearer I approached. . . ." Draper 16C, p. 52.

202– "I took very little interest. . . ." Harding, p. 35.

202– Harding had been commissioned to paint the portrait by the Reverends James E. Welch and Joseph M. Peck of St. Louis, who were well aware of Boone's place in Missouri history—Peck wrote one of the early Boone biographies.

204– "Of the great names. . . ." *Register*: vol. 5, no. 13 (1907), pp. 31–32.

Bibliography

This is far from an inclusive Boone bibliography which, with related published work on the early frontier, would fill a book of its own. The books, periodicals and manuscript collections listed here are those I have consulted; their relative usefulness will be apparent from the chapter notes.

My starting point and ultimate reference was the famous Draper Manuscript Collection at the State Historical Society of Wisconsin, now available on microfilm there and at several major libraries. Lyman Copeland Draper, that relentless amateur historian of the nineteenth century, who intended to write the definitive biographies of several notable frontier figures, covered more than sixty thousand miles on horseback and afoot in search of every last scrap of pertinent information. He sought out old woodsmen, hunters and pioneers, wrote down their stories and carried away letters, account books, family records—indeed, so much manuscript material that in Kentucky and Tennessee he became known as "the man who stole all our documents." But he ultimately gave them a safe home at the Wisconsin State Historical Society, where he became corresponding secretary in 1854, and spent the rest of his life adding to the collection, classifying and annotating it. Unfortunately, this work so preoccupied him that he lived to complete only one of the books he had projected, an account of the Revolutionary battle at King's Mountain; at the time of his death in 1891, his unpublished biography of Boone had only reached the period following the siege of Boonesborough. But his monumental effort has proven invaluable to writers and scholars down to the present day, and to countless numbers of people seeking information about their ancestors.

As finally organized, the Draper Manuscript Collection consists of 486 volumes divided into fifty series, each of which is identified by letter. The ones cited are those I used most extensively for this book.

For periodicals consulted only once or twice, I have included article titles and authors below; for those used more frequently, full information is provided in the chapter notes, as are the particulars of the county records and collections of other state historical societies which I have consulted. Finally, it ought to be said that anyone with special interest in the life and times of Daniel Boone would be well advised to study the indices of the *Filson Club Historical Quarterly*, the *Register* of the Kentucky State Historical Society, the *Missouri Historical Review* and the *Mississippi Valley Historical Review*; they are continuing sources of rich new material available nowhere else, the work of scholars, kinsmen and devoted history enthusiasts.

Abbott, John S. C. *Daniel Boone, Pioneer of Kentucky*. New York: Dodd, Mead, 1872.

American Heritage. "Ghost Writer to Daniel Boone," by John Walton. October, 1955.

———"Braddock's Alumni," by Robert C. Alberts. February, 1961.

American Historical Association. *The Regulators of North Carolina*, by John Spencer Bassett. Annual Report, 1894, Washington, D.C.

American Historical Review. "The Creative Forces in Westward Expansion: Henderson and Boone," by Archibald Henderson. vol. 20, 1914, Washington, D.C.

American History Illustrated. "Simon Girty: Beast in Human Form," by Paul B. Beers. December, 1968; National Historical Society; Gettysburg, Pa.

———"The Saga of James Smith." July, 1970.

Anonymous. *Heroes and Hunters of the West*. Philadelphia: Theodore Bliss & Co., 1853.

Arnow, Harriette S. *Seedtime on the Cumberland*. New York: Macmillan, 1960.

Bakeless, John. *Master of the Wilderness, Daniel Boone*. New York: William Morrow, 1939.

Bodley, Temple. *George Rogers Clark*. New York: Houghton, Mifflin, 1926.

Bogart, W. H. *Daniel Boone and the Hunters of Kentucky*. Philadelphia: Miller, Orton and Mulligan, 1881.

Boyd, Thomas. *Simon Girty, the White Savage*. New York: Minton, Balch, 1928.

Bradford, John, ed. "Notes on Kentucky," Kentucky *Gazette*, 1826–29. (Reprinted by Grabhorn Press, San Francisco, 1932; Douglas S. Watson, editor.)

Bruce, H. Aldington. *Daniel Boone and the Wilderness Road*. New York: Macmillan, 1910.

Bryan, Daniel. *The Mountain Muse; Comprising the Adventures of Daniel Boone* (in verse). Harrisonburg, Va.: Davidson and Bourne, 1813.

Bryan, William S. and Rose, Robert. *A History of the Pioneer Families of Missouri*. St. Louis: Bryan Brand & Co., 1876.

Butler, Mann. *A History of the Commonwealth of Kentucky.* Cincinnati: J. A. James and Co., 1836.

——"Valley of the Ohio." Frankfort: Kentucky Historical Society, 1971. (Reprinted from the 1834 edition).

Butterfield, Consul W. *History of the Girtys.* Cincinnati: Robert Clarke, 1890.

Caruso, John A. *The Appalachian Frontier.* Indianapolis-New York: Bobbs-Merrill, 1959.

Cattermole, E. G. *Famous Frontiersmen, Pioneers and Scouts.* Chicago: Donahue, Henneberry, 1884.

Chaffee, Allen. *The Wilderness Trail; the Story of Daniel Boone.* New York: T. Nelson and Sons, 1936.

Chinn, Col. George. *Kentucky: Settlement and Statehood.* Frankfort: Kentucky Historical Society, 1975.

Chitwood, Oliver Perry. *A History of Colonial America.* New York: Harper and Bros., 1931.

Clark, George Rogers. *The Conquest of Illinois.* Chicago: Lakeside Press, 1920.

Clark, Thomas D. *Frontier America.* New York: Charles Scribner's Sons, 1959.

——*A History of Kentucky.* New York: Prentice-Hall, 1937.

——*Kentucky, Land of Contrast.* New York: Harper and Row, 1968.

——*Simon Kenton, Kentucky Scout.* New York: Farrar & Rinehart, 1943.

Coleman, J. Winston, Jr. *A Bibliography of Kentucky History.* Lexington: University of Kentucky Press, 1949.

Collins, Lewis. *History of Kentucky.* Lexington: Henry Clay Press, 1968. (Facsimile of Maysville, 1847, edition).

Comfort, William Wistar. *The Quakers: A Brief Account of Their Influence on Pennsylvania.* Gettysburg: Pennsylvania Historical Association, 1948.

Commager, Henry Steele and Morris, Richard B., eds. *The Spirit of 'Seventy-Six.* New York: Harper and Row, 1958.

Cotterill, R. S. *History of Pioneer Kentucky.* Berea, Ky.: Kentucke Imprints, 1972. (Reprint of Johnson & Hardin, Cincinnati, 1917.)

Day, Sherman. *Historical Collections of the State of Pennsylvania.* Philadelphia: George W. Gorton, 1843.

De Voto, Bernard, ed. *The Journals of Lewis and Clark.* Boston: Houghton, Mifflin, 1953.

Doddridge, Rev. Dr. Joseph. *Notes on the Settlement and Indian Wars of the Western Parts of Virginia and Pennsylvania.* Albany, N.Y.; Joel Munsell, 1876. (Reprinted from edition of 1824).

Drake, Dr. Daniel. *Pioneer Life in Kentucky.* Edited by Dr. Emmet F. Horine. New York: 1948. (Reprinted from Robert W. Clarke, Cincinnati, 1870).

Draper, Lyman C. Manuscript Collection. State Historical Society of Wisconsin, Madison.

    B   Draper's Life of Boone

    C   Boone Papers

D   Border Forays
J   George Rogers Clark Papers
K   George Rogers Clark Miscellanies
S   Draper's Notes
U   Frontier Wars Papers
BB   Simon Kenton Papers
NN   North Carolina Papers
CC   Kentucky Papers
QQ   William Preston Papers
XX   Tennessee Papers
ZZ   Virginia Papers

Durrett, Rueben T. *Bryant's Station* (and the Memorial Proceedings). Filson Club Publication no. 12. Louisville: John P. Morton & Co. 1897. (Includes *The Story of Bryan's Station* by George W. Ranck, and *The Battle of Blue Licks* by Col. Bennett H. Young).

———*John Filson, the First Historian of Kentucky*. Filson Club Publication no. 1. Louisville: John P. Morton & Co.; 1884. (Includes an account of Filson's *Discovery, Settlement and Present State of Kentucke*, 1784.)

———Manuscript Collection. Joseph Regenstein Library, University of Chicago.

English, William Hayden. *Conquest of the Country Northwest of the River Ohio, 1778–1783*. Indianapolis: Bowen-Merrill, 1896.

Filson Club Historical Quarterly. The Filson Club, Louisville.

Flint, Timothy. *The Life and Adventures of Daniel Boone*. New York: Hurst & Co., 1868.

Forbes-Lindsay, C. H. *Daniel Boone, Backwoodsman*. Philadelphia: J. B. Lippincott, 1909.

Froncek, Thomas, ed. *Voices from the Wilderness*. New York: McGraw-Hill, 1974. (Contains Filson's *Boone Narrative*).

Funk, Arville. *Squire Boone in Indiana*. Chicago: Adams Press, 1974.

Goeller, Glen. *The Saga of a Man and a House*. St. Louis: Daniel Boone Shrine Association, 1957. (Boone in Missouri.)

Hale, Dr. John P. *Daniel Boone*. Some Facts and Incidents not hitherto published. His Ten or Twelve Years' Residence in Kanawha County. Wheeling, W. Va: L. Baker & Co., ca. 1882.

Haldimand, Sir Frederick. Manuscript Collection. British Museum, London. (Microfilm copy in Public Archives of Canada, Ottawa).

Harding, Chester. *My Egotistigraphy*. Cambridge: John Wilson & Co., 1866.

Harper, Mrs. Lillie DuPuy VanCulin, ed. *Colonial Men and Times*. Philadelphia: Innes and Sons, 1916. (Contains *The Journal of Col. Daniel Trabue*).

Harper's Monthly Magazine. "The Kentucky Pioneers" by John Mason Brown. vol. 75; June, 1887.

Hart, Albert Bushnell. *American History Told by Contemporaries*. New York: Macmillan, 1898.

Hart, Val. *The Story of America's Roads.* New York: William Sloane Associates, 1950.

Hartley, Cecil B. *Life and Times of Colonel Daniel Boone Comprising History of the Early Settlement of Kentucky.* Philadelphia: G. G. Evans, 1859.

Henderson, Archibald. *The Conquest of the Old Southwest.* New York: Century, 1920.

———*The Significance of the Transylvania Company in American History.* (Publisher, place and date unknown).

———*The Star of Empire: Phases of the Westward Movement in the Old Southwest.* Durham, N.C.: Seeman Printery, 1919.

———*The Transylvania Company and the Founding of Henderson, Ky.* Henderson, Ky. 1929.

Henry, Gypsy Gray. *History of Gallatin County, Ky.* (Privately printed). Covington, Ky.

Herrick, Francis Hobart. *Audubon the Naturalist; A History of His Life and Times.* New York: D. Appleton, 1917.

Higginbotham, Dan. *Atlas of the American Revolution.* Chicago: Rand McNally, 1974.

Hill, George Canning. *Daniel Boone, the Pioneer of Kentucky.* Philadelphia: Clayton, Remsen and Haffelfinger, 1875.

Historical Sketches of Southwest Virginia. "Frontier Forts by Emory L. Hamilton." no. 4, 1968, Coeburn, Va.

———*"Christopher Gist Did Not Go Through Pound Gap"* by L. F. Addington. no. 5, March, 1970.

———"The Long Hunters by Emory L. Hamilton." no. 5, March, 1970.

Howe, Henry. *Historical Collections of the Great West.* Cincinnati: Henry Howe, 1872.

Hulbert, Archer B. *Boone's Wilderness Road.* Cleveland: Arthur H. Clark, 1903.

James, James A. *The Life of George Rogers Clark.* Chicago: University of Chicago Press, 1928.

Jenkins, Howard M. *Historical Collections Relating to Gwynedd.* Philadelphia: Ferris Bros., Wilmington, Dela., 1884.

Jillson, Willard Rouse. *The Boone Narrative.* Louisville: Standard Printing Co., 1932. (A facsimile reproduction of Filson's *Kentucke,* and a new Boone bibliography).

———*The Kentucky Land Grants* (a systematic index). Louisville: Standard Printing Co., 1925.

———*Pioneer Kentucky.* Frankfort: State Journal Co., 1934.

———*Tales of the Dark and Bloody Ground.* Louisville: C. T. Dearing Printing Co., 1930.

Johnson, J. Stoddard. *First Explorations of Kentucky.* (Facsimile reproduction of) Filson Club Publication no. 13, John P. Morton and Co., Louisville, 1898.

(Contains *The Journal of Doctor Thomas Walker* and *The Journal of Christopher Gist*).

Josephy, Alvin M., Jr.; Lyon, Peter; and Russell, Francis. *The American Heritage Book of the Pioneer Spirit.* New York: American Heritage Publishing Co., 1959.

Journal of the Illinois State Historical Society. "The Daniel Boone Myth" by Clarence W. Alvord. vol. 19, April–July, 1926.

Kent, Donald H. *Contrecoeur's Copy of George Washington's Journal for 1754.* Pennsylvania Historical and Museum Commission (reprinted from Pennsylvania History, vol. XIX, no. 1, January, 1952), Harrisburg.

Kenton, Edna. *Simon Kenton, His Life and Period*, 1755–1836. Garden City, N.Y.: Doubleday, Doran, 1930.

Kentucky Highways—Daniel Boone's Kentucky. 1970: Kentucky Department of Highways, Frankfort.

Kentucky Historical Society. *Kentucky Ancestors.* Frankfort.

Kentucky School Journal. "The Ancestry and Boyhood of Daniel Boone" by William Boone Douglass. vol. 13, September, 1934, Kentucky Education Association, Louisville.

————"Daniel Boone as a Surveyor" by Dr. Willard Rouse Jillson. vol. 13, September, 1934.

Ketchum, Richard M. *American Heritage Book of Great Historic Places.* New York: American Heritage Publishing Co., 1957.

Kincaid, Robert L. *The Wilderness Road.* Harrogate, Tenn.: Lincoln Memorial University Press, 1955.

Lavender, David. *American Heritage Book of The Great West.* New York: American Heritage Publishing Co., 1965.

Lester, William Stewart. *The Transylvania Company.* Spencer, Ind.: Samuel R. Guard and Co., 1935.

Lincoln Lore. Bulletin of the Lincoln National Life Foundation; Editors (successively) Dr. Louis A. Warren, Dr. R. Gerald McMurtry and Mark E. Neely, Jr. Lincoln National Life Insurance Co., Fort Wayne, Ind.

Magazine of Albemarle County History. "Daniel Boone's Adventures in Charlottesville in 1781: Some Incidents Connected with Tarleton's Raid by John Cook Wyllie." vol. 19, 1960–1961, Albemarle County Historical Society, University of Virginia Library, Charlottesville.

Marshall, Humphrey. *The History of Kentucky.* Berea, Ky.: Oscar Rucker, Jr. 1971. (Reprinted from Henry Gore edition, 1812).

Mason, Kathryn Harrod. *Harrod of Kentucky.* Baton Rouge: Louisiana State University Press, 1951.

McClung, John A. *Sketches of Western Adventure Containing an Account of the Most Interesting Incidents Connected with the West, from 1755 to 1794.* Dayton: Ellis, Claflin & Co., 1847.

MacKnight, Charles. *Our Western Border, Its Life, Forays, Scouts, Combats, Massacres, Red Chiefs, Adventures, Captivities, Pioneer Women, One Hundred Years Ago.* Philadelphia: J. S. McCurdy & Co., 1875.

Metcalf, Samuel L. "A Collection of Some of the Most Interesting Narratives of Indian Warfare in the West." *Magazine of History* (Extra no. 26), New York, 1913. (Contains James Smith's account of his captivity by the Indians, 1755–59).

Miller, John C. *Origins of the American Revolution.* Boston: Little, Brown, 1943.

Miner, William Harvey. *Daniel Boone: Contributions toward a Bibliography of Writings concerning Daniel Boone.* New York: Didbin Club, 1901.

Mississippi Valley Historical Review—Richard Henderson and the Occupation of Kentucky, by Archibald Henderson. vol. 1, no. 3; December, 1914. Mississippi State Historical Society, Jackson.

Missouri Historical Review. State Historical Society of Missouri, Columbia.

Moore, Arthur K. *The Frontier Mind.* Lexington: University of Kentucky Press, 1957.

Morison, Samuel Eliot. *The Oxford History of the American People.* New York: Oxford University Press, 1965.

National Geographic Book Service. *America's Historylands.* National Geographic Society, Washington, D.C., 1962.

Niles Register. Philadelphia.

Norton, Frank H. *The Days of Daniel Boone.* New York: American News Co., ca. 1883.

Outdoor World. "Rivers of North America," Waukesha, Wisc.: Outdoor World, 1973.

Patterson, A. W. *History of the Backwoods; or, The Region of the Ohio.* Pittsburgh: A. W. Patterson, 1843.

Peck, John M. and Sparks, Jared. *Makers of American History: Daniel Boone, Robert Cavalier de LaSalle and Father Marquette.* University Society, New York, 1904.

Perkins, James H. *Annals of the West.* St. Louis: James Albach, 1850.

Phulbrick, Francis S. *The Rise of the West, 1754–1830.* New York: Harper and Row, 1965.

Ranck, George W. *Boonesborough: Its Founding, Pioneer Struggles, Indian Expeditions, Transylvania Days and Revolutionary Annals.* Filson Club Publication No. 16, Louisville, 1901. (Reprinted, Oscar Rucker, II, Berea, Ky., 1971). With an extensive appendix containing Felix Walker's narrative, Henderson's journal and other documentary material.

Register. State Historical Society of Kentucky, Frankfort.

Roosevelt, Theodore. *The Winning of the West* (2 vols., VIII and IX of the National Edition of Roosevelt's works). New York: Charles Scribner's Sons, 1924, 1926.

Sandburg, Carl. *Abraham Lincoln: The Prairie Years* (Vol. 1). New York: Harcourt, Brace, 1925.

Scalf, Henry P. *Kentucky's Last Frontier*. Pikeville College Press, Appalachian Studies Center, Pikeville, Ky., 1972.

Shane, John. Manuscript Collection. Presbyterian Historical Society, Philadelphia.

Skinner, Constance Lindsay. *Pioneers of the Old Southwest; a Chronicle of the Dark and Bloody Ground*. New Haven: Yale University Press, 1919.

Sosin, Jack M., ed. *The Opening of the West*. University of South Carolina Press, Columbia, 1969. (Contains the journal of William Calk).

———*The Revolutionary Frontier*, 1763–1783. New York: Holt, Rinehart & Winston, 1967.

Speed, Captain Thomas. *The Wilderness Road*. Filson Club Publication No. 2, Louisville: John P. Morton & Co., 1886.

Spooner, Walter W. *The Back-Woodsmen; or, Tales of the Borders*. Cincinnati: W. E. Dibble & Co., 1883.

Spraker, Hazel Atterbury. *The Boone Family*. Tuttle Co., Rutland, Vt., 1922. (Reprinted by Genealogical Publishing Co., Baltimore, 1974). Boone family records for eleven generations; *Biographical Sketch of Daniel Boone*, by Jesse Procter Crump.

Sutton, Margaret. *Jemima, Daughter of Daniel Boone*. New York: Charles Scribner's Sons, 1942.

Talbert, Charles Gano. *Benjamin Logan, Kentucky Frontiersman*. University of Kentucky Press, Lexington, 1962.

Tennessee Historical Magazine. "Richard Henderson: The Authorship of the Cumberland Compact and the Founding of Nashville" by Archibald Henderson. September, 1916.

Tennessee Historical Quarterly. "Cumberland Gap National Historical Park," by William W. Luckett. vol. XXIII, no. 4, December, 1964, Nashville.

Tennessee Valley Historical Review. "This is Boone Country" by Russell I. Todd. vol. 2, no. 2, Summer, 1973, Nashville.

Thwaites, Reuben Gold. *Daniel Boone*. New York: D. Appleton, 1902.

———and Kellogg, Louise P. *Documentary History of Dunmore's War, 1774*. Wisconsin State Historical Society, Madison, 1905.

Tipton, John. Manuscript Collection. John Grant Crabbe Library, Eastern Kentucky University, Richmond, Ky.

Turner, Frederick Jackson. *The Frontier in American History*. New York: Henry Holt, 1920.

———*Rise of the New West*. New York: Harper & Bros., 1906.

Tuttle, Charles R. *History of the Border Wars of Two Centuries*, Chicago: C. A. Wall & Co., 1885.

Van Every, Dale. *Ark of Empire: The American Frontier, 1784–1803*. New York: William Morrow, 1973.

Van Every, Dale. *A Company of Heroes: The American Frontier, 1775–1783.* New York: William Morrow, 1962.

——*Forth to the Wilderness: The First American Frontier, 1754–1774.* New York: William Morrow, 1961.

Van Noppen, John James and Van Noppen, Ina Woestemeyer. *Daniel Boone, Backwoodsman: The Green Woods Were His Portion.* Boone, N.C.: Appalachian Press, 1966.

Virginia Historical Magazine. "Reminiscences of Western Virginia, 1770–1790," by John Redd. January, 1900.

Virginia Magazine of History and Biography. "Daniel Boone at Limestone, 1786–1787" by David I. Bushnell, Jr., vol. XXV, no. 1, January, 1917.

Waitley, Douglas. *Roads of Destiny.* Washington, D.C.: Robert B. Luce, 1970.

Wall, James W. *History of Davie County in the Forks of the Yadkin.* Davie County Historical Publishing Assoc., Mocksville, N.C., 1969.

Wallace, Paul A. *Indians in Pennsylvania.* Pennsylvania Historical and Museum Commission, Harrisburg, 1968.

Walton, John. *John Filson of Kentucke.* University of Kentucky Press, Lexington, 1956.

Watlington, Patricia. *The Partisan Spirit.* University of North Carolina Press, Chapel Hill, 1972.

Western Pennsylvania Magazine of History. Historical Association of Western Pennsylvania, Pittsburgh.

Winsor, Justin, ed. *The American Revolution: A Narrative, Critical and Bibliographic History.* New York: Sons of Liberty Publications, 1972.

——*The Westward Movement: The Colonies and the Republic West of the Alleghenies, 1763–1798.* Boston: Houghton, Mifflin, 1897.

Wisconsin Magazine of History. "The Frontier Hero in History and Legend" by Kent L. Steckmesser. vol. XLVI, no. 3, Spring, 1963, Wisconsin State Historical Society, Madison.

Withers, Alexander Scott (edited and annotated by Reuben G. Thwaites). *Chronicles of Border Warfare, or a History of the Settlement by the Whites, of North-Western Virginia: and of the Indian Wars and Massacres.* Cincinnati: Robert Clarke Co., 1895.

Works Progress Administration. *Kentucky, A Guide to the Bluegrass State* (American Guide Series, Federal Writers' Project). New York: Harcourt, Brace, 1939.

——*Missouri, A Guide to the "Show Me" State.* (American Guide Series, Missouri Writers' Project). New York: Duell, Sloan & Pearce, 1941.

Wright, Louis B. *Culture on the Moving Frontier.* Bloomington: Indiana University Press, 1955.

Index